UNDERSTANDING CREATIVITY

UNDERSTANDING CREATIVITY

The Interplay of Biological, Psychological, and Social Factors

John S. Dacey and
Kathleen H. Lennon

With contributions by
Lisa B. Fiore

Jossey-Bass Publishers
San Francisco

Jossey-Bass books and products are available through most bookstores. To contact Jossey-Bass directly, call (888) 378-2537, fax to (800) 605-2665, or visit our website at www.josseybass.com.

Substantial discounts on bulk quantities of Jossey-Bass books are available to corporations, professional associations, and other organizations. For details and discount information, contact the special sales department at Jossey-Bass.

For sales outside the United States, please contact your local Simon & Schuster International Office.

 Manufactured in the United States of America on Lyons Falls Turin Book. This paper is acid-free and 100 percent totally chlorine-free.

"Teachers' Attitudes Toward Creative Students" in Chapter Four from D. J. Treffinger, R.E. Ripple, & J. S. Dacey, Teacher's attitudes toward creativity, *Journal of Creative Behavior,* 1968, 2(4), 242–248. Used by permission of the Creative Education Foundation.

"Isaksen's Guidelines" in Chapter Nine from S. Isaksen, Toward a model for the facilitation of creative problem solving, *Journal of Creative Behavior,* 1983, 17(1), 18–31. Used by permission of the Creative Education Foundation.

Library of Congress Cataloging-in-Publication Data
Dacey, John S.
    Understanding creativity : the interplay of biological, psychological, and social factors / John S. Dacey, Kathleen H. Lennon.
        p.   cm.
    Includes bibliographical references and indexes.
    ISBN 0-7879-4032-1 (hardcover)
    1. Creative ability.   2. Creative thinking.   I. Lennon, Kathleen.
    II. Title.
    BF408 .D325 1998
    153.3'5—ddc21   98-19770

FIRST EDITION

HB Printing   10 9 8 7 6 5 4 3 2 1

CONTENTS

Part Five: Integration

This book is dedicated to our respected advisor and cherished friend, Dr. John F. Travers.

PREFACE

AS THE STUDY of creativity in both ordinary and exceptional people has burgeoned in the past few years, it has become increasingly apparent that biological, psychological, and social factors all interact as this essential human ability emerges. We have sought to bring together insights from the most current research in these three areas of creativity scholarship so that knowledgeable general readers, students from many disciplines, and creativity scholars may all benefit from reading this book.

Understanding Creativity is divided into five parts. Part One includes an introduction to the many components of creativity, as well as a brief history that highlights what philosophers and scholars have thought and written about creative people and creative processes over the last 2,500 years.

In Part Two, we introduce the impact that social forces may have on one's creativity. First, we explore how the family into which a person is born may positively or negatively influence the development of creative potential. Then, in the larger world beyond the family, there are social forces such as the educational system's influence, the effects of having social rewards for creative behavior, and the culture's impact at large.

Part Three is devoted to psychological issues. The ten characteristics that most contribute to creativity are described, with special emphasis given to self-control, a trait that is especially essential to creative productivity. We address the roles that parenting and schools play in the achievement and growth of children's self-control, as well as peak periods during the life span when self-control may best be developed. The intellectual processes that are believed to be involved in creativity are then laid out. We summarize cognitive theory from the earlier models of associationism, the Gestalt school, and Piaget to the most current work on the use of metaphors and analogies and combination and expansion theories. We present several models of how creative people operate as successful and imaginative problem solvers, including the model proposed by J. P. Guilford, based on his ideas about the structure of the intellect.

Moving to an even more internal aspect of the creative process, we address the biological underpinnings of creativity in Part Four. We examine the latest discoveries about how the brain works on the neuronal and chemical levels, and we explore what is now known about the specialization of the brain's hemispheres and the special importance of the way they communicate and coordinate with each other.

Finally, in Part Five we examine an earlier biopsychosocial model of creativity and then present our own biopsychosocial model. We show in detail how it applies to Guilford's five stages of creative problem solving. In both text and tables, we show the biological, personality, cognitive, and social factors that we believe to be most essential to creative ability, and we discuss the contextual aspects of our new model and theory.

In our opinion, the comprehensive explanation that results from this compilation of ideas will have definite value to all who want to learn more about creativity in general and about their own creative ability in particular. Ultimately, we hope to inspire further investigation into the endlessly fascinating subject of human creative ability.

A number of people shared with us their ideas and criticisms about this book. We would like to acknowledge the contributions of Jennifer Allen, Susan Besemer, Stephanie Biziewski, Leslee Brooks, Bernard Cordts, Kristen Dacey, Lawrence deSalvatore, Ann Donaruma, Juliette Fay, Andrea Krasker, Holly Malin, Richard Ripple, Judith Robinson, Linda Schulman, Jep Streit, Robin Tartaglia, and Chris Wu. We also want to recognize the significant contributions of our editors: Leslie Berriman, Cathy Mallon, and Eve Kushner. Each helped us enormously, and Leslie Berriman's assistance was above and beyond the call of duty.

PART ONE

INTRODUCTION

THE MANY COMPONENTS
OF CREATIVITY

IT CAN BE ARGUED that throughout human history, our most valued ability has been intelligence—the capacity to learn and to use existing knowledge. In the new millennium, this will no longer be so. Creativity, the ability to produce new knowledge, will become our most cherished trait.

In the fast-changing world to come, the ability to deal with a vast range of complex problems and opportunities will be at a premium. Take, for example, the area of medical advances. In addition to their lifesaving qualities, these enrichments have introduced a plethora of dilemmas: Who should get what services? Should people be helped to die if they so desire? What are the implications of cloning?

A presidential commission was established recently to resolve the thorniest of these quandaries. Early in its investigation, the commission concluded that as distressing as these problems are, the medical ethics dilemmas we will face in ten years will be much more severe. They decided that they must abandon their assigned task in order to tackle these greater calamities.

This growing complexity exists in most aspects of human endeavor. It seems safe to say that in no other era of human history have we had so great a need for creative ideas. We will require not only a higher general level of innovative quality but also imaginative contributions from many more individuals. How can we hope to achieve such a monumental task? Before we can embark on the societal endeavors essential to such a lofty goal, we must collect the best knowledge about the nature of creativity that has been produced in recent decades. Here are some of the most important questions for which we must have answers:

- How can we tell if someone is creative?
- How do we judge the creative quality of products?
- Do highly creative people think differently, or are they just better at thinking than the rest of us?
- Are their brains different? For example, do they have higher levels of certain hormones? Do they have better memories? Are more of them left-handed (dominated by the right sides of their brains)?
- Are more of them homosexual?
- Are they more or less religious than the average person?
- Do they have unusual personality traits? For example, are they great risk takers or are they especially self-controlled?
- Do they work in unusual environments? For instance, do they tend to be self-employed?
- Did they have unusual childhoods? Did their parents treat them differently than most parents treat their children? Did they attend schools that foster creativity? Did they have enriched opportunities? What about their parents' educations, talents, and careers?

Research on these questions offers an excellent overview of the level of complexity that a truly useful description of creativity must reach. As an example of the nature of studies of creativity, let us examine the early psychological and economic environments of creative people.

The Early Environments of Creative People

In a review of major studies, Ochse (1991) found that with few exceptions, in both the past and present, most people who have demonstrated exceptional creativity come from professional-class backgrounds. The parents and other role models for these creative individuals, such as teachers and other adult acquaintances, value intellectual and artistic pursuits and provide a climate conducive to the fullest development of the young person's talents. In such homes, books, stimulating conversation, and other cultural advantages are readily available.

Gardner (1993a) has made a detailed study of seven individuals whose work in the twentieth century has changed the foundations of their respective fields. All of these creators had childhoods that were privileged in some way. For example, the father of psychoanalysis, Sigmund Freud, had many advantages as a child. He was firstborn and enjoyed special attention from his mother, as well as from an especially loving nurse. He also showed great academic talent very early in life, and the adults around him responded positively to his giftedness. The young Freud did exceptionally well in school. At home, much of the family routine was tailored to suit his needs. He was not required to eat with the rest of the family but had a special room where he could eat alone and continue his studies. When he became annoyed because his sister was practicing piano, his father had the instrument removed from the house.

There is some evidence that Albert Einstein had some problems in childhood because he was not fond of the lockstep regimentation of the German schools of his day. He did poorly in subjects that did not pique his interest. Nevertheless, supplied with his family's and friends' support and encouragement, as well as with numerous books, young Einstein avidly learned subjects that interested him, especially mathematics and physics.

Pablo Picasso's father was a painter, and young Pablo began to draw before he learned to speak. Like Einstein, he disliked school and did poorly in academic subjects. His family began an extensive collection of his drawings and notebooks when he was nine, however. This collection reflects that he worked hard at perfecting his drawing ability and at abstracting from and experimenting with the forms he had mastered. In addition, it shows that his family consistently held his work in high esteem.

Igor Stravinsky's family belonged to the Russian landed gentry, and the atmosphere of his family home was both intellectual and musical. Stravinsky's father was an actor and opera singer, and the young Igor often went to concerts and operas. Almost from the beginning of his musical education, he had a penchant for creating his own improvisations and compositions, although his family and teachers did not encourage this particular activity.

The three other examples in Gardner's study were T. S. Eliot, whose poetry was pivotal in modernizing English letters; Mahatma Gandhi, the leader of India's anti-British revolution; and Martha Graham, who revolutionized American dance. All were raised in financially comfortable and intellectually supportive homes (although Gardner does not say that this finding should be generalized to every highly creative person).

Other studies of persons who have been eminent in their fields do not conclude, however, that financially privileged childhoods are prevalent in this population. Take, for example, the ninety-six people noted for their creative ability whom Csikszentmihalyi (1996) interviewed. This group included philosopher Mortimer Adler; astronomer Margaret Burbidge; psychologist Donald Campbell; biologist Barry Commoner; paleontologist, geologist, science historian, author, and teacher Steven Jay Gould; prizewinning author Madeleine L'Engle; psychologist Jane Loevinger; social scientist and adult development pioneer Bernice Neugarten; social scientist David Riesman; musician Oscar Peterson; and pediatrician, psychiatrist, author, and activist Benjamin Spock. Almost all of Csikszentmihalyi's interviewees described childhoods in which parents and families supported and encouraged their creative talents and efforts. Many of them, however, felt they had attained their achievements in spite of limited financial resources. Their parents had made numerous and sustained efforts to expose their children to learning and to the life of the mind. They also imbued their offspring with a solid sense of values—including self-respect, self-discipline, and especially honesty—in both their work and their dealings with others.

In his "psychohistorical" study of eminent people, Simonton (1994) produced a prodigious list of variables that, in his opinion, contribute to eminence:

○ Psychobiological factors, such as genes and ethnicity

○ Learning and cognition

○ Problem-solving strategies

○ Motivations

○ Early experience and the impact of aging

○ Intelligence

○ Personality traits

○ Psychopathology

○ Personal experience of violence and trauma

○ Public opinion

○ Attitudes and beliefs

○ Imitation, affiliation, group dynamics skills, and leadership

He found that each of these factors plays a role in the early lives of eminently creative people. Some evince a positive environment (intelligence, affiliation); others indicate obstacles that had to be surmounted (psychopathology, trauma).

The research briefly reviewed in this section indicates that some highly creative people have had privileged childhoods. Other people are creative in spite of, or perhaps because of, early hardships. The difference between these two groups may depend on other factors that were also present in their childhoods.

Other Factors That Affect Creative Ability

Studies like the ones produced by Ochse, Gardner, Csikszentmihalyi, and Simonton are of well-known creative individuals. By what criteria do we categorize a person as creative? To be awarded such a label, must a person's achievements bring national or international recognition? We do not think so. As Schank and Cleary (1995) point out, simply getting through a typical day in the modern world requires some degree of creativity. "These small acts of creativity, though they differ in scope, are not different in kind from the brilliant leaps of an Einstein. Creativity is commonplace in cognition, not an esoteric gift bequeathed only to a few" (p. 229). So what about more ordinary creativity, which may make a greater cumulative contribution to society than more famous achievements? What other factors are involved?

Most researchers in cognitive science agree that no single process can be identified as the one kind of thinking that leads to creativity. Instead, creative thinking consists of combinations and patterns of the same cognitive processes that are used in ordinary pursuits (Perkins, 1981). Thinking and producing creatively do not necessarily involve a major restructuring of acquired knowledge. Quite often, these processes use reproductive methods—that is, the application of past methods to a present task (Weisberg, 1995). Most humans are far more alike than different in their cognitive abilities, and individual differences in creativity often depend on acquired knowledge and the way in which that knowledge is used (Ward, Finke, & Smith, 1995; Smith, Ward, & Finke, 1995a, 1995b). According to Bailin (1994), rather than being mysterious, irrational, or unique, creativity involves "the excellent use of our ordinary processes of thinking" (p. 85). In fact, it is even possible for some people who have been identified as learning disabled to be quite creative (Torrance, 1995a).

Although the details of how the human brain works neurobiologically are still not fully understood, there is so far no evidence that the structures (as opposed to the functions) in the brains of highly creative people are significantly different from those of more ordinary individuals (Gardner & Wolf, 1994; Herrmann, 1991). Although creativity is often thought of as being parallel to intelligence, it is different from intelligence in that it encompasses much more than cognitive functioning (Feldhusen & Goh, 1995).

A classic study by Getzels and Jackson (1962) showed that intelligence in the normal range was sufficient for high-level creativity and that, above an IQ of 120, creativity and intelligence were not correlated. Recent research has continued to confirm that extraordinary intelligence is not necessary for creativity and, in some cases, may even be a hindrance (Csikszentmihalyi, 1994; de Bono, 1992, Gardner, 1988a; Gardner & Wolf, 1994). It is now clear that such noncognitive factors as personality traits, brain function, intrinsic motivation, and the ability to recognize and act on opportunity are also involved.

Hence, this book is not primarily about extraordinarily creative geniuses. In fact, the ideas presented here are generally not restricted to highly creative persons. Instead, this book describes creativity as a cognitive, attitudinal, personal, and genetic trait that every person has to some degree. Newborn infants do not exhibit creativity. Clearly it is a trait that develops over time. Our goal is to review the best research thoroughly to explain as well as possible how people develop creativity. Our major premise is that all people may be helped to move from their present level of creative ability to a much higher one. The greater a person's initial ability, the more she or he may hope to grow. Although this is not a self-help book, studying the principles presented here should help all intelligent people make significant gains in their creative ability. The best way to cultivate creativity, we have found, is to learn more about the components that comprise it. An improvement in creative contributions is almost certain to result from this knowledge.

The Biopsychosocial Point of View

One of the main reasons we have written this book is to publicize the advances being made in creativity research and theory by applying the principles of the biopsychosocial perspective. This view of human behavior is based on the belief that all human capacities have biological, psychological, and social elements. This perspective, we believe, comes closer than others to producing causal explanations that will stand the test of time. Now, we will briefly introduce our own biopsychosocial model of the creative process. Then, after summarizing research in each of the areas that make up the model in the next ten chapters, we will describe it in much more detail in Chapter Twelve.

The biopsychosocial outlook is an enhancement of the long-held premise that all of human nature is created through genetic and environmental processes. The biopsychosocial model offers a better solution to the old "nature versus nurture" controversy. More sophisticated research designs and measurement techniques have made us aware of the complex interactions of human functioning. From this newer standpoint, three interacting factors—biological, psychological, and social elements—are involved in virtually all human abilities. Biological elements range from the role our genes play in our development to adult health issues. Psychological elements include all aspects of cognitive and personality development. Social elements involve such influences as family, school, peers, and culture. The biopsychosocial position is being featured more and more in all human sciences research.

The list below offers examples of the model's components. As this table shows, every single example affects and is affected not only by the element under which it is listed but also by the other two elements. This concept of multidirectional interaction is central to the model. As diverse as these elements are, each nevertheless plays some role in the creative act at some time in the creator's life.

Biological: fertilization, pregnancy, handedness, temperament, physical development, motor development, health, puberty, menopause

Psychological: personality, information processing, problem solving, motivation, perceptual development, language development, moral development, self-efficacy, body image

Social: maternal attachment, sibling relationships, success in school, friendships, media influences, medical interventions, cultural stresses, marital relationships, atmosphere in the workplace

Biopsychosocial research is new, however. In most areas of social science (including creativity), it is necessary to review a literature that, until recently, has been almost entirely composed of studies with biological, psychological, or social emphases. This means that we will mostly report research results that have been broken down into one of these constituent parts. This research has been conducted by specialists in such diverse fields as molecular biology and cognitive psychology.

Some people strenuously object to studying creativity by analyzing its components. Take, for instance, an experience that this book's senior author had some years ago. He was writing a book on creative thinking and, hoping to receive suggestions on it, he sent the manuscript to a colleague who was noted for her talents as a composer and a writer. She returned it with a short but blistering review: "Who do you think you are to assume that you or anyone else is capable of explaining the mysterious intricacies of the creative mind? Even the greatest geniuses in the arts and sciences shrink from so audacious a task!"

Eastern thinkers have long denigrated the analytical method. For instance, a Japanese Zen master compared Eastern and Western thought processes. As examples, he used two poems, each describing a lily. The one written by a Western poet spoke of its stalk, its petals, its stamen and pistil, its root system, and the corm from which it grows. This poet explained the lily's nature by theorizing about how its elemental parts contributed to and indeed defined its beauty. But to describe the flower in such a way, the poet had to uproot it and pull it apart. The Eastern poet, on the other hand, described only the flower's overall effect. This poet wrote of the flower's impact on the senses—its delicate curves, its satiny surface, its evocative odor. The Zen master maintained that only the Eastern poet could capture the flower's true essence, for the whole is greater than the sum of the parts.

Flowers are complex, it is true, but even they are not as complex as creative thought, the human mind's highest function. Nevertheless, at this relatively early stage of scientific investigation, we are forced to conduct our inquiries analytically. Only in this way can we gain an overview of the parameters of this convoluted subject. Validating the use of scientific principles to analyze creative products, Besemer and O'Quin offered this argument: "We do not want to kill the Muse by overscrutinizing her, but magic as an answer in science is less than satisfactory. Perhaps it is in the area of product analysis that the arts and sciences may join forces. In doing so we may enable ordinary folk to make their products more creative" (1993, p. 398).

We begin this book by looking separately at the three broad types of variables that make up creativity: its biological, psychological, and social elements. By the end of the book, however, when we have a clearer idea of the pieces that make up the puzzle, we will describe creativity more holistically.

A New Model of Creativity

Our primary goal in writing this book has been to determine the salient factors that collectively make creativity most likely to develop. From this compilation, we have constructed a model of the creative process. The model highlights five sources of creative ability, from the smallest environment (the brain cell) to the largest (the world culture). These sources are as follows:

- Biological features (including microneurons, hormones, IQ, regulatory genes, brain development, hemispheric dominance, and interhemispheric coordination)
- Personality characteristics (for example, tolerance of ambiguity, risk taking, and delay of gratification)

○ Cognitive traits (for instance, remote associations, and lateral thinking)

○ Microsocietal circumstances (such as relationships with family and friends and type of living quarters)

○ Macrosocietal conditions (including type of neighborhood and work, educational, religious, ethnic, legal, economic, and political environments)

This graduation from smallest to largest is not meant to represent the factors' relative importance. Each of the five plays a significant role. The roles differ according to the type of creativity involved, the various characteristics of the creative person (such as age and gender), and the stage of the creative process.

Each factor influences the others bidirectionally. For example, the flow of the neurotransmitter ACTH (see Chapter Ten) enhances the cognitive ability to produce high-quality remote associations (see Chapter Eight). Simultaneously, the cognitive activity of producing remote associations spurs the flow of ACTH. In fact, more than just influencing each other, the five main variables are embedded in each other uniquely in every individual. None of the variables can be understood except in the context of the others. Once again, take the example of remote associations. Whatever is remote about a person's associations cannot be objectively defined. Their peculiarity can only be truly understood in the context of the person's family background, ethnic group, socioeconomic class, and so on. For example, it is not surprising if a pilot understands the principles of aerodynamics; on the other hand, a farmer who discovers these principles through his own experiments would demonstrate a highly innovative mind!

Conversely, a term such as *family background* only has meaning when one considers each neighborhood's peculiarities. To take a simple case, being African American in an African American neighborhood is quite a different experience from living in a mainly Latino area. Thus, each variable contributes to the definition of the other variables.

At any one time, our creativity model is like a snapshot of a moment in a person's creative life. Lives don't stand still, however. The whole is always in flux, so the level of creative output will vary greatly with the passage of time. It is also clear that the atmosphere has a cumulative effect on any particular historical period. Could the Declaration of Independence have been written so brilliantly fifty years earlier or later? Probably not. It could not have come about unless the right thinkers—those with the necessary biological and psychological endowments—associated with each other under the right social circumstances.

In the process of summarizing creativity, we have discovered that this array of information has important implications for another explanatory model that is highly esteemed in the field—J. P. Guilford's creative problem-solving model. Briefly, Guilford's model is a five-step process of going from an unconscious awareness that a problem exists to producing a highly creative solution for it. The model recognizes that creativity seldom takes an orderly, sequential path. According to Guilford's view, there are several points in the course of creative thinking at which the thinker may abort the search for truly useful and appropriate solutions. His model is noted for its insight into the variables that interfere with the quest for high-level creativity.

Our model, we believe, suggests concepts that enrich each of Guilford's five stages of problem solving. We feel that understanding how biopsychosocial factors affect the creative problem-solving process as Guilford described is the best way to improve one's own level of creative functioning. Insight into this complex procedure does not only affect the conscious mind; as we will demonstrate, it also permeates unconscious thinking in such a way that more original and useful ideas are likely to occur. The application of our model to Guilford's is also detailed in Chapter Twelve.

The Organization of This Book

Before we examine research and theories about the elements of creativity, we think it will prove helpful to provide readers with a history of the concept. Thus in Chapter Two, we chronicle the strikingly different ways in which creativity has been viewed over the centuries.

In the chapters that follow, we categorize information according to the three factors of our model: social, psychological (personality and cognition), and biological. We will do this in the reverse order from that implied in the word *biopsychosocial,* but we believe that proceeding from the very large to the very small will make it easier to understand the roles that these elements play in the process.

When one considers the social aspect of creativity, the family immediately comes to mind. Early theorists recognized that "genius," as they called it, tends to run in families. They mistakenly assumed that this was solely due to genetic inheritance. We know now that there are elaborate systems and subsystems within all families that powerfully affect the ways in which a person thinks, feels, and behaves. In Chapter Three, we look closely at the role of the family.

As we will demonstrate, the environment does not merely affect individuals; rather, individuals are "embedded" in their environments. Ultimately, one cannot understand human behavior except within the context of the circumstances in which that behavior takes place. Chapter Four expands on the role that the social context plays in creativity. This includes schools and the larger cultural environment, as well as the historical events that can powerfully influence the creative process.

From social variables, we turn to those that are considered to be mainly psychological. In Chapter Five, we look at traits that contribute to the creative personality. A review of the literature reveals that more than fifty traits have been studied for their contributions. Based on our judgment of the quality of this research, we have chosen ten characteristics for which we found the most solid evidence of a contribution to creativity.

Chapter Six examines the special contribution of self-control. Contrary to the popular stereotype, creative individuals are usually not slovenly, wrapped up in their own deep thoughts, or given to long periods of unproductive "writer's block." In fact, they tend to be among the most self-controlled people. In this chapter, research on this fascinating aspect of the creative nature is explored.

Theorists have asked not only what traits matter most but also how they are formed. In Chapter Seven, we examine several well-established explanations of the formation of the creative personality.

Closely associated with personality traits are the cognitive processes typical of the creative person. Research on these mental operations has become quite sophisticated in recent decades. Chapter Eight considers a number of new models, based both on the older schools of thought such as behaviorism and information processing.

As a category within the field of cognition, the specific ability known as creative problem solving has received a great deal of attention from researchers. Given the exponential growth in the number, complexity, and interactivity of problems in our world as we move into the twenty-first century, there are few human capacities that are more vital to understand thoroughly. Chapter Nine focuses on problem solving.

The next two chapters treat biological aspects. Chapter Ten considers such physical influences as the roles that neurotransmitters, memory, and microneurons play in facilitating original thinking. Chapter Eleven deals with laterality (the domination of various functions by the brain's right and left hemispheres), as well as interhemispheric coordination.

In the last chapter, we move away from our elemental examination of the three causative components of creativity to a more integrated point of view. We believe that this book makes two major contributions to a new, more integrated model of creativity. The model we espouse is based on the concepts of biopsychosocial causation and contextual explanation. The goal of this model will be nothing less than a succinct integration of the collected wisdom gathered in the preceding chapters. The second contribution is an elaboration of its applications to the five stages of Guilford's creative problem-solving model. We are convinced that readers who familiarize themselves with this body of information will have not only a clear grasp of the interplay of factors that make up creative ability but also the best chance of significantly enhancing their own creative powers.

2

A BRIEF HISTORY OF THE
CONCEPT OF CREATIVITY

WHAT IS CREATIVITY, and how does it work? Answers to these two questions have ranged as far as creative thought itself often does. In one sense, the story is simple. From earliest times until the Renaissance, it was widely believed that all desirable innovations were inspired by the gods or by God (depending on the creator's religious orientation). Sometime during the Renaissance, this view began to give way to the idea that creativity is a matter of genetic inheritance. In the beginning of this century, the debate turned to an argument over the relative contributions of nature versus nurture. In recent decades, there has been growing acceptance of biopsychosocial theory—the belief that all creative acts are born of a complex interaction among biological, psychological, and social forces. The way these changes in the popular conception of creativity emerged, however, is far from simple and is not without controversy.

Prior to the nineteenth century, very little was written about the nature of creative thinking. Although there had been extensive theorizing about other human capacities, conjecture about the origins of creative productivity was impeded by the belief that it is too obscure, multifaceted, and ethereal to allow for intellectual analysis of its process. The first effective scholarly inquiry was undertaken only a little more than a century ago. Research on the creative process was deterred not so much by ignorance as by the conviction that the nature of innovative thinking was already understood; it was thought to be a gift from above.

15

The Bicameral Mind

The earliest explanation, one that is largely inferred from the writings of Homer and the Bible's authors, was that the mind is composed of two entirely separate chambers. (This concept is unrelated to the current knowledge that the brain has two hemispheres.) The first scholarly treatise to document this view was written by psychologist Julian Jaynes. He coined the term *bicameral mind* as a label for this phenomenon. Throughout early human history, Jaynes posits, people uniformly believed that the gods controlled the chamber of the mind in which new thoughts occur. Thus, they thought that all creative ideas come from the gods, usually through the mediation of a muse, a sort of intermediary for the gods. A person who felt a creative impulse would invoke the appropriate muse for assistance: Calliope for epic and heroic poetry, Clio for history, Erato for love poetry, Euterpe for music and lyric poetry, Melpomene for tragedy, Polyhymnia for songs or hymns to the gods, Terpsichore for dance, Thalia for comedy, and Urania for astronomy. A major function of the mind, then, was to serve as a receptacle for supernatural innovations. It was believed that the gods projected their ideas from Mount Olympus by inspiring (literally, "breathing into") this first chamber.

People deeply believed that this was the origin of creative thought, as reflected in this quotation from the epic Greek bard Hesiod. He described what some muses said to him one day: "'Listen, you country bumpkin, you swag-bellied yahoo, we know how to tell many lies that pass for the truth, and we know, when we wish, to tell the truth itself.' So spoke Zeus' daughters, masters of word-craft, and from a laurel in full bloom they plucked a branch, and gave it to me as a staff, and breathed into me divine song, that I might spread fame of past and future, and commanded me to hymn the race of the deathless gods, but always begin and end my song with them."

The purpose of the mind's second chamber was to express inspiration through the more ordinary mechanisms of speech and writing. It was considered to be the public representative of the first chamber. The second chamber was also used to express such mundane thoughts as "I am hungry."

The workings of the bicameral process are exemplified in Homer's tales, in which the characters were able to accomplish great acts, but only as directed by the gods. In their most important achievements, Homer's heroes did as they were inspired to do, carrying out the strategies given them. This was no passive act, however. They could choose not to follow the inspiration they received, and some did. Thus, when they effectively followed a god's instructions in battle, they were credited with great bravery but not with the idea for the act. When they wrote a beautiful poem or play, they were admired for having produced it, but mainly because they had been chosen for the honor.

Many early thinkers, Plato and Aristotle among them, believed that the "creativity" chamber also housed madness when the muse's spirit was present. Hans Eysenck (1995) has cited Plutarch's description of Archimedes, the great geometrician: "how, continually bewitched by some familiar siren dwelling within him, he forgot his food and neglected the care of his body, and how, when he was dragged by force, as often happened, to the place for bathing and anointing, he would draw geometrical figures in the oil with which his body was anointed, being overcome by great pleasure and in truth inspired of the Muse" (p. 126).

This "madness" was not the same as insanity, however. As Eysenck (1995) points out, "In Latin there is no linguistic distinction between *madness* and *inspiration*. *Mania* and *furor* are terms that cover many different non-rational states like anger, passion, inspiration and insanity" (p. 130).

Perhaps the first to challenge the concept of the bicameral mind was the philosopher Aristotle in the fourth century B.C.E. Although he agreed with his predecessors that inspiration involved madness, he suspected that great insights begin as the result of a person's own thoughts, through a process that has become known as *associationism*. This view proposes that the mind consists entirely of ideas (words, images, formulas, and so forth), each of which is associated with other ideas. Thinking, therefore, is simply a process of moving from one idea to another by way of a chain of associations. Aristotle suggested that people form mental associations between events and objects that occur in the same place or at the same time and that are similar or opposite.

For example, with the associationist view, one might speculate that the prehistoric builder who thought of moving huge blocks of temple stones by repeatedly placing wooden rollers in front of the stones got the idea by remembering the childhood experience of playing with toy blocks and sticks. Even though the situations are different, the method of transportation is similar. Another example would be an imaginative chef's ability to create a delicious new dish by combining ingredients from another recipe in a different way. At any rate, Aristotle did not spend much time pursuing this insight, and belief in the bicameral mind lived on for several more centuries.

Jaynes states that by the end of the medieval period, speech, writing, and other mental operations grew more complex. As a result, it was recognized that thought could actually originate within a person's mind, and the notion of the bicameral mind eventually broke down. In its place came the idea of self-awareness and, thus, insight into the human potential to create. After many divergencies, this insight provided the opportunity for the development of scientific discovery.

For this monumental achievement to occur, however, other innovations were required. So many of these innovations come to us from the Greeks in the three centuries before the ascendancy of the Roman Empire, and so few come from the medieval Europeans. Both cultures accepted the concept of the bicameral mind, so why was there such a great disparity in the creative output of the two periods? It appears that although they shared the conscious concept of creativity (the "gift from above" view), the two cultures held very different unconscious concepts.

The Greeks

During the so-called golden age (500 to 200 B.C.E.), the Greeks invented most of our Western literary and political forms, developed many innovations in the arts, and shaped the disciplines of history, medicine, mathematics, and philosophy. Only portions of their written output still exist, perhaps about a fifth. Not one of their public buildings and only a few of their statues remain standing. Yet their speeches, plays, and histories are still considered to be worth reading in the world's colleges and universities, and their buildings and sculpture are emulated more than any other. Historian Daniel Boorstin compares the Greek civilization to others: "Inquiry for its own sake, merely to know more, philosophy on the Greek model, had no place in [a worldview such as the Confucian, Incan, Buddhist, or Christian] tradition. Greek philosophers, beginning with Thales, were men of speculative temperament. What was the world made of? What are the elements and processes by which the world is transformed? Greek philosophy and science were born together, of the passion to know" (1992, p. 46).

To what may we attribute this flourishing of passionate imagination? Historian Moses Hadas (1965) offered an insightful hypothesis. He suggested that the Greeks were prolifically creative because they were free of many of the cognitive restraints that afflicted other major civilizations. It is true that they were economically secure and had ample assistance in their daily lives by virtue of their slave system. Hadas argued, however, that their main asset was not having the religious beliefs that fettered most other societies. They believed that their ideas were inspired by the gods, but they thought these gods existed in proliferation and cared little about the lives of humans. Although they were concerned about displeasing their gods, the Greeks did not think that self-expression would distress the deities. After all, the more beautiful or original their creative product was, the more likely that it was given to them by their pleasure-loving gods.

In making this case, Hadas compared classical Greece and its pagan beliefs to medieval Europe and its fundamentalist Christian orientation. He argued that it was not so much early Christianity's restrictive teachings or its "otherworldliness" that inhibited creative thought throughout the medieval period (the end of the fourth through the twelfth centuries) but its claim to exclusive validity. In its struggle to gain acceptance and then dominance, early Christianity was harsh in its rejection of deviant ideas, which were considered heretical. Beginning with the execution of Arias and extending through the use of several forms of Inquisition, the Church dealt harshly with the progenitors of such thinking.

The polytheistic Greek religion, on the other hand, allowed the individual to choose among various classes of deities. The scope of individual autonomy was infinite. In addition, the Greeks believed that the gods' actions were unpredictable; they could never presume to know what the gods thought or felt.

Hadas (1965) buttressed his case for a sharp distinction between the attitudes of Greek paganism and Christianity by pointing out what Greek paganism did *not* have:

- Churches
- Family allegiance to one point of view (members of Greek families were free to choose any god to worship, or none at all)
- Strong prejudices against older or newer beliefs
- Dogma
- Sacred books revealed by a spiritual being detailing a dogma
- Priests
- Claims to infallibility
- Epic religious stories (for example, the Garden of Eden, the escape from Egypt)
- A clear concept of sin
- True villains (because many religious views were simultaneously acceptable, persons with diametrically opposed views could still respect each other; there were no heretics)

Perhaps the clearest view of the Greek ideal can be seen in that culture's emulation of heroes, as compared with Christian attitudes toward saints.

A Greek hero was "any deceased person worthy of a cult, that is, of receiving offerings of flowers or wine on his special anniversary" (Hadas, 1965, p. 201). The offerings were not meant to appease him or her but to serve the people. For example, Hadas noted, "We eat cherry pies and chocolate hatchets" on George Washington's birthday "to serve ourselves, not our first president" (p. 201). The main distinction, he argued, is that "a man approaches sainthood to the degree that he *suppresses* the impulses of ordinary humanity and assimilates himself to a pattern outside humanity. A man becomes a hero to the degree that he emphasizes his human attributes" (italics his). Hence, Greek pagans were encouraged to perceive excellence as a more readily attainable goal than medieval Christians were.

The single "sacred source" that the Greeks did have was Homer's poetry. This was the one origin of information that all Greek children studied, and it was therefore accepted with as little question as we accept the facts of the multiplication table. Their immersion in Homer's works apparently explains the relentless drive toward excellence in all aspects of Greeks' lives and the quality of their production in the arts and crafts. A person composed music or wrote poetry not merely for self-expression or profit but as an entry in the national contest for society's approbation. The main objective was honor. Even the potters who fashioned the cheapest household bowls took pains to sign their work. When the vases were artfully crafted, both potter and painter signed the bottom. All Greeks knew who designed the Parthenon, but the builders of the great Christian cathedrals remain anonymous. Cathedral architects chose not to put their names on their work because the work was for the greater honor and glory of God, so it would be prideful and disrespectful to display authorship.

From Homer through the Epicureans (who believed, as many Romans did, that seeking pleasure and avoiding pain are the supreme goods), we can see that significant and persistent value was placed on the self-sufficient individual. To quote Hadas (1965, p. 208), "The Homeric warrior [knew that] what was decreed for him by a power outside himself he could not alter and need not bother to understand; he was definitely the captain of his soul, but made no pretense of being master of his fate. So the hero of tragedy knew that he must behave well as a man; the disasters that might befall him had no relationship with his own excellence."

Because the gods played so small a role in their daily existence, the Greeks were free to do whatever they wished, as long as it was honorable. A heavenly source may have breathed life into a Greek person's creative process, but the credit went to the individual responsible for the creation. Hence the fabulous three-hundred-year-long cornucopia of creativity that was the golden age.

The Medieval Europeans

A squelching of free thought began in the late Hellenistic period as pagan Rome came to accept its all-powerful emperors' claims that they themselves had become gods. Under them, Rome became famous for its "universal" codes of behavior, which covered one's duty to the state. On the other hand, the Romans were not so different from the Greeks in their attitudes toward religious imperatives. It was not until the rise of Christianity, with its fervent devotees, that we see a strict code of behavior, enforced by powers in this world who were exclusively backed by the Power of the next.

This extensive change in philosophy was accompanied, and probably abetted by, another sweeping event. Barbarian tribes began attacking the Roman Empire from several sides in the fifth century and systematically ravaged huge territories. This onslaught eventually destroyed faith in the Roman belief systems and prepared the ground for a new one.

The most notable group of invaders, the Vandals, deeply penetrated the empire and nearly destroyed Rome. The Vandals were a Teutonic tribe that governed their North African kingdom from 439 to 534. Other tribes, such as the Huns, Vikings, and Visigoths, also invaded and pillaged large tracts of the empire. While rampaging the lands, especially the cities they wished to conquer, they destroyed any books or other written materials they could find. They had a savage disregard for intellectual or spiritual enlightenment, being interested only in the spoils of battle and the domination of their victims.

An exception to this was Alaric. Along with his horde of Goths, he smashed through Rome's gates at midnight on August 24, 410. He prevented his men from torching everything, saying that although he wished to destroy the Roman Empire, he had no desire to harm the many Christians who inhabited the city. Soon, a few treasured works hidden in the city were spirited off to Muslim strongholds. Throughout the medieval period, other precious tomes were rescued by an unlikely source—the reclusive Christian monks based on secluded islands off Ireland's west coast. They secretly made it their business to locate the hidden writing of Christians as well as pagan thinkers. Not only did the monks preserve these works but they also painstakingly and artistically copied the writings by hand in an attempt to perpetuate these obscure pockets of intellectualism.

The efforts of these monks must be considered a critical contribution to human creativity, for although the marauders were frequently successful in ravaging the lands, they were never able to destroy the words that would stimulate thinkers in centuries to come.

The work of these monks is an example of how the Dark Ages were not totally devoid of creative achievements. The famous *Book of Kells,* which the monks produced over many years, is an example of the level of their creativity. Another such example is the work of Saint Augustine, bishop of Hippo, early in the fifth century. In his brilliant treatise *The City of God,* written between 413 and 426, he argued that Plato and the Greeks were wrong to believe that life is a series of repetitious cycles. He offered the life of Christ and the subsequent new view of humanity offered by Christianity as arguments against that position. He was probably one of the first to discredit the idea that all creative ideas come straight from God, devout though he was. He was, in fact, awed by the creative powers of his fellows, although he couldn't resist chastising them for the purposes to which they often put such gifts: "Man's invention has brought forth so many and such rare sciences and arts (partly necessary, partly voluntary) that the excellency of his capacity makes the rare goodness of his creation apparent, even when he goes about things that are either superfluous or pernicious, and shows from what an excellent gift he has those inventions and practices of his.

"What millions of inventions has he against others, and for himself in poisons, arms engines, stratagems, and such like" (cited in Boorstin, 1992, p. 51).

Further evidence of medieval creativity was the work of the Roman Boethius, who served as counselor to Theodoric, king of the Visigoths. This ingenious scholar single-handedly produced the quadrivium, which offered explanations of the four "mathematical" disciplines: arithmetic, music, geometry, and astronomy. Together with the trivium (grammar, rhetoric, and logic), which others later assembled, the quadrivium formed the basic curriculum for the handful of scholars who struggled to keep knowledge alive during the Middle Ages.

Such contributions notwithstanding, the situation in the Western world in the fifth century was rather grim, as Christopher Dawson (1954) so succinctly described it. He disagreed, however, with Hadas's position that fundamentalism primarily caused the lack of creative output. After all, Dawson argued, the Muslims were as rigidly fundamentalist as the Christians, and yet the Muslims made many creative contributions. In his view, the creative output of the Greek and Muslim cultures was superior to that of the medieval Christian culture because numerous invasions by outsiders reduced the Christians to having a simple agrarian society. People may have allowed the Church to have such a tight grip on their minds because it afforded a consoling relief from the fear of vandalism and starvation, but, as is so often the case at the macrosocial level, establishing causation is perilous. For example, the medieval Church's fundamentalist posture and the low level of creative output in medieval times might have both resulted from the destabilized political and economic environments brought about by the widespread vandalism. As Dawson stated:

> While there is no reason to suppose that the Dark Ages were dark [solely] because they were religious, it is nonetheless difficult to exaggerate their darkness, both as regards scientific knowledge and the completeness of the break between the science of antiquity and the science of modern times. Here the traditional view is justified, and it only becomes false when this judgment is extended from the early to the late Middle Ages so as to make the scientific development of Western Europe begin with the Renaissance. In reality the recovery of Greek science and the restoration of the contact with the main tradition of Greek thought was one of the most striking achievements of medieval culture. And it is even more than this: it is the turning point in the history of Western civilization, for it marks the passing of the age-long supremacy of oriental and eastern Mediterranean culture and the beginning of the intellectual leadership of the West. It is, in fact, a far more important and original achievement than anything that the Renaissance itself accomplished. For the Renaissance scholars, in spite of their originality, were carrying on a tradition that had never been entirely lost: the tradition of humanism and classical scholarship that was founded on Cicero and Quintillian. But the rediscovery of Greek thought by the medieval scholars was a new fact in the history of the West: it was the conquest of the new world [pp. 246–247].

The Renaissance and the Beginnings of Humanism

As dark as the medieval period was, nothing that happened during its eight hundred years could compete with the catastrophe of the Black Death. By the time it ended around 1350, it killed one-third of the Western population. As a result, however, a new emphasis on the individual developed. With this shift came a loosening of reflexive obedience to clerical rule. Because workers had become so scarce, they also found that they were in a much stronger bargaining position vis-à-vis the feudal hierarchy. This change shook up the entire social structure and brought about a widespread challenge to the belief system of the previous millennium.

For example, artisans began to win acclaim and patronage. This is similar to the attitude of the ancient Greeks, who exulted in all their creations from the minimal to the most spectacular. Painters once again signed their work, abandoning pious humility for personal pride in their craft. Guilds were formed to foster the growth of individual crafts and skilled trades. The principal source of patronage was no longer the Church but rather wealthy princes and merchants whose pride in artistic possessions was no longer considered sinful. In their work, poets, painters, and philosophers still emphasized God's glory, but as it was reflected in the countless joys of *human* existence.

At this time, there was also widening criticism of what has been considered the acme of Church power—the Inquisition. This tribunal, with its witch-hunt for heretics and its infamously murderous auto-da-fé ("prove your love of God by admitting your guilt!"), had exerted a chilling influence over independent thought for many years. As the Inquisition lost its power, the Holy Roman Empire declined in importance and the papacy was weakened by schism. Among the major causes of this breakdown were the burnings of such popular Church critics as Jan Hus and Girolamo Savonarola and the publication of Martin Luther's ninety-five theses, which began the Protestant Reformation. There was a reformation of the Church itself at this time, but it came too late to stave off the winds of change. Simultaneously, the national monarchies increased in strength and prestige. At the beginning of the 1400s, Europe's population was better off financially than at any time since before the fall of Rome.

The attitudes in this era mark the inauguration of humanistic philosophy, the belief that we ourselves are responsible for much of what happens to us. This view was not generally antimonotheistic but rather co-monotheistic. The resurgence of creative production on so grand a scale was inspiring and piqued the curiosity of those who wished to understand the complexities of minds that were capable of such accomplishments.

The term *renaissance* originally referred to the revival of the classical age's values and artistic styles. By the 1500s, the word acquired a broader meaning; the Renaissance was becoming known as one of the great ages of human cultural development, a distinct period signaling the dawn of the modern era. Essentially, the rigid social order that had so dominated European societies broke down, leading to cultural and intellectual advances. The style of Renaissance music, literature, and arts is quite distinctive. Ultimately, this intellectual and spiritual revolution motivated people to release themselves from medieval traditions. The historian Nicolas Berdyaev describes the period this way: "In the creative upsurge of the Renaissance there occurred such a powerful clash between pagan and Christian elements in human nature as had never occurred before. In this lies the significance of the Renaissance for the world and for eternity. It revealed the activity of the pagan nature of man in creativeness, and at the same time the activity of his Christian nature" (1954, p. 116).

Christian ideas had been accepted for a long time, but pagan ideas were rapidly being reintroduced. This came about through the influx of scholars from Muslim countries and the circulation of magnificent books that the Irish monks had produced and kept safe for centuries. Spurred by these "new" old ideas, the best minds experienced a sense of freedom that encouraged an inquiry into everything, even the most cherished beliefs. From this resurgence sprang the scientific, artistic, philosophical, and political revolutions that came to be called the Age of Enlightenment.

The Age of Enlightenment and a Flourishing Humanism

By the beginning of the eighteenth century, the spate of knowledge born of the work of such giants as Copernicus, Galileo, Hobbes, Locke, and Newton solidified belief in the scientific process. Faith in *humanism,* or humans' ability to solve problems through their own mental efforts, grew rapidly. Spiritual works such as the Bible waned in their authority; some scholars viewed them with impunity as literary efforts rather than as the word of God. The right of individuals to come to their own conclusions began to gain acceptability.

In 1767, the first major inquiry into the creative process took place. William Duff was one of the first to write about the qualities of original genius (as distinguished from talent, which is productive but does not necessarily break new ground), and his insights were strikingly similar to more modern attempts to unravel the creative mind's mysteries. What set Duff apart as an important figure in the study of creativity is that he was the first to suspect the process's biopsychosocial nature.

Duff was principally interested in determining the cognitive traits that caused the variance he observed in people's accomplishments. He was concerned not only with hereditary influences but also with the eras in which his subjects lived. As we shall see, it would be quite some time before others would agree that social influences play a role in creativity.

The main qualities that Duff considered fundamental to genius were imagination, judgment, and taste. Any one of these three characteristics alone would not result in Shakespeare's caliber of genius; rather, he thought that the combination of the three ingredients was essential. He argued that imagination contributed the most, in that the mind not only reflects on its own functions but also organizes its ideas into an infinite variety of new associations and combinations. Duff felt that all discoveries and inventions in science and art were the result of imagination. Judgment, he asserted, is the ability that evaluates ideas or options and that acts as a counterbalance to the imagination's influences. Taste supplements judgment, adding a sense of aesthetics to the cold, evaluative nature of judgment.

The publication of Duff's work was one of several events that set the stage for scientific research on human thought, which would later prove essential to the demystification of the creative act. His brilliant analyses created an atmosphere whose hallmark was that people questioned everything. The act of asking hard questions was itself considered "enlightened." Here is a brief list of major Enlightenment milestones that helped break the path for this more open mind-set:

○ The spread of social and philosophical opposition to Church and state authority

○ The institution of the British Royal Society, the first research organization

○ A plethora of developments in the natural sciences

○ Separation of the idea of creativity from more ordinary notions of genius (as in "He has a genius for poetry")

○ The doctrine of individualism

○ Three enormously influential books: Francis Bacon's *Advancement of Learning,* Adam Smith's *The Wealth of Nations,* and Thomas Malthus's *Essay on Population*

Robert Albert and Mark Runco have summed up the ways in which this period contributed to a new concept of creativity: "Tedious and tangential as they were at times, nevertheless, the debates through the eighteenth century eventually came to four important acceptable distinctions, which were to become the bedrock of our present-day ideas about creativity: 1. Genius was divorced from the supernatural; 2. Genius, although exceptional, was a potential for every individual; 3. Talent and genius were to be distinguished from each other; 4. Their potential and exercise depend on the political atmosphere at the time (this last distinction would not be recognized for many years, however)" (1997, p. 26).

The Debate About Associationist and Gestalt Views

Throughout the nineteenth century, there was a major shift in the conception of the creative act. With the renunciation of divine inspiration as the sole cause of creativity came a transmigration to what may be the opposite extreme—the idea that great men (decades would pass before the recognition of women of genius) are great because they have inherited from their forebears a serendipitous combination of genes, which produce a mind of intensely fine acuity. This assumption grew as medical science produced evidence that physical traits are heritable. Moreover, this concept seemed to jibe with the recognition that high-level mental ability runs in families.

For a while, a debate raged over just how specific inherited traits might be. Jean Lamarck believed that learned traits could be passed on genetically. Charles Darwin demonstrated that he was wrong, confirming that genetic change occurs not as the result of practicality but through random mutation over aeons.

So what explanation did nineteenth-century science offer as to how geniuses formulate their brilliant ideas? A subordinate question was, does a genius search for knowledge elementally (from a problem's parts or elements to the whole) or holistically (from a sense of the whole problem to its parts)? Two scientific camps formed. They have become known as the associationist (a branch of behaviorism) and the Gestalt positions. From this seemingly academic debate came one of the greatest advances in our understanding of the creative act itself.

Research on the history of creativity often cites Sir Francis Galton (1870, 1879) as having conducted the first scientific research on the nature of genius. He was the second great associationist, after Aristotle, and was highly respected in nineteenth-century England as a multifaceted scientist. He was a eugenicist, meteorologist, evolutionist, geographer, anthropologist, and statistician, and he probably should be credited as the world's first cognitive psychologist. Building on his friend Charles Darwin's groundbreaking insights about evolution, natural selection (survival of the fittest), general diversity, and adaptation, he made inestimable contributions to our thinking about creativity.

One of his most interesting experiments was his attempt to measure the workings of his own mind. The descriptions of his findings have been insightfully analyzed by Crovitz in his book *Galton's Walk* (1970). The walk referred to is one that Galton took down London's Pall Mall while meticulously recording every thought that crossed his mind. His goal was to "show how the whole of these associated ideas, though they are for the most part exceedingly fleeting and obscure, and barely cross the threshold of our consciousness, may be seized, dragged into daylight, and recorded. I shall then treat the records of some experiments statistically, and shall make out what I can of them" (Galton, 1879, p. 148).

He was awestricken by his tabulations: "The general impression they left upon me is like that which many of us have experienced when the basement of our house happens to be under thorough sanitary repairs, and we realize for the first time the complex systems of drains and gas- and water-pipes, flues, and so forth, upon which our comfort depends, but which are usually hidden out of sight, and of whose existence, so long as they acted well, we had never troubled ourselves" (Galton, 1879, p. 149).

His most important conclusion: "The actors on my mental stage were indeed very numerous, but by no means as numerous as I had imagined. They now seemed to be something like the actors in theatres where large processions are represented, who march off one side of the stage, and going round by the back, come again at the other" (Galton, 1879, p. 162).

At first glance, this conclusion may not seem earthshaking, but Galton had actually discovered two principles that have had an enormous impact on our thinking about thinking. The first is his notion of *recurrence,* which holds that the conscious mind is like a plenum. A *plenum* is a space that is completely filled with objects. An example would be the ball-bearing ring that supports the fluid motion of a wheel. Little balls fill two concentric rings and roll around in the wheel's hub, making the wheel spin much more freely than it otherwise would. Each ball can only move by taking the place of the ball in front of it. There is nowhere else for it to go. The only possible movement is cyclical.

Galton argued that this is what happens in the conscious mind. It is always filled at any one point in time, and thoughts can only follow each other around. He found this positive, because otherwise, he believed, conscious thought would be random and would have no order. Orderliness is essential to logical thought.

If this were the only way the mind could process information, however, there could be no new thoughts and therefore no creativity. The second and more important discovery Galton made was that new input can come into this plenum from another part of the mind. The source of this input is the unconscious, the mind's "basement." Most important, the unconscious can be made conscious through association of thoughts. Thus was discovered the critical notion of *free association.* The concept was certainly revolutionary: "Ideas in the conscious mind are linked to those in the unconscious mind by threads of similarity" (Galton, 1879, p. 162). At the turn of the century, Sigmund Freud and his associates would bring this notion to fruition.

Of particular note in Galton's research is his use of statistical analyses in his study of individual differences among geniuses. The modern statistical principles of correlation and regression evolved from Galton's findings, gleaned from biographical sources for his subjects in various fields and from their families. This methodology was incorporated into the studies of other researchers who pursued the study of creativity at the onset of the twentieth century and in the years to follow.

Galton was convinced that mental capacities are inherited. He believed that these capacities follow certain laws of transmission that can be determined through observation. In an attempt to show that genius is inherited in the same way that physical features are inherited, he examined the hereditary nature of mental abilities in people who had been recognized by society as "geniuses." In Galton's view, geniuses possess a natural intellect and disposition that lead to this reputation and are urged on by some internal stimulus that strives to overcome any obstacles.

This definition of *genius* originated with Galton. Historian Jacques Barzun (1964, p. 147) then described several iterations in the meaning of *genius:*

> In ancient and medieval times, a genius or a demon was a person's guardian spirit, giving good or evil advice on daily affairs. Then genius came to mean a knack of doing a particular thing—a gifted person was said to "have a genius" for calculation or public speaking. It gradually acquired a more honorific sense. By the 1750s genius was defined by the poet Edward Young as "the power of accomplishing great things without the means generally reputed necessary to that end." This notion fitted Shakespeare's case, for he was thought lacking in discipline, learning and art. He had a wild, untutored genius.
>
> In the next generation came the subtle shift from "having" genius to "being" a genius, with no limitation such as Young included in his praise. A genius was now a fully conscious, competent and original "creator," and only two classes of artists were recognized: the geniuses and the non-geniuses, the second group being dismissed as "talents." Unable to create, they followed the path blazed by the geniuses.

Galton agreed with this last view. For him, genius resides in persons who inherit exceptional qualities, especially in the brain cells. He refused to believe that early experiences or the immediate environment played much of a role in the creative act.

Galton and his associates began to be opposed by a group of German theorists who were known collectively as Gestalt psychologists. They held that creative thinking results from the formation and alteration of *gestalts,* which is German for "mental patterns or forms." The elements of gestalts have complex interrelationships; they are not merely "associated" with each other. Great paintings are made up of elements, all of which are interrelated so that the whole is greater than the sum of the parts.

For example, creative musicians do not write down musical notes in hopes of achieving new associations. Rather, they form half an idea of a finished piece of music and then work backward to complete the idea. They develop an overview of the entire structure and then rearrange its parts. People often obtain creative solutions by seeing an existing gestalt in a new way. This can happen when they change the position from which they view a scene or problem or when the personal needs that affect perception change.

Gestaltists argued that being creative is much more complicated than merely associating ideas in new and different ways. They believed that the whole of any idea always amounts to more than the mere sum of its parts, and they referred to associationism as "brick-and-mortar" psychology. Gestalt psychology started with the work of von Ehrenfels in the latter half of the nineteenth century. It was originally founded on the concept of "innate ideas"—that is, thoughts that entirely originate in the conscious or unconscious mind and that do not depend on the senses for their existence.

As is often the case in scientific inquiry, the disagreements between the advocates of the associationist and Gestalt positions produce wonderful new insights into the process even today. In many ways, the current field of cognitive psychology represents an amalgam of these two positions. The struggle to understand the workings of genius coexisted with the zealous effort to reveal the workings of the brain itself. This endeavor also contributed to a new, more scientific understanding of the creative act.

Nineteenth-Century Knowledge of the Brain's Biology

It should be no surprise that our knowledge of the way the human brain works is quite recent in the history of medical research. Less than two hundred years ago, no one was sure that the various areas of the brain had isolable functions. The first person to suggest this was Franz Gall, a German anatomist, who did so early in the nineteenth century. His research led him to believe that speech is located in the frontal lobes, those sections of each hemisphere that are located toward the front of the head.

This is the doctrine of *cerebral localization*. Unfortunately, most scientists dismissed his report, because it included the argument that the skull's shape reflects the person's personality traits and that it would therefore be possible to study those traits by examining bumps on the head. This idea became known as *phrenology* and has long since been discredited.

Although most doctors branded Gall a quack, he did have some followers. Jean Bouillard, a French professor of medicine, offered a large sum of money to anyone who could produce a patient with damage to the frontal lobes but with no loss of speech. The knowledge of the brain's landscape was so primitive in those times, however, that the question remained unresolved for some years.

In 1861, the stalemate ended dramatically. A young French surgeon, Paul Broca, learned of cerebral localization at the meeting of the Society of Anthropology and remembered a patient of his who had long suffered from speech impairment and some right-side paralysis. Two days after the meeting, the man died. Broca quickly got permission to autopsy his brain and found what he was looking for—a region of tissue damage (a lesion) on his left frontal lobe. Some months later, a similar paralysis occurred in another patient, and frontal lobe lesions were again found. Broca brought this patient's brain with him to the next society meeting and created a furor. Many were impressed, but those who dismissed localization accused him of lying.

Interestingly, while everyone noted that in both cases the lesions were frontal, no one seemed to see the left-side link. Only after eight more autopsies did Broca publicly announce this finding. The notion that the brain's left side could more powerfully direct mental processes in some persons and that the right side could do this in others was put forth even later. This idea came about mostly because it was learned that equal degrees of brain lesion do not produce equal degrees of disruption. By 1868, John Hughlings Jackson, the eminent British neurologist, was guessing that one side might "lead" the other. Increasingly, there was evidence that the interactions between the brain's halves are complex, as well as different in various people. It was learned that the areas involved in speaking are not the same as areas given to understanding others' speech. The discovery of *apraxia* (the inability to perform coordinated physical functions such as combing one's hair), which can result from a number of causes, led to many new hypotheses.

Eventually, it was accepted that most people are right-handed because the left side of their brain is dominant. It was concluded that the right side has few important functions, serving mainly as a backup to the more powerful left side. In the nineteenth-century biological battles, we see the

dim beginnings of the debates about how the two hemispheres' interactions across the corpus callosum contribute to creative thinking. The
general position of those students of genius and of brain biology was that
genetic inheritance rules creative ability. The first scholarly questioning of
this position came at the turn of the century from William James, the man
some have called the first true psychologist.

Nature *and* Nurture

William James (1880, 1890) was the first scientist to make a case for the
interaction of the environment and genetic inheritance. As James put it,
"The only difference between a muddle-head and a genius is that between
extracting wrong characters and right ones. In other words, a muddle-
headed person is a genius *spoiled in the making*" (1880, p. 442, italics
his). Thus, James argued that environment is a more powerful influence
than genetic inheritance in determining ability. Whereas Galton claimed
that creative ability frequently occurred within certain well-known families because of genetics, James believed that the conditions of one's upbringing, such as the parents' philosophy, were more important than
genes. In his time, he was virtually alone in putting forth this idea.

Along with Galton and Freud, James was a leader in thinking that the
ability to get in touch with one's unconscious ideas is a vital part of being
original. This is how he described the process:

> Most people probably fall several times a day onto a fit of something
> like this: the eyes are fixed on vacancy, the sounds of the world melt
> into confused unity, the attention is dispersed so that the whole body
> is felt, as it were, at once, and the foreground of consciousness is filled,
> if by anything, by a sort of solemn surrender to the empty passing of
> time. In the dim background of our mind we know meanwhile what
> we ought to be doing: getting up, dressing ourselves, answering the
> person who has spoken to us, trying to make the next step in our rea-
> soning. But somehow we cannot start; the *pensée de derrière la tete*
> [literally, "thought in the back of the head"] fails to pierce the shell of
> lethargy that wraps our state about. Every moment we expect the spell
> to break, for we know no reason why it should continue. But it does
> continue, pulse after pulse, and we float with it, until—also without
> reason that we can discover—an energy is given, something—we
> know not what—enables us to gather ourselves together, we wink our
> eyes, we shake our heads, the background-ideas become effective, and
> the wheels of life go round again [1880, p. 447].

James clearly recognized the importance of thoughts "in the back of the head" in the creative process, but he did not pursue that idea. If he had, he might have added the third piece to the modern concept of creativity—the psychological element.

In the twentieth century, theorizing and eventually research on creativity became increasingly specialized. In retrospect, we can see that these more recent investigations can be divided into four areas. Some writers have referred to the four areas as "the four Ps": personality, cognitive processes, physiology, and product. Most of the work that has been done on the physiology of creativity is relatively recent; it will be reviewed in Chapters Ten and Eleven. The research on the creative product is quite extensive and is beyond the scope of this book. Therefore, the remainder of this chapter will examine views of the roles that cognitive factors and the personality play in creativity. These views were produced in the first half of the twentieth century.

Early Twentieth-Century Views

In both the cognitive and personality fields, the contributions of German and Austrian psychologists were outstanding. American dominance was not established until later in the century.

Cognitive Processes

By the early 1900s, a number of scientists became interested in studying the processes that make up human cognition. Three of the most significant contributors were Max Wertheimer, Wolfgang Köhler, and Graham Wallas.

MAX WERTHEIMER. Reorganized "mental patterns or forms" were the focus of psychologist Max Wertheimer (1945), who continued the work of the Gestalt school of thought. In his perspective on creative thinking, gestalts form and change in complex relationships, ones that far exceed the mere "associations" proposed by Galton and his followers. Wertheimer proposed that four principles affect the organization of gestalts: proximity, similarity, closure, and *pragnanz* (the tendency to see any figure or concept as "good" if it is symmetrical, simple, stable, and orderly).

Wertheimer wrote this stinging indictment of his opponents: "In [the associationists'] aim to get at the elements of thinking, they cut to pieces living thinking processes, deal with them blind to structure, assuming that the process is an aggregate, a sum of those elements. In dealing with [creative] processes, they can do nothing but dissect them, and thus show a dead picture stripped of all that is alive in them" (1945, p. 162).

He contended that getting a new point of view on the whole of a problem, rather than rearranging its parts, is more likely to produce creativity. Why is a new point of view so hard to achieve? Many impediments exist. For example, most people do not like to face problems, because they cause stress and tension. To avoid problems, people become rigid and stifle their creativity.

WOLFGANG KÖHLER. The concept of *instantaneous insight* was espoused by Wolfgang Köhler, another gestaltist. Köhler gained his most important insight while conducting research on the island of Tenerife during World War I. He had gone there to study chimpanzees in 1913 and was unable to leave the following year because World War I had begun. He spent seven years there on his studies.

His classic experiment, described in his book *The Mentality of Apes* (1925; see also 1929), involved putting bananas out of the reach of caged chimpanzees. He gave the chimps two sticks. Each one was too short to reach the bananas, but they could be fitted together to make one stick that was long enough to reach the fruit. The chimps experimented with the sticks unsuccessfully, even occasionally pushing one stick with the other so that it touched the bananas. Giving up, they would play with the sticks until they noticed that the sticks could be fitted together. This appeared to provide a *flash of insight,* for they would immediately go to the side of the cage and drag the fruit within reach.

Köhler emphasized that the problem-solving process produced behaviors that

- ○ Represent complete wholes rather than individual responses
- ○ Appear suddenly rather than being gradually reinforced
- ○ Were not practiced earlier in the individual's life and were therefore not reproduced from prior experience (Mayer, 1995)

Many psychologists in the first quarter of the twentieth century used Köhler's research to reinforce the contention that learning and creativity involve a reorganizing or restructuring of gestalts.

GRAHAM WALLAS. Graham Wallas introduced his theory of the creative process in his book *The Art of Thought* (1926). Wallas suggested that there are four distinct stages in the creative process.

1. *Preparation.* At this first stage, the problem solver begins to gather information about the problem to be solved. Some say that the best way to do this is to learn as much as possible about the problem area. Learn the essence of the problem, and gather all the basic materials related to it. Others contend that too much familiarization, especially "book learning," may discourage original thought. As George Bernard Shaw put it, "Reading rots the mind." In other words, knowing a great deal about a field makes a thinker incapable of challenging the rules. Herbert Crovitz offers a most reasonable perspective on this matter:

> There are forms as well as content to be learned in preparation. The more varied the problem-solving experiences one has had, the greater the chances of trying a variety of attacks on a problem. It is not that one fails—he can try, try again—it is that he can try different things. As we shall see, and learn to regret deeply, the natural tendency is to keep trying the same old thing when illumination requires more flexibility than that. . . . The "good idea" is the confrontation of the problem by the knowledge that makes a solution rather easy. The "good idea" is a verbalization of what now must be verified; it springs from importing the appropriate knowledge into the problem [1970, p. 80].

Where exactly does the necessary information come from? It does not come from the conscious mind. New thoughts must be produced, and they usually come from one's unconscious mind. This is better explained in Wallas's second stage.

2. *Incubation.* In this stage, gathering more information or mulling over the problem further will prove counterproductive. Efforts to solve the problem must be abandoned and allowed to sink into the unconscious mind. Therefore, the problem solver must not intentionally work on the problem. Rudyard Kipling described in one short sentence how he got ideas for his work: "Drift, wait, and obey" (cited by Crovitz, 1970, p. 54). This is not an easy task, for usually there is a strong drive to solve the problem as soon as possible. Nevertheless, a problem solver will eventually give up conscious effort, at least temporarily, and then the real search for new ideas can begin. If the second stage is a success, then the third stage occurs.

3. *Illumination.* In this stage, the problem solver suddenly experiences insight into the problem when a new idea, solution, or relationship emerges. There is no clear explanation as to why this phenomenon happens. For some reason, vital new methods, data, or relationships become clear to the thinker. Crovitz (1970) speaks of this phenomenon as the

"Oh! There's something now" phenomenon. This leads the thinker to a conscious process of naming or labeling a previously unnamed thought.

Occasionally, the sense that something new is about to emerge does not always signal a solution. Rather, it indicates that some more conscious work is needed. Other times, nothing comes at all, and these unsuccessful instances tend to be forgotten quickly, which explains why the phenomenon is given so much credence. Regardless, when this "Aha!" or "Eureka!" feeling occurs and yields a true insight, the fourth stage may be entered.

4. *Verification.* This is the stage in which the thinker tries and checks the solution (Mayer, 1995). This is really the most crucial aspect of creativity, despite the romantic reputation that incubation and illumination have. Long ago, it was suggested that if a million monkeys were taught to type and if they all typed for a million hours, one of them would probably type *Hamlet.* The difference between monkeys and humans who type at random is that monkeys would never *know* that they had typed a classic. The ability to recognize when a solution fits a problem is a vital part of the creative process (Rothenberg & Hausman, 1976).

Wallas certainly improved on the theories of his predecessors, but like their theories, his is not without weaknesses. For example, incubation is depicted as a passive process, whereas creativity is usually seen as dynamically active.

The Creative Personality

The first half of the twentieth century produced some of the finest thinking about the nature of personality. Some of this work recognized the importance of creativity in this complex set of traits. Among the most notable such advances are the research and theories about the creative personality by Sigmund Freud, Ernst Kris, Alfred Adler, Carl Jung, Otto Rank, Abraham Maslow, Carl Rogers, Erich Fromm, Herbert Lehman, and Wayne Dennis.

SIGMUND FREUD. The chief proponent of the view that creative ability is a personality trait that tends to become fixed by experiences in the first five years of life was Sigmund Freud. In general, he and his early psychoanalytic followers thought that creativity resulted from overcoming some traumatic experience, usually one in childhood.

Often such an experience is buried in the unconscious. Although hidden from conscious awareness, this material could nevertheless have a powerful impact on a person's behavior. In his 1895 book with Josef Breuer, *Studies on Hysteria,* Freud discussed his discovery that one could reveal the contents of the unconscious by suggesting certain key words to patients (as well as by hypnosis). The contents of their unconscious minds would come forward through their seemingly random associations with those words. These contents can then be dealt with by allowing conscious and unconscious ideas to mingle in an innovative resolution of the trauma. Transforming an unhealthy psychic state into a healthy one is seen as a creative act.

Freud characterized the unconscious mind as having a weak concept of time and space and as being largely involved with images rather than words. He saw the unconscious as using a more primitive language that is likely to surface in dreams and in so-called Freudian slips. He was also adamant that creativity almost always stems from ideas first produced in symbolic form in the nebulous world of the unconscious mind.

Freud's explanation of the creative process depended heavily on his ideas about *defense mechanisms,* which are unconscious attempts to block awareness of unpleasant or unacceptable ideas. The psychoanalytic literature describes almost fifty different kinds of defense mechanisms. Because they prevent an accurate perception of the world and because they use up psychic energy, they usually interfere with creative productivity. There are, however, a few defense mechanisms that can often lead to creative insights. Briefly defined, they are as follows:

> *Compensation:* An attempt to make up for an unconsciously perceived inadequacy by excelling at something else (for example, if one is unable to be a superior athlete, one becomes a highly regarded sportswriter)
>
> *Regression:* A reversion to previously successful behaviors when current behavior is unsuccessful (for example, acting childishly silly about a problem when one becomes frustrated with it)
>
> *Displacement:* The act of taking feelings out on someone without much power (for example, one's son) when one is afraid to express feelings to a more powerful person (for example, one's boss)
>
> *Compartmentalization:* The simultaneous commitment to two incompatible beliefs (for example, "I am above average in my schoolwork" and "Most of the kids are a lot smarter than I am")
>
> *Sublimation:* Creative expression in some artistic pursuit (for example, playing the violin well) to make up for an inability to fulfill one's sex drive

Freud firmly believed that people are most motivated to be creative when they cannot directly fulfill their sexual needs. Hence, he believed that sublimation is the primary cause of creativity. The link between unconscious sexual needs and creativity begins in the early years of life. Although many people do not think of children as having sexual needs, Freud argued that at the age of four, children typically develop a physical desire for the parent of the opposite sex. Because this need is virtually never met, sublimation sets in and the first vestiges of a fertile imagination are born.

He traced many specific artistic works to the artist's sublimation. For example, he suggested that Leonardo da Vinci's many paintings of the Madonna resulted from a sublimated longing for sexual fulfillment with a mother figure, as he had lost his own mother early in his life. As Freud (1917/1957, p. 21) put it, "Should we not look for the first traces of imaginative activity as early as in childhood? The child's best-loved and most intense occupation is with his play or games. Might we not say that every child at play behaves like a creative writer, in that he creates a world of his own or, rather, rearranges the things of his world in a new way that pleases him?"

Some of his followers disagreed with his emphasis on sublimation, insisting that other defense mechanisms were the source of creative thought. For example, Ernst Kris (1952, p. 2) argued that only people who are able to "regress in the service of their egos" into a more childlike mental space are likely to be creatively productive.

ERNST KRIS. For Kris, regression was the most productive defense mechanism. He stated that when a person is able to regress to a childlike frame of mind, the barriers between the unconscious and conscious mind are weakened, and the unconscious material is more readily available to awareness (1952, 1965a, 1965b). He noted that regression causes the ego to relax, which in turn promotes creative functions. This type of relaxation occurs in fantasy, dreams, states of intoxication, and states of exhaustion.

When there is a free interchange between the conscious and unconscious mind, creative people are able to retrieve material in the unconscious and to look at problems in a fresh, innovative way. Kris believed that creative people are those who are uninhibited enough to be childlike in their thinking and to maintain a playful attitude about the most serious concerns in life. Kris lamented that psychoanalysts were unable to gain full insight into the mechanisms of the creative personality because of the boundaries imposed by the therapeutic situation.

ALFRED ADLER. Another defense mechanism—compensation for feelings of inferiority—is the basis of the theory of Alfred Adler (1870–1937). Adler departed from the Freudian adherence to sublimation by arguing that the creative act is primarily an attempt to compensate for some perceived inferiority. The perception of this inferiority often begins in early childhood. Thus, Adler posited that creativity is motivated by a conscious idea (the perception of inferiority), not by unconscious feelings, as argued by the other Freudians.

Adler thought that each individual's uniqueness is evident in that person's lifestyle and is rooted in his or her specific inferiorities (Taylor & Getzels, 1975). He originally explained compensation by focusing on physiological deficits (for example, deafness or a clubfoot). He later came to the view that the deficit could be either physical or psychological and saw creativity as the result of dealing effectively with the deficit.

CARL JUNG. Carl Jung, a close associate of Freud's, concurred that the unconscious is deeply involved in high-level creativity. Whereas Jung acknowledged that the individual's sexual experiences are important, however, he believed that great ideas typically come from an even deeper source (1933, 1956).

Jung suggested that personal experiences that are now only vaguely remembered form each person's unconscious mind. In addition, the unconscious contains primordial images and feelings that he called archetypes. These contents are even vaguer, and they result from the experiences of the entire human race (1933, 1960, 1966). We unconsciously "remember" the most influential knowledge of our ancestors, and it is from this collective unconscious that the greatest inventions, theories, art, and other new achievements are drawn. The creative individual is somehow able to connect this unconscious knowledge with conscious ideas. The whole then becomes an unusual, appropriate, transformed, condensed product (to use Jackson and Messick's criteria [1965]). Jung believed that this process lends continuity to human existence while providing progressive advances to the human journey.

OTTO RANK. A student of Freud's, Otto Rank suggested that the supreme act of creativity is the realization of an individual's will. Through that will, a person is able to resolve guilt feelings and integrate personality (1945, 1965). Rank hypothesized that people are born with no will of their own, and that the development of a will is a function of the ego. He agreed with Freud's contention that personality forms in the first five years of life. Therefore, without parental support in early childhood, one could never be truly creative. Rank noted that when children begin to develop a will of their own, their parents respond in one of three ways.

He estimated that 75 to 80 percent of all parents tend to find themselves threatened by their child's wishes and demands, because they consider it their job to control the child. When parents say "No!" to a child, they do so out of a feeling that the child was wrong and that having a individual will is inappropriate. When this occurs, the child typically becomes an "acquiescor." A child acquiesces to parental will for fear that with too much deviation, the parents will abandon him or her. This fear is intolerable to the vulnerable youth, who then fails to develop a sense of personal free will. Such children (that is to say most children) come to anticipate the desires of those in authority and quickly choose to align their own goals with those of their "superiors." This all happens at an unconscious level, so such children tend to get along fine in the world. They simply avoid ever being innovative and are therefore seen as cooperative "good citizens."

A second group of parents (much smaller in number) tends to be inconsistent, sometimes acceding to their child's will and sometimes arbitrarily criticizing the child for being impudent and willful. Such a child cannot predict whether parents will reject or approve of the requests he or she makes. This uncertainty causes the child to become "neurotic"; the child will often develop phobias in an attempt at self-protection. Neurotic people, like acquiescors, cannot be truly innovative.

The very small remaining group of parents typically responds to their children's wishes in a supportive manner. This type of parent does not believe in opposing their children unless they are endangering their own safety or that of others. This philosophy is different from that of the permissive style of parenting, according to which children are allowed to do as they please either because the parent is disinterested or believes in permissiveness for ideological reasons. Children raised by Rank's third type of parent tend to develop what he called a "creative personality." They feel that their desires are worthy; they dare to put themselves out on a limb. Thus, they are the only people who have a chance of being truly creative.

Departing from the psychoanalytic view, the theories of several other psychologists adhered to a "humanistic" approach. The role of the unconscious is much smaller in humanistic theories, which place a greater emphasis on positive, self-fulfilling tendencies. The psychologist who most strongly argued that creativity is a healthy reaction to the environment and that it can be fostered throughout the life span was Abraham Maslow.

ABRAHAM MASLOW. Known as the founder of humanistic psychology, Maslow contended that human beings have six basic instincts that manifest themselves as needs. These needs must be met in a sequential order. The most basic or primitive needs are present at birth, and the higher-order needs develop as maturation proceeds (1954, 1962). Maslow called this the "hierarchy of needs," with the first four called *deficiency needs* and the highest two called *being needs*. Deficiency needs are requirements that may be completely satisfied, at least for a while. The four lowest levels are the needs for physiological essentials (food, warmth, and so on), safety, belonging and love, and the esteem of one's associates. Being needs are so-called because nurturing them makes them even greater, which in turn enriches our being. The two highest levels are needs for self-actualization (fulfilling one's potential) and aesthetic needs (the desire to have a deeper understanding of one's world and one's purpose in life).

In Maslow's opinion, psychoanalysts like Freud and Adler overemphasized deficiency needs and saw motivation as a drive to eliminate lower-level requirements. He attributed this bias to the fact that most psychoanalysts are psychiatrists or otherwise medically oriented persons who normally treat ill people. In industrialized countries, however, where most people have little trouble meeting their lower-level needs, they spend at least some of their time attempting to meet their self-actualization and aesthetic needs.

The process of self-actualization is closely linked to creativity. According to Maslow, self-actualized people are independent, autonomous, and self-directed. Because they are not distracted by lower-level needs, they are free to strive for optimal health and well-being. They are likely to experience an occasional *peak experience,* which is a momentary flash of insight that brings great joy and gratitude for being alive. The peak experience is self-forgetful, a moment of unselfish ecstasy. Maslow's concepts were expanded on by another humanistic psychologist, Carl Rogers.

CARL ROGERS. Carl Rogers studied creative individuals to determine the personality traits that are most closely associated with the potential for creative production (Rogers, 1938, 1959). He found three characteristics that other researchers have come to document.

o An openness to experience that prevents rigidity. This quality is the opposite of the defensiveness that occurs when people unconsciously protect themselves from potential criticism. Furthermore, this openness involves a tolerance for ambiguity, as well as the ability to receive conflicting information without closing one's mind to the situation. Rogers stated

that the "more the individual has available to himself a sensitive awareness of all phases of his experiences, the more sure we can be that his creativity will be personally and socially constructive" (1959, p. 40).

○ The ability to evaluate situations according to one's own personal
standards. This is an important quality because the value of one's creative
work is established not by others' feedback but ultimately by one's own
opinion. The creative person certainly considers others' evaluations but
chooses to draw on himself or herself for the final judgment.

○ The ability to experiment with and engage in unstable situations.
This condition is associated with the lack of rigidity described above. Creative people are able to explore possibilities and to toy with concepts,
which allows them to generate hypotheses, express the ridiculous, translate from one form to another, and transform concepts into improbable
equivalents. From this exploration arise hunches that often lead to creative ways of seeing life.

The person who possesses these traits, stated Rogers, is also likely to be
in excellent psychological health.

ERICH FROMM. It is extremely important to possess the right set of attitudes, according to Erich Fromm. He believed that there are five relevant
traits, each of which can be fostered at any point in life (1941, 1959):

1. The capacity to be puzzled or surprised

2. The ability to concentrate

3. An objective knowledge of self

4. The ability to accept conflict and tension resulting from polarity

5. The willingness to let go of security, such as paternal support

Fromm viewed creativity as stemming from the basic human need to
rise above one's instinctive nature, a perspective that resembles Maslow's
notion of a hierarchy of needs. This need orients the individual toward
productivity and away from self-centeredness. The essence of this concept
of self-transcendence is derived from Fromm's belief that there are two
perspectives from which a person may perceive God—transcendence and
immanence.

The transcendental God is viewed as knowing and controlling all
things. Although Fromm allowed that this perception may be correct, he
saw little evidence of it. The idea of an immanent God—the notion that
God is manifested within us—was much more obvious to him. This idea
echoes the sentiment of the creative boom during the Renaissance. We are

in touch with God's immanent manifestation when we do or feel something that seems somehow greater than ourselves. In those moments, we temporarily rise above our ordinary natures. We are communicating with the wellsprings of our very essence, and it is inevitably an ecstatic feeling. In this sense, immanent godliness and creativity are synonymous. This euphoric feeling results when we achieve our creative potential.

Thus far, the theories and models described in this section on personality have sprung from the theorists' personal experiences and from work with their therapy clients. The next two researchers derived their ideas from data provided by biographies.

HERBERT LEHMAN. Herbert Lehman carried out a series of studies of highly creative persons. The age at which these individuals were most productive was the main variable under study, and personality characteristics such as motivation and perseverance were inferred to be intervening variables (1953, 1962, 1966). Lehman examined biographical accounts of the work of several thousand individuals born since 1774. He examined the age ranges in which the major contributions of deceased persons were typically made, as compared with the contributions of those still living. On the basis of this study, Lehman concluded that scientists in both past and present generations seemed to have produced their best research no later than age thirty-nine. He found that creative output tended to decrease as the individuals aged.

WAYNE DENNIS. Lehman's findings were criticized by Wayne Dennis, who conducted his own research on this subject. Dennis stated that Lehman's work included many individuals who died before they reached old age (Dennis, 1956, 1966). Thus, any opportunities that they may have had to produce creatively were not afforded them. We cannot know what contributions the deceased people would have made had they lived.

Dennis studied the biographies of 738 creative persons, all of whom lived to be seventy-nine years old or older and whose contributions were considered valuable enough to have been reported in biographical histories. He looked at the percentage of works that these people performed in each decade between the ages of twenty and eighty. When he evaluated creative productivity this way, his results were quite different from Lehman's. Dennis found that scholars and scientists (with the exception of mathematicians and chemists) usually had little creative output in their twenties. The peak period for most was between their forties and sixties, and most produced almost as much in their seventies as they did in their early years. For artists, the peak period tended to be their forties, but they were almost as productive in their sixties and seventies as they were in their twenties. Hence, youthful vigor does not appear to be an essential trait in creativity.

Dennis offered an interesting hypothesis to explain the difference in productivity among the three groups (artists, scholars, and scientists). He suggested that because productivity in the arts depends primarily on individual creativity, peak periods occur earlier and decline earlier and more severely. Scholars and scientists require a longer period of training and a greater accumulation of knowledge than others. Employing research assistants allows scholars and scientists to make more contributions in later years than those in the arts. Most of the productive people in Dennis's study were males. It would be interesting to examine the patterns of productivity among a comparable all-female group.

For many centuries, it was believed that human creativity resulted from forces outside the individual's control. Throughout our early history, the gods (or, in the monotheistic view, God) were credited with all innovations. For example, the authors of the Bible were not thought to have *authored* it—they just religiously copied down the ideas that Yahweh gave them. In the pagan view, muses mediated between the gods and humans.

From the Renaissance through the nineteenth century, the creative source slowly came to be seen as genetically inherited genius, which was as mysterious as previously accepted supernatural influences. Only in this century have we come to believe that virtually all humans manifest some level of creativity, just as we possess some level of intelligence, and that the environment (especially childhood experiences) plays a significant role in that manifestation.

Twentieth-century speculation on the creative personality first centered on defense mechanisms, according to theories put forth by psychoanalytically oriented psychiatrists. Then humanistic psychologists moved away from "compensatory" models and began to emphasize the personalities of mentally sound innovators. Cognitive research was motivated in large part by the conflicting views of associationist and Gestalt psychologists. Wallas's overly rational view held sway for several decades. J. P. Guilford's watershed speech to the American Psychological Association in 1950 changed everything. The rest of this book will explain what we mean by that.

PART TWO

SOCIAL FACTORS

3

THE ROLE OF THE FAMILY

AS EMINENT CREATIVITY researcher Frank Barron has noted, "The story of a family is the story of a system, perhaps the most complex and important system we know" (1995, p. 218). In this chapter, we examine how the family influences creative development.

A purely genetic explanation for creative achievement in the arts and sciences was considered sufficient earlier in the century. Now, however, it is clearly inadequate, as John-Steiner (1997) and others have noted. "The intensity with which most creative individuals approach their work is frequently nourished by a highly supportive and stimulating environment in one's home, although at times, loneliness or conflict may contribute to the lure of a world of one's own making" (p. 35). Simonton (1995b) estimated that although a large number of the infants born each year may begin life with the potential for developing exceptional creativity, perhaps only 1 percent of these will have the opportunity to realize this potential. Clearly, the environment in which children grow will have a strong influence on how much of their latent ability will be developed and how much will be wasted.

"I am sometimes asked," stated Gardner (1997a), "why I do not just accept the power of an individual's biological heritage and let it go at that" (p. 48). When this happens, he then asks the questioner to take part in a short "thought experiment," which he calls "Five Experiences a Day." This involves thinking of any two organisms that are very alike, such as twins, and imagining that one of them goes through five positive experiences per day and that the other goes through an equal number of negative experiences. Then think of them in five years' time. Gardner asks, "Can one really expect these individuals—with a disparity of 20,600 experiences—to be anything but radically different from each other" (p. 49)?

Albert's Theory

Robert Albert, in his presidential address to the Division of Psychology and the Arts of the American Psychological Association (1996a), presented his theory of family characteristics, especially as they relate to creativity. He has been researching this theory for many years. Albert has defined a family not in the legal sense but as two people who have one or more children and who stay together. In his view, the family is an ongoing system that has its own agenda and that resists change. When a creative child is born into such a family, the family will change "in terms of what the family wants and has been doing" (p. 309).

As an example, Albert used the Mozart family: "Mozart did not change his family. He accelerated some of the interest in it. But he was absorbed in it as a prodigy, and also for his commercial value. The other point about Mozart is that when Mozart (the son) came along, the older daughter was dropped. The daughter was a very talented pianist and the father just simply said, 'I'm going to pay attention to this boy, not you'" (p. 309).

Based on extensive studies of families in general, and the Brontë family in particular, Albert (1996a) ascribed six major characteristics to families: they are historical, systematic, informational, self-similar, and self-organized, and they possess family transfer processes, both transgenerational and intergenerational. The family's "historical" aspect involves its attention to experiences in the past, ideas, people they honor, and traumas they have suffered, as well as their own method of deciding whom they will accept. The family's "systematic" nature means that although its members may be unpredictable, they do not operate randomly; they have particular familial ways that mesh at some level that works for them. The family's "informational" function is to take in and interpret the culture for its members and to define for them what the family believes is important and unimportant. Also included in the informational function are the family's tactics and strategies for solving problems. "Self-similarity" in a family refers to the observation that family members form part of a pattern and that they tend to stay within that part. The family's "self-organized" facet is seen in the way its members allocate the resources available to them in order to survive in the environment in which they find themselves. Finally, "family transfer processes" are the family's way of passing on what they know; these can be both "transgenerational" and "intergenerational." Transgenerational transfer processes refer to the passing on of ideas and values that have persisted in the family for several generations; this phenomenon explains the existence of musical families, for example. Intergenerational transfers are the socialization processes that all children go through, but Albert noted that even these are based on what earlier generations passed down to the parent.

These ideas may be illuminated by what happened in the Brontë family. Patrick, the father, was the oldest son in a poor family that owned only two books, which he memorized. Fourteen years before Patrick's birth, however, his uncle had published a book. When Patrick had his own children, he often told them the story in this book and informed them that the book had been published. This act formed a link across three generations of this family—a link that emphasized stories and writing.

The family suffered a series of losses, beginning with Mrs. Brontë's death after the birth of her last daughter. The oldest daughter, who may have been the most intellectually gifted of all the children, had to take the mother's place in caring for the home and children. This daughter died a little more than three years later. The family then became reorganized, with the father as the only parental figure.

Branwell, the only son, was the father's obvious favorite, which led the three daughters to band together. Charlotte has left us records of the great resentment she felt because of her father's obvious preference for the one boy in the family. The father became a mentor to Branwell and placed all his hopes in this son. "His father protected Branwell from a series of failures as he let the girls kind of float for themselves" (Albert, 1996a, p. 313). Eventually, Branwell failed so often and so badly that his father stopped supporting him.

When the father learned that his daughters' writing had been published, he was astonished and said that he had never expected this to happen. "He didn't really look for it. He didn't care that what they were doing was that important. It was Branwell that he was highly attached to and looked at. So when Branwell fails, he is alerted" (Albert, 1996a, p. 314).

In terms of Albert's theory, the Brontë family had a history of reverence for writing and publishing, which was transferred to the children. The systematic and informational aspects of a family are illustrated by the expectation that the oldest daughter had to take on her dead mother's parental duties and ignore the loss of her own creative potential. The father's obvious favoring of the son informed the girls that they were not important. The Brontës were self-similar in that the daughters formed an alliance in the face of the father's virtually ignoring them. The father wished to allocate all of the family resources to the son and believed that this was the correct thing to do.

Albert argued that the most important element in families in terms of the nurturing of creativity is whether they are primarily concerned with conventional success, acceptability, and status or whether they are willing to take risks and allow children to learn from experience what sparks their interest and leads them to be creative. The families that can allow for this kind of risk taking and allow children to "bump their noses, . . . a critical developmental antecedent for creativity" (Albert, 1996a, p. 312) are very different from those that cannot. The children in non-risk-taking families may be very bright, but they will probably not be very creative.

Research of Dacey and Colleagues

According to Amabile (1996), one of the more comprehensive recent studies on the family lives of highly creative young people was that conducted by Dacey and his colleagues (Dacey, 1989b). This study demonstrated that creative people's family lives do differ from those of people of ordinary ability in many important ways and that their lives bear out many of the contentions of the research presented above.

Fifty-six families of one hundred New England area adolescents participated in this study. Half of the families were selected after members of a profession identified one parent as being in the top 5 percent of creative people in that profession. The other half were included after knowledgeable staff members identified one of the teenagers as being in the top 5 percent of creative people in his or her school system.

The actual creative achievements of these nominees were then scrutinized and scored by a team of Boston College faculty and graduate students who specialize in this field. Then, the nominees' families were invited to participate. Of the sixty-one families nominated, three were eliminated by this procedure, and two decided not to participate. Data for the fifty-six participating families were compared with analogous data gathered from twenty other families in which no members were identified as creative.

Almost all research sessions were held in the evening at the families' homes. The research consisted of fifty minutes of tests administered to the teenagers, followed by two hours of interviews with the family members on topics concerning the family's lifestyle. All interview sessions were conducted so that no family member was aware of the other members' responses. The responses were later compared and were found to be surprisingly in accord.

To determine the creativity levels of the study's participants, researchers asked each person to describe and provide evidence of her or his own creative productions, as well as those of the other family members (the latter as a means of cross-validation). Such evidence included publications, awards, and media articles describing their achievements. No test data were used as evidence. For each case, the research team rated the assembled evidence (interscorer reliabilities averaged .83). This method is the same as that defined by Amabile (1983a): "A product or response is creative to the extent that appropriate observers independently agree it is creative. Appropriate observers are those familiar with the domain in which the product was created or the response articulated. Thus, creativity can be regarded as the quality of products or responses judged to be creative by appropriate observers" (p. 31).

Four types of creativity (Guilford, 1975) were rated from 1 to 9. These four types, along with examples of each, are shown in Table 3.1. The points on the rating scale are described in Table 3.2, in which 9 represents the highest possible score.

The quality of the person's products and the level of recognition received for them were jointly considered in making the four evaluations.

Table 3.1. Types and Examples of Creativity Rated in This Study.

Type of Creativity	Examples
Figural	Sculpture, architecture, cabinetmaking
Symbolic	Mathematics, music, ballet
Semantic	Journalism, playwriting
Social (behavioral)	Psychology, teaching, school politics

Based on Guilford, 1975.

Table 3.2. Rating Scale Criteria.

Score	Level of Recognition
9	National
8	
7	Regional
6	
5	Local
4	
3	No recognition
2	
1	

Based on Guilford, 1975.

Table 3.3. Illustrative Achievements of Highly Rated Youth.

Age	Gender	Achievement
13	F	Choreographed and starred in a junior high school assembly ballet program
12	M	Wrote and produced a half-hour radio play
19	F	Had the lead in university plays two years in a row
11	F	Organized and led several clubs in school; organized and led summer day care for twelve preschool children
15	F	Directed Shakespeare's *Tempest* in junior high; received districtwide acting award
20	M	Wrote and illustrated three children's books for a major publishing company, all of which are selling well
18	M	Won scholarship to Harvard University for innovative approach to mathematics in regional science fair
14	M	Won regional architecture contest for drawings of buildings
15	F	Won regional short story contest
18	M	Was hired by advertising company because of imaginative drawings
14	M	Had music written for the saxophone published in regional music magazine
20	F	Had two poems published in college poetry magazine and one in national magazine

Based on Guilford, 1975.
Note: *All of the above participants had other
achievements, which were too numerous to mention here.*

As might be expected, the quality and the level of recognition are highly correlated. Therefore, joining them caused few problems. A total score, composed of the sum of these four scores, was also computed. Table 3.3 describes examples of achievements that received scores of 8 or 9, as well as the ages and genders of subjects who received those ratings.

In drawing conclusions from this study, Dacey and colleagues used the following types of data:

○ Correlations among creativity tests and ratings of creative achievements.

○ *T* tests of differences of means for high and low creative samples.

○ Qualitative analyses of answers to forty-two interview questions.

○ Qualitative analyses of taped conversations among the parents of twenty-five of the most creative youth. These parents were invited to spend an evening talking about ways to produce creative children. There were five three-hour sessions, and five different families participated in each.

The next sections will discuss the principal conclusions of this research.

Genes Versus the Environment

In families that were selected because one parent had clearly demonstrated high creativity, slightly more than half of the children were also above average in creativity. In the group of families chosen because a school system had nominated a teenaged family member as being extremely creative, only one-third of the parents were above average in creative achievement. Although this finding cannot be considered definitive in the "nature versus nurture" debate, it does support the position that environmental factors such as parenting style and home atmosphere play a greater role than genetics in determining creativity.

Rules for Behavior

The parents of creative teenagers had, on average, less than one specific rule (such as a required number of study hours, a specific bedtime, or restrictions on sexual activity) for their children's behavior. The group of twenty families with no highly creative members averaged six rules.

The parents of the creative youth were not permissive, however (Goertzel, Goertzel, & Goertzel, 1978; Taylor, 1964). Baumrind (1989) defined three styles of parenting. "Permissive" parents exert little control over their children's behavior and fail to discipline them. "Authoritarian" parents exert control over their children that is as strict as possible, expect unquestioning obedience, and apply stern disciplinary measures. "Authoritative" parents strive to strike a balance between these two extremes and seek to guide rather than direct their children. Dacey and Packer (1992) have delineated a fourth parenting style, that of the "nurturing" parent. The parental approach in this study most resembled this nurturing style. Most parents put forth and modeled a clear set of values and encouraged their children to decide which behaviors exemplify those values. As one Jewish man put it, "I can't think of any rules we've had for our kids. We just wanted each to become a *mensch,*" meaning a truly admirable person (Dacey, 1989b, p. 193). Most of these parents remarked that they had surprisingly few problems with discipline.

Paper-and-Pencil Tests as Poor Predictors of Creativity

Six abbreviated versions of creativity tests were administered to the youth in this study. Although some of the tests' correlations with the creativity ratings were significant, all the correlations were rather low. It was hoped that at least one of these short tests would prove to be a good predictor of the much more laborious rating method, but this did not occur, probably because the shortened adaptations were used. Thus, it would be inappropriate (and probably unfair) to discuss them further here.

Of course, although the achievement ratings may themselves lack validity, their high correlations with other factors in this study offer encouraging evidence of construct validity. Several studies have found that creativity is a relatively unstable trait as compared with, for example, shyness, and that creativity is most unstable during adolescence (Dacey, 1986; Ripple & Dacey, 1969).

Critical Periods

Many subjects spoke of a "critical moment" in their lives, a time when, for various reasons, their self-image was unusually open to change. At this moment, if the right event occurred, they became inspired to think more imaginatively and to take greater risks in acting on their thoughts. The right event might include encouragement by a teacher or parent or rare good fortune in some endeavor.

On the basis of these subjects' testimony, as well as on the basis of other research on personality development (Gould, 1978; Levinson, 1978, 1997; Vaillant, 1977), it seems that six periods in life can be pinpointed as having the greatest opportunities for such critical moments (Dacey, 1989c; Jaquish & Ripple, 1980; Ripple & Dacey, 1969). These periods are as follows: the first five years of life, the early years of adolescence, early adulthood (around twenty), from twenty-nine to thirty-one, the early forties, and sixty to sixty-five. Unfortunately, it appears that such opportunities become less likely with each succeeding period.

Humor

Joking, playing tricks, and "fooling around" take an important place in these families, a finding buttressed by other authors (Derks, 1985; O'Quin & Derks, 1997; Torrance, 1979; Wicker, 1985). Family members often have comical names for each other and use a vocabulary that only they understand. Both parents and children in this study were asked to rate thirteen traits, such as "having a high IQ" and "being popular with peers," as they pertain to the child (Getzels & Jackson, 1962). "Sense of humor" was ranked much higher by the creative people's families than by the comparison families. It was in the top half for most of the responses.

Type of Housing

Most of the families of the creative youth live in decidedly different kinds of houses from other people. Some are modern; for example, quite a few were located on rocky ledges in the woods. Others are ancient; one family lives in a converted nineteenth-century town hall. Another bought a two-room eighteenth-century home, then added ultramodern bedrooms and a kitchen to the back of it.

The insides of their homes are usually quite different, too. Many are unconventionally furnished. Several were decorated with surprising collections, such as Turkish teapots. In one home, a room was devoted to housing forty-seven unusual birds. (It should be noted that most of the families were middle-class or upper-middle-class. It is difficult to find successfully creative people who are also poor, as they often lack the space, education, and material resources to do creative work.)

Recognition and Reinforcement at an Early Age

Parents in the study were asked to say at what age they first suspected that their child had unusual abilities and what made them think so. Most noticed signs such as distinctive thought patterns or high problem-solving abilities before the child had turned three. Although few parents had set out to foster these traits in their children, most reported that they found it exciting and tried to encourage these tendencies. Furthermore, they usually provided a wide range of opportunities (lessons, equipment, contacts, and situations) that cultivated the traits. Without exception, they were delighted to find that their children were exhibiting signs of high creativity. Most of the children said that they felt strong encouragement from their parents.

Parents' Lifestyle

Most of the parents in these families were able to note some aspect of their lives which is uncommon. For instance, most of the mothers work at jobs that few women have; they were attorneys, surgeons, or artists, for example. Virtually all the parents have well-developed interests aside from work, and many of these are unusual. In a substantial number of the families, the children share in their parents' interests, too.

Trauma

Creative children suffer a larger number of traumatic incidents than ordinary children do. These are occurrences that cause grief, anger, or both and that seriously disrupt the children's lives. The parents of the creative youth in this study remember from two to nine of these incidents, as opposed to one to three in the comparison group of families. Several theorists believe that dealing with childhood trauma is a major spur to creativity, particularly among writers (Adler, cited in Ansbacher & Ansbacher, 1956; Albert, 1996b; Goertzel, Goertzel, & Goertzel, 1978; Kris, 1965a).

Insignificance of Schools

The youth and parents in this study see the children's schools as ranging from the highly traditional to the highly innovative, but they all agree on one thing—few of the schools have any effect on creativity. This is buttressed by the finding that the correlation between the researchers' creativity ratings and the school's innovativeness was quite low. Perhaps certain schools or individual teachers help students expand their creativity, but there was little evidence of it in this study. (The next chapter treats this problem in much greater detail.)

Importance of Hard Work

Subjects in this study agree with Thomas Edison that creativity is "one part inspiration and ninety-nine parts perspiration." Almost without exception they say that they work considerably harder than their schoolmates and that they have done so since starting school. This was true in a wide range of work, such as jobs, homework, and chores.

Left-Handedness or Hemispheric Dominance

Several theorists have suggested that left-handedness should be more common among the highly creative because it is an indication that they are dominated by the right sides of their brains, which in turn causes more interhemispheric communication. Some see the left side as the "logical" side and the right as the "intuitive" side. It is now clear that the situation is much more complicated than that (Springer & Deutsch, 1993), but this study does offer some support for the theory.

In the general population, 5 to 10 percent of people are left-handed. Of those who scored in the lower half of the creativity scale in this study, this percentage is 8, whereas 20 percent of those who scored high in creativity are left-handed.

Gender Difference

Although their fathers had higher scores than their mothers in almost all categories, the youth's gender in this study made no significant difference in their creativity ratings. This appears to be accounted for by changing perceptions of the female gender role in our society, which in turn may be encouraging female productivity more than in the past.

Both mothers and fathers agreed that almost twice as many of the highly creative teenagers have a strong sense of identification with their mothers. From the interview data, it seems likely that these youth imitate their fathers' successes but rely more on their mothers for encouragement.

Parents' Judgment of Children's Creativity

In every family, the parents were asked to evaluate each child's level of creativity, given the four types outlined. These ratings were then compared to those that the research team gave. Mothers and fathers were in strong agreement with each other and with the panel's overall ratings on all but the social ratings.

Number of Collections

The more highly creative adolescents were more likely to have a larger number of collections, and these collections were unusual for the children's ages, such as campaign buttons and models of prehistoric birds.

Other Outstanding Traits

Contrary to the stereotype, the creative children in this study saw themselves as getting along well with others, and they ranked this trait highly (it also appeared in the top half of the ranking most of the time). They regarded themselves as being "different" and said they thought so at an early age (usually before six). Most felt that this has been an asset.

To describe themselves, the adolescents most often chose "best able to look at things in a new way and discover new ideas" and gave lowest rankings to "healthiest" and "has the most energy." Most of the parents agreed that "having outstanding traits of character, such as honesty and trustworthiness" best described themselves, followed by "best able to look at things in a new way and discover new ideas." Parents gave the lowest rankings to "best-looking" and "healthiest."

"Getting highest grades" and "having the highest IQ" were ranked moderately low by most parents in a 1977 study by Stanley, George, and Solano. Several other studies (Getzels & Jackson, 1962; MacKinnon, 1978; Taylor & Getzels, 1975) have found that internal states such as imagination and honesty are much more valued by creative people and their family members than such readily observable traits as grades and health.

Because this study is based primarily on self-reporting and retrospective case study data, no claims for causal relationships between the family's lifestyle and its creativity may be made. The number of strong, clear differences found between the families with high and low creativity, however, are powerful indications that the family is an important force—very likely the most influential one—in the development of creative ability.

Other Empirical Studies

Several recent empirical studies have addressed the family's impact on children's creativity (Gardner & Moran, 1990; Michel & Dudek, 1991; Urban, 1991; Grzeskowiak, 1996; Mendecka, 1996; Swietochowski & Poraj, 1996). In contrast, other observers have directed attention to the effects that a highly creative child has on the family (Keirouz, 1990; John-Steiner, 1997; Moon, Kelly, & Feldhusen, 1997).

To assess students' level of creativity, Gardner and Moran (1990) tested eighty undergraduates on the Davis How Do You Think instrument, which asks for self-reports on such traits as curiosity, risk taking, self-confidence, adventurousness, sense of humor, creativity, and originality, in addition to information about hobbies and creative activities that students have pursued in the past. The students were also administered the Family Adaptability and Cohesion Evaluation Scales to measure their family environments.

The highest creativity scores were obtained by those whose families were seen as highly adaptable, whereas family rigidity characterized those with the lowest creativity scores. Gardner and Moran suggested that within highly adaptable families, children are allowed to make their own mistakes as part of the learning process. Family cohesion was not a significant contributor in predicting creativity scores. This is consistent with previous research that has often found that creative individuals have come from families that are far from harmonious (for example, Albert, 1992, 1996b; MacKinnon, 1992).

Mother-child relationships were the focus of a study by Michel and Dudek (1991). It involved thirty mothers and their children, who had been selected from an initial sample of 133 eight-year-old public school children as the fifteen highest and fifteen lowest scorers on the Torrance Tests of Creative Thinking. The children's level of differentiation was assessed by the Draw-a-Person Test and by the Kinetic Family Drawing Test, whereas the mothers' encouragement of the children's differentiation and their level of emotional involvement with the children were evaluated with the Family Relations Test and through interviews. It was found that children who tested high on creativity had mothers who were less emotionally involved with them and who encouraged them to be independent. These mothers were more self-confident and had higher occupational levels outside of the home than the other mothers. Michel and Dudek interpreted this as being beneficial to the children, in that it allowed them more freedom to explore their world and to develop their imagination and creativity. It appears that the mother's overinvolvement with the child is likely to curb, rather than foster, the independence and curiosity that can lead a child to be creative.

Mendecka (1996) conducted a biographical survey of sixty-five successful inventors and compared them to a control group of uninventive individuals. Extensive interviews were conducted, which yielded complete biographies of the subjects, according to the study's author. These were written down and analyzed by three qualified judges. It was found that inventors' parents were accepting of them as children, were cooperative with them, and demonstrated love and high expectations, but also respected their subjectivity and autonomy. Parents of those in the creative group were less closely involved with their children because they were more absorbed in their own professional pursuits, and this did not appear to be detrimental to the offspring's creativity.

Many in the uninventive group had parents who were controlling and restrictive in their attitudes toward and treatment of their children. They also were reported as believing that family problems should be hidden from the children so as not to undermine the parents' authority and their need to be good examples for their children.

Another study conducted by Grzeskowiak (1996) showed that the more mothers set strict limits on children's behavior, the less independent and curious the children acted. Twenty mother-child pairs participated. The children, ages two to four years, were observed in free play. The researcher noted the amount of manipulated material (puppets, animal figures, and so on) that children used. Differences in the extent of exploration were age- and sex-independent among the group. The researcher assessed the mothers' childrearing styles in two ways—by asking them about their views on raising their children and by analyzing videos of mother-child interactions made in the homes. In terms of the mothers, the investigator was most interested in the degree to which they controlled the children's behavior.

As stated earlier, the stricter the mother's limits on the child's behavior, the less independent exploratory behavior the child showed in a new situation. One striking result was that both too much and too little control appeared to confine the child's explorations. Thus, a U-shaped relationship between control and exploration was observed. The author concluded that finding the "narrow path that lies between insufficient attention from the mother and a permanent limiting of the child's behavior by excessive control" (p. 426) is a difficult task for a parent who does not want to inhibit the child's curiosity. Although most of the mothers declared in their interviews that they wanted their children to develop autonomy and creativity, their actual behavior as observed in the videos was often at odds with this goal. Grzeskowiak suggested that the mothers likely derived their stated positive views toward curiosity from popular childrearing ideals but that it was often not possible for them to translate these ideals into appropriate behavior.

Harrington, Block, and Block (1992) empirically evaluated Rogers's (1954) theory that three internal psychological conditions are most apt to foster the development of constructive creativity. These conditions are openness to experience, an internal locus of evaluation, and the ability to play with elements and concepts. According to Rogers, such internal conditions are most likely to occur when two external conditions are present in the child's life: psychological safety and psychological freedom. Psychological safety is created when the child feels unconditionally accepted as worthwhile, empathically understood, and free from external evaluation. Psychological freedom results when the child has permission to engage in unrestrained symbolic expression.

Although Rogers explicitly requested that his theory be empirically tested, Harrington, Block, and Block believe that theirs is the first investigation to do so. Their study included 106 families who are part of an ongoing longitudinal study of ego and cognitive development begun by Block and Block in 1968. When the families joined the main study, their children were three or four years old. In the 1992 study, fifty-three boys and fifty-three girls and their families were observed. These selected families were of above-average educational levels, most of the parents having completed more than four years of college.

The researchers examined six key indexes: preschool creative potential, preschool intelligence, adolescent creative potential, mother's childrearing, father's childrearing, and combined parents' childrearing. These last three were indexes of Rogers' prescribed childrearing practices. All three indexes of Rogers' recommended childrearing practices were positively and significantly correlated with the adolescent creative potential index, as well as with the preschool creative potential. Creative potential in adolescence was also correlated significantly with preschool intelligence and with preschool creative potential.

To ensure that these observed correlations were not spurious, the investigators conducted three multiple regression analyses, one for each index of Rogers's prescribed practices. The results of these regression analyses consistently rejected the spurious correlation explanation and supported Rogers's theory. The authors cautioned that although the index of creative potential used here was presumed to measure important facets of creative potential in early adolescence, creative activity and creative achievement were not measured, so no conclusion could be drawn about actual creative production in adulthood.

As part of a longitudinal study she has been conducting with a sample of 141 women, Helson (1992) reported on the actualization of creative potential of 31 of these women. These 31 women were nominated by faculty members for their creative potential when they were seniors at a women's college in 1958 or 1960. If these women were considered successful in a career that drew on their creative abilities by the time they were in their early forties, they met the criterion for actualization. Of the 31 women, 13 qualified and were designated "successful careerists." Most of them were practitioners in music, dance, writing, visual arts, or psychotherapy, with a few in planning or administration. Of the other 18 women in the sample, some gave up or lost careers that they had begun. Others never worked after marriage or childbearing, or they worked without career aspirations. These 18 women were designated "other nominees."

The participants were asked, at ages forty-two to forty-five, to describe a recurrent positive and recurrent negative feeling that they held toward their mothers in childhood. They were asked the same question about their fathers. The modal response for the successful careerists was that they appreciated their mothers' love and encouragement but disliked their dependence. The fathers were most often admired and perceived as the stronger parent. The modal response for the other nominees was that they admired their mothers' abilities but resented their coerciveness and their inability to recognize their daughters' individuality. Fathers were most often described as the more understanding parent but also as the less dominant one. Helson interpreted these results to mean that the successful women felt conflicted about separating from their mothers but that they partially identified with their fathers and were thus able to forge their own way and actualize their creativity better than the other nominees. In some ways, the women in that second group remained too tied to their parents and failed to live up to their putative creative potential.

Helson (1992) did caution that this particular cohort of women was subjected to a series of especially sharp changes in environmental support for the achievement of creativity, making it particularly difficult to separate family influences from other elements in the social environment. When they were college students, "They lived in a milieu in which creativity was admired and encouraged. When they entered the adult world, they encountered—as anticipated—the pressure to marry, have children, and subordinate their lives to the career of husband and needs of children. Then in the late 1960s and 1970s, expectations for women changed radically" (p. 222). Therefore, the results reported are not necessarily generalizable beyond this group.

In a longitudinal study of adolescents who were talented in mathematics, science, art, music, and athletics, Csikszentmihalyi, Rathunde, and Whalen (1993) found that the students' families fell into four categories: differentiated, integrated, complex, and simple, according to the amounts of stimulation and support they provided for their children. "Differentiated" families were high on stimulation but low on support, whereas "integrated" families provided much support but little stimulation. Children from "complex" families were given both stimulation and support, and those from "simple" families were given neither stimulation nor support. Except for those in athletics, who seemed to thrive best in a "differentiated" family, the adolescents from "complex" families enjoyed the most positive environment for the development of their talents. They were happier and more alert, had higher energy and skill levels, and spent more time studying than those from the other types of families. They also had higher levels of achievement in their domain of talent.

Finally, Swietochowski and Poraj (1996) conducted a study of 249 adolescents designated as "high creative" or "low creative" by their scores on the Urban and Jellen Test for Creative Thinking-Drawing Production. These investigators were interested in learning whether parents' attitudes contributed to their teenagers' developing type A behavior—the pattern of being tense, driven, and impatient that is known to contribute to coronary disease. Findings indicated that if mothers exhibited rejecting or demanding attitudes, it was not significantly related to type A behavior in creative teenagers, but if fathers showed rejecting attitudes, this type of behavior was more prevalent in creative adolescents. The results for the uncreative individuals showed that the attitudes of either parent had little influence on type A behavior. This suggests that creative adolescents are more cognizant of and sensitive to the attitudes of their parents than those who are uncreative.

Csikszentmihalyi (1996) pointed out that in any retrospective report of childhood, "It is inevitable that what we see is colored by what happened in the years in between, by present circumstances, and by future goals" (p. 172). He noticed an intriguing pattern in some of the interviews he conducted with fine artists over a twenty-year period. When one particular artist was an extremely successful young man, he described his childhood as almost idyllic. Ten years later, however, when the artist was having professional problems, the story of his childhood took on darker tones. In yet another ten years, this man's career as an artist was virtually finished, and he was having problems with alcohol. At that time, his description of his childhood was darker still, including both physical and emotional abuse at the hands of an alcoholic father and other relatives. Csikszentmihalyi suggested that successful creative adults might remember their childhoods as warm and supportive because of the very fact that they are now successful people. More than the objective facts, what seems to matter is how people interpret these facts and imbue them with meaning.

The results of the above studies appear to be congruent with many of the views on family put forth by Albert (1996a), as discussed at the beginning of this chapter. That is, family influences are extremely complex and difficult to separate from other circumstances that impinge on the development of creativity from childhood through adolescence and beyond. There is much that parents can do to nurture whatever creative gifts their children are blessed with, however.

Family Facilitation of Creative Growth

Recent studies confirm that many parents of creative children are greatly concerned with how best to encourage and nurture the development of their children's talents (for example, Keirouz, 1990; Meckstroth, 1990; Moon, Kelly, & Feldhusen, 1997). The retrospective interviews collected by Benjamin Bloom (1985) with successful scientists and artists also showed an enormous amount of parental investment in the development of their children's talents.

Based on findings in Dacey and colleagues' 1989 study of families of creative adolescents (described earlier in this chapter), as well as extensive experience with children, adolescents, and parents, Dacey and Packer (1992) went beyond Baumrind's authoritarian, permissive, and authoritative styles of parenting (1989) to define a fourth style, which they call "nurturing parenting." These are parents who show trust in the child's fairness and good judgment; respect for the child's thoughts, feelings, and autonomy; support of the child's interests and goals; enjoyment of the child's company; an ability to protect the child from doing injury to self or others; and a tendency to model values that the child needs, including self-control and sensitivity. Dacey and Packer suggested more than a hundred activities for parents to carry out with their children to foster the ten most salient traits of personality and thinking that nourish creativity.

Teresa Amabile, whose work on the social psychology of creativity will be discussed in Chapter Four, also identified characteristic attitudes of parents whose children become creative (Amabile, 1989). Her list of such attitudes agrees in many places with that of Dacey and Packer. From both field and laboratory research, Amabile concluded that parents should convey the following attitudes to their children: freedom, respect, moderate emotional closeness, values rather than rules, achievement rather than grades, appreciation of creativity, the importance of having parents be actively involved in their own pursuits, vision for the future, and humor. Amabile stressed the importance of the parents' being models for the child's creative inclinations, and she offered a number of activities to stimulate creativity.

Vera John-Steiner (1997) gave many examples of how the family environment affects the creativity of the successful creators she interviewed. A photographer stated that he came from a very visual background, where he was surrounded by his father's collection of paintings and his own collection of postcard reproductions of paintings. An artist described his home life by saying, "There was always this kind of striving to become artists, writers, within the whole family. Though my father was a writer, he could draw. And he actually would draw for us when we were children. He even taught us to draw" (p. 34). Author Margaret Drabble remembered "a joyously literate childhood" (p. 35) as the beginnings of her extraordinary facility with language. Her family's joint activities included playwriting and the publishing of family magazines. A sculptor whose stepfather was a blacksmith stated that he made all his own toys as a child.

The picture that emerges from the studies we have reviewed shows parents as being highly encouraging of their creative children's freedom, as opposed to forever attempting to control them. Although some psychologists have lamented that most American children are not held to high enough standards (Damon, 1995), others have observed that some parents expect too much of their children at too early an age (Elkind, 1989). Winner (1996) agreed that high standards should be set for children but warned that parents who are overly involved in their children's abilities and who fail to nurture children as whole people can cause disengagement, depression, and resentfulness in their children, as well as loss of their creative talents. She made the point that although such retrospective studies as Bloom's (1985) show that high parental expectations and even some pushing are often associated with high achievement, those studies cannot show us where to draw the line between "just enough" and "too much" parental involvement. Children who are pushed too hard and who are emotionally deprived may never recover from such an upbringing and therefore may not realize their potential in adulthood. The case of William James Sidis gives a stark illustration of these dangers (Montour, 1977; Wallace, 1986).

Sidis was born in 1898 to Russian immigrant parents, who named him after William James, the famed Harvard psychology professor. William Sidis's father, Boris, wholly embraced James's ideas. Boris believed that he could make his son into anything he desired, in accordance with the then-prevalent idea that with the "right" education, any child could be molded into a young genius. Although it is clear that William was born with extremely high potential, his father pushed him relentlessly from the time he was an infant, so that the child could spell and read before the age of three. By the age of six, William could read Russian, French, and German, as well as English, and he could type. When he entered public school, as required by law, he passed all seven grades of its curriculum in six months. His father then taught him at home for two years, and William enrolled in Brookline High School at the age of eight. After three months, his parents took him out of school again to teach him at home for another two years. By the time he was ten, William knew algebra, geometry, trigonometry, and differential and integral calculus. From the time

William was nine, his father began petitioning Harvard to admit him, and he was finally accepted as a special student at the age of eleven. That year, he delivered a lecture on the fourth dimension before the Harvard Mathematical Club, an event that received front page coverage in the *New York Times*. When he was sixteen, William became the youngest man ever to receive a Harvard bachelor's degree.

Unfortunately, from this time onward, his life story is one of decline. He began graduate studies at Harvard on two different occasions but never completed a degree. He failed at a teaching position at Rice that his mentor at Harvard obtained for him, and he got into trouble with the law. Soon, he became a bitter and disillusioned young man, for which he blamed both his father and academia. For the remainder of his life, he worked at low-level jobs and was totally estranged from his parents. He refused to attend his father's funeral in 1923 and was not mentioned in the obituary. In 1944, William himself died of a brain hemorrhage. He died alone in the Brookline, Massachusetts, boardinghouse, where he lived, destitute and unemployed.

What is known about William Sidis's upbringing is that his father used him to illustrate his theory that any child could be made into a genius. He was very harsh with his son, never allowing any play or social contact with other children and thoroughly exploiting the boy for his own ends. Boris was certain that his son's phenomenal abilities were due not to heredity but to his own expertise and unrelenting efforts in educating the boy. When William began to get into trouble after his Harvard graduation, his father disowned him. Neither parent had ever given him any emotional support. "It was not extreme educational acceleration that destroyed William James Sidis emotionally and mentally, but instead an interaction of paternal exploitation and emotional starvation" (Montour, 1977, p. 276).

It appears that although parents must supply support and encouragement, their most important contribution to the development of creative children is willingness to follow the children's leads and the sensitivity to discern which goals are truly those of the children.

Effects of Marriage and Parenthood

All of the research we have discussed so far in this chapter examines the impact that the family of origin can have on a child's creative potential, as most of the work in this area has addressed parental influences on the young creator. Recently, however, some attention has been given to the effects that marrying or having children may have on creative productivity.

Csikszentmihalyi's study (1996), based on the histories of more than eighty contemporary creators, found that most of the individuals were involved in long-term, stable, and satisfying marital relationships. Some of the interviewees related youthful involvements in promiscuous sexuality, but most married early and stayed married for many years. Many men and women in this sample reported that their spouse's help had been indispensable in the realization of their creative goals. "These accounts of the relationships of creative individuals are so diverse that they cannot prove any one point. But they can *disprove* a generally held notion that people who achieve creative eminence are unusually promiscuous and fickle in their human ties. In fact, the opposite seems closer to the truth: These individuals are aware that a lasting, exclusive relationship is the best safeguard of that peace of mind they need in order to focus on their creative pursuit" (p. 192).

Pohlman (1996) interviewed twenty creative writers to explore the relationship between being creative and having a family. She found that writers were affected by family in three ways: gender expectations, material and symbolic constraints of parenthood, and social support provided by their spouses.

For the male writers, it was found that although they often rebelled against the image of men that was often associated with marriage and parenthood, being husbands and fathers actually brought them the stability and partnership that made it possible for them to write. All but one of the men worked at home but tended to stay in their offices most of the day. They also strove to provide financially for their families through their writing, preserving their image of masculinity in this way.

In contrast, the women did not try to preserve traditional sex-role expectations. Instead, they rebelled against many aspects of this role, especially passivity. They also tended to weigh their choices about having a family in terms of how they would or would not be able to get their creative work done. Two of the women chose to remain childless specifically in order to create. Some of the women were prevented from beginning their writing careers until after their children were grown and gone because of the expectation of being a good wife and mother.

For the men, parenthood did not detract from the privacy and solitude they needed in order to write, usually because their wives provided child care. Having children was likely to give men a greater sense of meaning in life and a focus for their work. Women found that children both disrupted the physical and psychological space they needed for their writing and isolated them from the adult world.

In terms of spousal support for the creative enterprise, Pohlman found that men acknowledged less help from their wives than they actually received. They insisted on the autonomy of their achievements but often revealed through examples in interviews that they had received a great deal of emotional and instrumental support from their wives. This included the wives' financial support and sacrifices, as well as their ongoing child care and management of the home. The women writers, on the other hand, acknowledged more spousal support than they actually received. Much of the emotional support from their husbands was tolerant rather than proactive. The women deemed instrumental support, including help with household maintenance and child care, to be moderate. Most of the women writers had to balance both their writing careers and the management of their homes and children.

Pohlman concluded that the study of family relationships' impact on adult creators has been neglected and needs to be expanded to explore further the ways in which the marital and parental relationships both constrain and enable creativity.

4

THE ROLE OF THE
SOCIAL CONTEXT

THE EVIDENCE PRESENTED in the last chapter clearly indicates that the family is a major influence in creative development. Is this also true of the larger society? In this chapter, three societal elements are examined: the typical school experience, societal rewards across the life span, and the overall cultural environment.

The Educational System

Schools suppress creativity.

How can we say this so categorically? The reasoning goes as follows. Most young children are naturally curious and highly imaginative. On the basis of his research at Harvard's Project Zero, Gardner (1991) stated that the period from age two to about age seven is a crucial time for creativity and artistry to be unleashed or blocked. After children have attended school for a while, most become more cautious and less innovative. Worst of all, they tend to change from being participators to being spectators. Unfortunately, it is necessary to conclude from the investigations of many researchers (for example, Csikszentmihalyi, 1996; Torrance, 1995a), that our schools are the major culprits. Teachers, peers, and the educational system as a whole all diminish children's urge to express their creative possibilities.

What would cause a school and its teachers to squelch students' imagination and originality? Some light was shed on this problem by psychologist E. P. Torrance's study of first graders (1963, 1979), which is described in Chapter Five. Scores for boys and girls were similar in first grade, but when the same test was given to the children as they were about to enter third grade, boys outperformed girls in all categories. Current research (Orenstein, 1994; Sadker & Sadker, 1994) confirms that however inadvertently, many teachers are still passing on the same gender bias to yet another generation of children: "After almost two decades of research grants and thousands of hours of classroom observation, we remain amazed at the stubborn persistence of these hidden sexist lessons" (Sadker & Sadker, 1994, p. 1).

Another element may be deduced from the classic research of Adorno and colleagues (1950). They devised a test of "authoritarianism." It is known that people with this personality characteristic become quite angry when those in an "inferior" position fail to behave in a subservient way. Authoritarians want instant obedience from those "below" them. The researchers learned that authoritarian people also feel that they themselves should be subservient to those they perceive as being above them. Thus, the "authoritarian" is someone with an exaggerated sense of social hierarchies, of "pecking orders." Dominance and subordination are the key factors in life for them. The test was administered to hundreds of persons in nearly four hundred American occupations. Not surprisingly, state police scored highest in authoritarianism, followed closely by army officers (soldiers in general were in the bottom half). Teachers ranked third.

Let us look at what the first two occupations have in common.

o Both bear arms and are allowed by society to use them to enforce their orders.

o Both wear uniforms with abundant signs of rank: collar pins, arm patches, hat bands, and "scrambled eggs" (gold decorations) on the visors of senior officers.

o If the orders of police and army officers are not obeyed, the public or military court system will dole out punishments.

o Those in an inferior station must salute them. This custom developed in the Middle Ages, when serfs were forced to grasp the forelocks of their own hair and pull their heads down as a gesture of respect for the lord of the manor as he rode around inspecting his fields.

o Those who rank below them must call them "sir." This derives from "sire," the medieval term for the lord of the manor.

Students and school personnel do not have such overt insignia, but the differences between students and teachers and between students and administrators are there. Not many teachers are seen publicly disagreeing with the principal, superintendent, or school committee on important issues. Furthermore, in most school systems, they can expect relatively complete obedience in their classrooms. Teachers can assume that serious infringements will be duly punished by their superiors. When teachers close classroom doors, their reign is more or less supreme (although there are admittedly more exceptions today than when the Adorno study was done). Even now, however, a student who occasionally asks original and unexpected questions or suggests alternative answers to an authoritarian teacher may be devalued and labeled as disruptive (Sternberg & Grigorenko, 1997).

Torrance (1995a) suggested another reason for the shortage of teachers who recognize and encourage creativity in their students. His thesis is that there is excessive risk involved in being such an outstanding teacher: "The creative teacher is involved in discovery, risking, pushing the limits, and taking a step into the unknown. This is serious business—dangerous business. When you challenge students to be creative, you lose control" (p. 107).

The way in which children receive instructions may also affect their creative freedom. In a study by Koestner, Ryan, Bernieri, and Holt (1984), children were randomly assigned to two groups to paint. Both groups were given instructions about neatness. One group received controlling instructions and a set of rules for neatness. The other group received informational instructions about neatness; in that set of instructions, the reasons for the rules were explained and children's natural reluctance to follow such rules was recognized. The children in the informational instructions group produced paintings that were judged to be more creative than those done by children in the other group. The authors concluded that children who were given some autonomy by not having heard rules for neatness were more motivated to be creative in their paintings.

Another study found that children's perceptions of their autonomy within the classroom environment can significantly affect their motivation and performance. The study determined large individual differences in terms of autonomy within classrooms (Ryan & Grolnick, 1986). Newer research has found systematic differences between classrooms in children's perceptions of how much self-determination they are allowed to have (Picariello, 1994).

Sternberg and Lubart (1995) suggest that schooling also inhibits creativity by imparting a low tolerance for failure; schools therefore make students risk averse. It is easy to see how this risk aversion develops and escalates as a student progresses through school. For one thing, failure is often punished in some way, whereas good work is rewarded. Failure might result in students' having to do makeup or remedial work or might cause them the humiliation of appearing unmotivated or dull-witted. Risk taking in school is discouraged, both explicitly and implicitly. All the way through college and graduate school, students often opt for safe courses rather than challenging ones. Sternberg and Lubart stated, "One of the problems with the culture of the schools . . . is that students never learn how to take sensible risks, a skill that will be needed if they are going to do genuinely creative work" (pp. 48–49).

A child's classmates may also have a negative impact on creative drives. This has been confirmed by older research, as well as by the latest studies. Torrance (1968) found that creativity scores for both sexes became consistently lower after third grade. He labeled this the "fourth grade slump" and suggested that pressure to conform with peers increases at this age. Other studies by Torrance (1970, 1988) also demonstrated the importance of peer influence in supporting or discouraging creative efforts. Teresa Amabile (1989, 1996), who has been investigating the social psychology of creativity for more than twenty years, agreed that peer pressure is a major inhibitor of children's willingness to take risks and discourages them from articulating or presenting creative ideas.

Teachers and peers are not the only culprits in this issue. Clearly, the whole educational system is involved. Stories abound about teachers who have attempted to organize innovative school projects, only to have the principal or school committee block them for being too risky (Torrance, 1995d). As an example of an impediment at the national level, it may be noted that there are currently far more educational services for the retarded than for the gifted. American ideals of egalitarianism and anti-elitism also play a part in this neglect of students who have the potential to become important innovators. Almost half of the states require no special educational provisions for gifted and talented students (Winner, 1996).

Hallman (1967) discovered several obstacles to creativity in the schools he studied. Both students and teachers contribute to pressure to conform (including inflexible rules, standardized routines, and the quashing of original ideas as the most salient inhibitor), the ridiculing of unusual ideas, intolerance of a playful attitude, and excessive questing for success in terms of extrinsic rewards. Dacey and Packer (1992) reported that these problems continue to characterize many school systems.

John-Steiner (1997) pointed out that Western schooling methods emphasize what she calls "seated learning." These methods discourage young children's natural tendencies to use all their senses in learning. The physical organization of most schools encourages a reliance on language as the major means of learning, especially in having students listen to the teacher. This prevents students from being fully engaged and is especially deleterious to those who require a more active approach to learning. John-Steiner cited many eminent creators who did not do well in school as children. Howard Gardner (1997a) identified eight types of intelligence: linguistic, logical, spatial, musical, kinesthetic, introspective, influential, and apprehensive of the natural world. He defined intelligence as "the ability to solve problems or fashion products that are valued in at least one cultural setting or community" (p. 35) and stressed that American schools only recognize and highly value the logical and linguistic types of intelligence.

Nevertheless, the question of why some teachers are so authoritarian (and thus anticreativity) remains. Several studies have indicated that teachers are likely to come from families in which the father has an extremely powerful personality. With such a model, a bright young woman is naturally attracted to a vocation in which she can imitate her father's power. Adorno and his colleagues did their research some years ago, and no doubt the teaching profession has changed significantly since then. Furthermore, there are a greater number of jobs and professions available to women today that offer positions of power, and women have far more education and more opportunities to pursue work outside the home (Ochse, 1991). Teaching still has a strong attraction for the authoritarian personality, however. Clearly, some people go into teaching in order to dominate others, whereas others do it in order to help their students flourish. There may be more of the former, as evidenced by the fact that the longer children are in school, the more creativity scores decline.

A study carried out by Dacey and his colleagues at Cornell University (Dacey, 1976; Ripple & Dacey, 1969) suggested ways in which the process eventually suppresses the creativity of both genders. They studied the creative abilities of twelve hundred seventh and eighth graders in forty-five school systems located in three states. One of the main instruments they used was the Story-Writing Test described in Chapter Five. The results of this test appear in Figure 4.1.

As you can see, the largest group of students scored in the bottom third of the possible range of scores (the top score on this test was 22). Students in this group had an average score of 7. A smaller group of students scored in the top third and averaged around 18. Although the overall mean score was 10.2, very few students actually got that score.

Such a finding surprised the researchers. It has long been known that almost all human traits and abilities are "normally distributed" if enough people are tested. This means that most people are average, with only a

Figure 4.1. Distribution of Junior High School Creativity Scores.

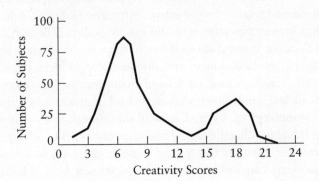

few getting the lowest or highest scores. A normal distribution of scores produces a bell-shaped curve on a graph. Figure 4.2 illustrates how IQ scores are typically distributed.

Why, then, are the creativity scores shown in Figure 4.1 distributed so differently? One obvious explanation would be that creativity reflects genetic inheritance; most people inherit only a little creative ability, and a few lucky people inherit a lot. If this were so, it would produce a graph such as is seen in Figure 4.1. There are several problems with this hypothesis, though. For one thing, it does not explain *why* creativity should be different from all other traits. In addition, as was discussed in the last chapter, there is little other evidence that creativity is that highly influenced by genes.

The Cornell researchers came to a different conclusion. They asked themselves, What would happen if, at birth, creativity naturally falls into a normal distribution just like IQ, but then is affected adversely by some major experience such as attending school (Dacey & Ripple, 1967). Over time, such an effect could move everyone's score lower on the graph. It would not affect the *shape* of the distribution, however; it would still be bell-shaped, but with a lower average.

Suppose, though, that the suppressing effect of school is only powerful enough to affect some of the students—the bottom three-fourths, for example. Suppose those in the top quarter of creative ability are relatively impervious to the effect. They would go on being creative no matter how they are treated by the school system. If this situation were true, then we would expect a curve just like the one we see in Figure 4.1. Hence, our educational system's suppression of creativity in all but the most gifted students appears to be the most likely explanation for the Cornell results.

Figure 4.2. Typical Distribution of IQ Scores.

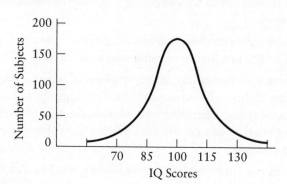

Finally, Dacey's research on families, reported in Chapter Three (Dacey, 1989b), bolstered the conclusion that schools generally do not reinforce creative thinking. As was noted, neither the parents nor the children regarded the children's schools as having any real impact on their talents. This was true whether the school was viewed as traditional or innovative.

Whichever dynamics are causing the problem in schools, no amount of money will correct them as long as teachers maintain their current attitudes toward creativity. Obviously, most teachers do not intentionally suppress creativity, but apparently they need to avoid what seems to be a natural impulse to "correct" nonconforming ideas, rather than examining or encouraging them.

Training Teachers to Cultivate Students' Creativity

A number of efforts have been made to encourage teachers to overcome this problem. E. P. Torrance (1975) has been a leader in this endeavor. He and his associates at the University of Minnesota conducted twenty studies of ways to help teachers cultivate creativity in their elementary school students. Unhappily, the studies' results indicate that the efforts were unsuccessful. Torrance hypothesized a number of causes:

- Teachers' personality characteristics and their beliefs about what is expected of them make it difficult for them to change their teaching styles.
- Change is difficult because the average teacher is preoccupied with critiquing and correcting students' work instead of being open to unusual ideas. It was found that the average teacher frequently

interrupts students as they are speaking, in order to make evaluative remarks about their thinking and attempt to improve their work.

o Teachers fail to reinforce interesting, original responses, perhaps because they just do not recognize them as such.

o Teachers may also fail to protect students of superior creative-thinking ability, who often experience pressures to reduce their productivity and originality and who are frequently given less credit than they deserve for their positive contributions to the group's success.

o Students need vehicles for creative writing, such as a class newspaper or school magazine, which motivate them to do high-quality work. These opportunities are seldom provided, as they can be very time-consuming for staff.

Treffinger, Ripple, and Dacey (1968) reasoned that a teacher's inability to cultivate creativity probably results from deeply ingrained attitudes and values. Thus, it would take substantial time and effort to overcome these unconscious biases. The researchers designed an extensive program of lectures, exercises, and discussions, which required a full week of day and evening sessions. They measured teacher attitudes before and after the experience by rating their responses to the statements below. These statements come from the surveys they filled out before the sessions. They have been reproduced here because those that show negative attitudes toward creativity are deemed to be still representative of many teachers' attitudes today. The researchers presented the statements to the teachers and rated the responses on a scale from 1 to 5; 1 meant strong agreement, 2 meant agreement, 3 meant no opinion, 4 meant disagreement, and 5 meant strong disagreement.

TEACHERS' ATTITUDES TOWARD CREATIVE STUDENTS

1. The creative child is a liability to my classroom because of his disruptive manner.

2. A creative problem-solving ability is probably a natural strength that some students have and that others lack, so most of our efforts to improve it in our students would be in vain.

3. The creative child is not likely to be well liked by his or her classmates.

4. It is possible to improve pupils' ability to think creatively and to solve problems through direct instruction in creativity.

5. Only a few people in every thousand can truly be considered creative.

6. Because of the explosion of knowledge in the world, children cannot be taught how to cope with every situation they will ever meet; this indicates the need for teaching creative thinking if we can.

7. I think I could identify the most creative children in my class.

8. Most paper-and-pencil tests of creativity do not really measure pupils' creative abilities.

9. The most typical creative person is the "nonconformist" type who may well be in need of a bath.

10. Even if it is possible to teach children to become more creative, there are serious questions about the necessity or wisdom of doing so.

11. Creative people are made, not born.

12. "Creativity" is something found among only a few people; most of us lack it almost entirely.

13. There is a very thin line that divides the very creative act from the pathological.

14. If we try teaching pupils to become more creative, we run the risk of creating a nation of nonconforming individuals who will be unable to maintain normal social relations.

Statements seen as favoring the likelihood of fostering creativity are 4, 6, 7, and 8.

At the end of the weeklong series of sessions with the teachers, it was found that significant changes in their attitudes had occurred. They had adopted much more positive feelings about creativity and those who have it in abundance. No follow-up of the teachers' classroom performance was possible in this study, but it did offer some hope that with sustained methods, schools can become places that enhance creative talent.

In defense of teachers, it is undeniable that by their very nature creative students demand more of their teachers than average students do (Torrance, 1995d; Zimmerman, 1997). It is also important to appreciate that teachers increasingly have more and more things to manage during the school day, making it difficult for even the most willing of them to teach consistently in the manner they might prefer. Perkins (1992) cited Lee Shulman of Stanford University on this dilemma: "Teaching is impossible. If we simply add together all that is expected of a typical teacher and take note of the circumstances under which those activities are to be carried out, the sum makes greater demands than any individual can possibly fulfill. Yet, teachers teach" (p. 51).

Evaluating Schools

Let us hasten to add that negative findings about the impact of educators apply only to schools in general. Certainly there are some schools and many teachers about whom this description is untrue. Based on their research, Dacey and Packer (1992) listed criteria that parents can use to investigate a school before allowing their child to enroll in it. This list is reproduced below in simplified form as an indication of the kinds of practices and values that mark schools in which a child's emerging creativity is likely to be supported.

CRITERIA FOR SCHOOLS THAT
SUPPORT THE CREATIVELY GIFTED

Acceptance in the existing gifted program depends on measurement of creative abilities. There is a mentor program (in which specialists in the community volunteer time to advise and encourage those interested in their field) for talented and creative students.

The school provides adequately for intrascholastic and interscholastic competitions (for example, science fairs, math games, poetry and debating contests, "Olympics of the Mind," and so forth).

The school has set aside physical spaces for long-term projects and research.

The school offers students instruction in what creativity is and how they may nurture it.

Specialists on the staff hold degrees or other training in teaching the creatively gifted.

These specialized personnel belong to state or national organizations for the creatively gifted.

The principal is committed to the program, as seen in his or her economic policy toward it, for example.

There is a generous field trip policy.

Psychology staff members (counselors, school psychologists) cooperate well with the program. Teachers who are not involved in the program say they believe it is a good one.

Student program members say that they like it.

Societal Rewards as Help or Hindrance

Amabile, Hennessey, and Grossman (1986) cite the story of the young Albert Einstein as an example of how motivation affects creativity. From childhood to young adulthood, he was so deeply fascinated with his self-chosen work that little else was important to him while he was engaged in it. Amabile has been a leader in researching the social influences on creativity and has proposed the "intrinsic motivation principle," explaining this idea as follows: "When people are primarily motivated to do some creative activity by their own interest in and enjoyment of that activity, they may be more creative than they are when primarily motivated by some goal imposed on them by others. . . . Sylvia Plath, for example, appeared to be crippled for long periods of time by a concern with evaluation and competition and the demands that others made on her" (Amabile, 1983a, p. 15). Plath's concern with possible external rewards, such as winning competitions, required her to try working without intrinsic motivation. Recently, Amabile has expanded, refined, and revised her earlier research, especially as it pertains to the workplace (Amabile, 1996, 1997; Amabile, Goldfarb, & Brackfield, 1990; Amabile, Hill, Hennessey, & Tighe, 1994) as will be discussed later in this chapter.

Amabile is not the first to study the effects of incentives on creativity. Lepper, Greene, and their associates (Greene & Lepper, 1974; Lepper & Greene, 1975; Lepper, Sagotsky, Dafoe, & Greene, 1982; Lepper, Greene, & Nisbett, 1983) have researched what they call the "overjustification effect." They found that when too much extrinsic motivation is present (such as pay, praise, or promotion), creativity is dampened. This is also true when a person's natural interest in a project is undermined by, for instance, unnecessary rewards or motivational instructions or choices (Amabile, 1982a, 1982b; Amabile & Gitomer, 1984; Amabile, DeJong, & Lepper, 1976; Amabile, Hennessey, & Grossman, 1986; Berlas, Amabile, & Handel, 1979; Garbarino, 1975; Greene & Lepper, 1974; Lepper & Greene, 1975; Lepper, Greene, & Nisbett, 1983; Kernoodle-Loveland & Olley, 1979). These researchers have learned that rewards can cause a narrow focus on the task, turning the goal into one of getting it done quickly and taking no risks. People begin to be controlled by the payoff and gradually come to lose whatever intrinsic interest in the task they may have had.

As a result of this research, Amabile (1982a, 1982b, 1983a, 1983b) originally proposed her own theory of the impact of the social environment on creativity and a way of measuring creativity by judging creative products. This method of measurement is called the Consensual Assessment Technique (CAT). It employs appropriate judges—usually people with formal training in the domain under study—to assess the creativity of study participants' products, such as collages, paintings, or computer programs.

Amabile's 1983 model had two purposes: (1) to supply a frame of reference for understanding social influences on creative behavior and (2) to advance the field of creativity research. The model was one of the earliest to include cognitive, personality, motivational, and social influences on the creative process and was the first to propose an explanation of how each of these factors might modify different steps in the creative process. The model was also original in its particular emphasis on the function of motivation in the creative process and of social influences on creativity.

In 1983, Amabile believed that intrinsic motivation alone was paramount and that extrinsic motivation was inevitably detrimental to creativity (Amabile, 1983b). She has modified her position as more empirical evidence has accumulated (for example, Amabile, Goldfarb, & Brackfield, 1990), asserting that this statement is inaccurate. Certain types of extrinsic motivation can add to creative incentive, or at least not hamper it: "We now have considerable evidence that extrinsic motivation need not undermine intrinsic motivation and creativity. Indeed, it appears possible that some types of extrinsic motivation may enhance creativity" (Amabile, 1996, p. 117). Nevertheless, she and Hennessey now hold that most research evidence indicates that "working for reward, under circumstances that are likely to occur naturally in classrooms and workplaces every day, can be damaging to both intrinsic motivation and creativity" (Hennessey & Amabile, 1998, p. 675).

These types of extrinsic motivation that enhance creativity are called "synergistic extrinsic motivators" because they have a positive effect in combination with intrinsic motivation. Synergy includes the idea that the whole is more than the sum of its parts. In this case, extrinsic and intrinsic motivators each gain strength from their relationship to one another. Amabile proposes two psychological mechanisms that create such synergy: (1) "extrinsics in service of intrinsics," which are extrinsic factors that make the creator feel competent or that allow more task involvement, such as rewards like better equipment and supplies that enable a person to do exciting work, and (2) "stage-appropriate motivation," which includes any external motivators that occur at a stage of the creative process in which they are particularly useful. The four-stage process of problem identification, preparation, response generation, and validation and communication that originated with Wallas (1926) offers many opportunities for idea validation, which is a reward. For example, it is most important to determine the novelty of an idea at the problem-identification and response-generation stages (Amabile, 1997).

Although some researchers continue to maintain that extrinsic motivation is always detrimental to creativity, often insisting that competition is particularly harmful (Kohn, 1993a, 1993b; Schwartz, 1990), others have become convinced, as has Amabile, that this may be true in some instances but definitely not in all (Bernstein, 1990; Cameron & Pierce, 1994; Eisenberger & Cameron, 1996; Eisenberger & Selbst, 1994). Cameron and Pierce's meta-analysis (1994) of ninety-six studies seems to offer particularly convincing evidence that external reward does not necessarily decrease intrinsic motivation and may in some instances augment it. Although this work has recently been criticized for the statistical methods it used (Lepper, 1998), Eisenberger and Cameron (1998) remain convinced of the validity of their original results.

In *Creativity in Context* (1996), Amabile revised her 1983 model and terminology (see Figure 4.3). Amabile's theory of the three components of creativity suggests that any creative performance or production requires domain-relevant skills, creativity-relevant processes, and task motivation.

1. "Domain-relevant skills" refer to what we commonly call talent or expertise. A certain degree of technical skill is required before one can perform in any given domain of activity. One must have extensive familiarity with the relevant domain, including necessary factual and technical skills. For example, a good working knowledge of language, the ability to use metaphor and imagery, and a mastery of the principles of scansion might be considered domain-relevant skills for the poet.

2. "Creativity-relevant processes" include all those strategies or dispositions that an individual uses to facilitate the creative process. Examples include the ability to break functional fixity (see Chapter Five), to suspend judgment (Chapter Two), and to take risks (as discussed earlier in this chapter).

These first two components have been considered in different ways by many creativity researchers. Amabile's original contribution came with the prominent role she gave to task motivation in creativity. Here, she has expanded on earlier work by social psychologist Edward Deci (1971, 1975) and others.

3. "Task motivation" can be seen as the most important determinant of the difference between what people can do and what they will do. The former is determined by the level of domain-relevant skills and creativity-relevant processes; the latter is determined by these two in conjunction with an intrinsically motivated state. According to Amabile's framework, task motivation is responsible for determining whether the creative process will begin at all and whether it will continue. Domain-relevant and creativity-relevant processes make their contribution after the process has begun and is being sustained by the motivated individual.

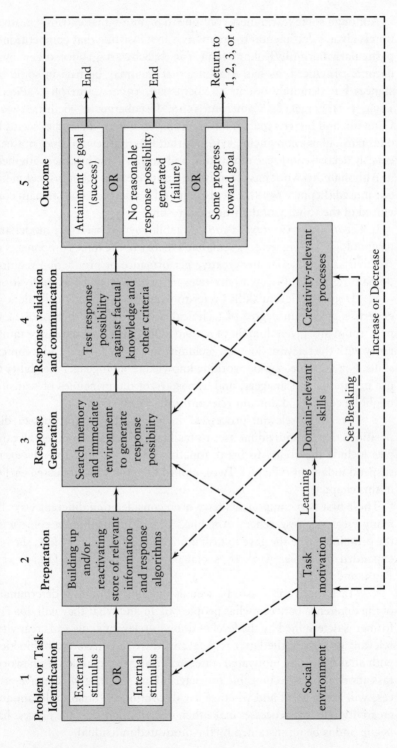

Figure 4.3. Amabile's 1996 Revision of the Componential Model of Creativity.

Source: *Amabile, 1996, p. 113. Copyright © 1996 by Westview Press. Reprinted by permission of Westview Press.*

The most noticeable and important change is the prominent addition of the large rectangle at the lower left representing the social environment. Amabile (1996) has stressed that even though the only direct line shown in the graphic is between social environment and task motivation, the social environment also influences the other components, as clarified in Figure 4.4, which gives additional details about the social environmental influences on creative processes.

Amabile's research has great implications for cultivating and supporting children's creativity. Some of the most useful are discussed in detail in Amabile's *Growing Up Creative* (1989). As we have seen, promoting intrinsic motivation, especially among gifted children, remains a major focus. Amabile (1996) has summarized three basic ideas.

1. Encourage autonomy by respecting children's individuality and by avoiding anxious control of their activities. In the socialization

---

**Figure 4.4. Detailed View of the Componential Model:
Direct and Primary Social-Environmental Influences.**

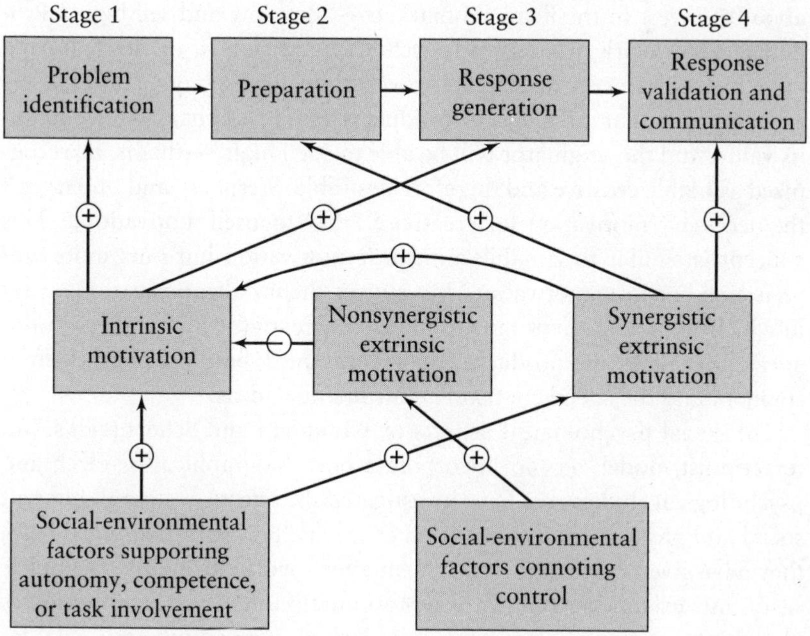

Source: *Amabile, 1996, p. 119. Copyright © 1996 by Westview Press.
Reprinted by permission of Westview Press.*

process, emphasize guiding principles and the reasons for them, rather than rules.

2. Teach children to focus on the intrinsic joy of learning and of developing competencies. Help them to achieve a cognitive distance from the extrinsic constraints placed on them without ignoring those constraints completely. The point is to teach children to keep rewards, competition, evaluation, and other constraints in perspective so that these factors do not overwhelm children's intrinsic enjoyment of their work.

3. Model independent engagement in creative activities and provide children with opportunities to discover their own creativity through a variety of activities and experiences.

Other recent research supports these principles, including Conti, Coon, and Amabile (1996), Gerrard, Poteat, and Ironsmith (1996), Hennessey (1989), Kemple, David, and Wang (1996), Meador (1992), and Runco (1996b). Several other theorists are currently studying motivational and social aspects of creative behavior from different perspectives. Sternberg and Lubart (1992, 1993a, 1993b, 1995) state their "investment approach" to creativity in the common advice given to a person who is about to invest in the financial markets—"Buy low and sell high." Producing good work in an already well-accepted vein is, in effect, buying high. Investing energy in developing something new is buying low, but the expectation is that if the idea or product is valuable, others will recognize its value, and the originator will be able to "sell high"—that is, be recognized as highly creative and therefore desirable. Sternberg and Lubart call the necessary motivation for creativity "task-focused motivation." This concept is similar to Amabile's intrinsic motivation but puts more emphasis on extrinsic motivation. Investment theory also posits three ways in which the social environment influences creativity. First, others evaluate creative ideas and products. Second and third, both the physical environment and the social context can inspire new ideas.

The social psychological aspects of Woodman and Schoenfeldt's "interactionist model" (1990) incorporate both biographical research and psychological studies that have investigated the effects of several different social and physical environments on creativity. For their theoretical base, they have given particular credit to Amabile's work, including its emphasis on intrinsic motivation. In their formulation, however, more stress is placed on interactive social influences, such as competition and social facilitation, as well as the physical environment and cultural aspects. According to Woodman and Schoenfeld, "Individual differences in creativity are a function of the extent to which the social and contextual factors nurture the creative process" (p. 287).

Feldman, Csikszentmihalyi, and Gardner (1994a) also have an interactionist orientation. Their framework, which they call Domain-Individual-Field Interaction (DIFI), proposes that three subsystems interact to generate a creative product: the individual, the domain, and the field. The *domain* is "a formalized body of knowledge that is associated with a given field" (p. 20). For example, in the study of creativity, "art" is too large to be considered a single domain. One of its branches, such as painting or sculpture, would be considered a domain. A *field* is made up of the persons who support and contribute to the domain. The persons in the field will decide what new ideas or products become accepted into the domain. They therefore determine which efforts will be rewarded. "The easiest way to define a field is to say that it includes the following: art teachers and art historians . . . art critics . . . collectors . . . gallery owners and museum curators . . . and, finally, the peer group of artists whose interaction defines styles and revolutions of taste" (p. 22). Feldman, Csikszentmihalyi, and Gardner also believe that an understanding of the historical and social context is necessary to valid knowledge about creativity.

Two creativity theorists are working on what they call ecological models. Harrington (1990) saw the role of the social system in the creative process as capable of creating or destroying, of extending or limiting the potential of particular acts. He suggested that unlike biological ecologists, psychological ecologists must examine not only the objective ecosystem but also the subjectively perceived ecosystem. He argued that individuals seek psychosocial benefits that are thought to be intrinsic to or extrinsically associated with creative activities and projects and that this motivates them to engage in such activities. Harrington included four sets of factors in the objective ecosystem: the individual's personal resources, the distribution and complementary nature of those resources, the relevant resources residing in the rest of the ecosystem, and the functional relationships among creatively active persons and between these persons and the remainder of the ecosystem's resources.

Barron's ecological perspective on creativity (1995) focuses on stability, flexibility, and a systems approach. Barron has placed particular importance on balancing the conscious and the unconscious, as well as the male and female aspects, in both the individual and social forms. This balance is especially true for an acceptance of what he calls "contra-sex behavior" (that which is not sex-role stereotyped) and the capacity for spiritual or religious experience to take place, either individually or socially. Barron has noted that what is especially researchable is the relationship between, on the one hand, the increasing use of telecommunications and other such technologies and, on the other hand, increased population density and crowding.

An "evolving systems" approach to creativity (Gruber, 1988, 1995; Gruber & Davis, 1988) posits that many kinds of social relationships influence whether a creative individual's efforts will meet with success and reward. They stress that not only does the historical, societal, and institutional context affect creative people but creators themselves actively construct the society around them.

Creativity Across the Life Span

Although much of the research we have discussed so far is largely concerned with the preservation and nurturance of creativity in children, some investigators have been more concerned with how it continues to progress or fails to develop across the life span.

Dacey (1989c) has suggested that there are certain critical periods in life during which creative ability can be cultivated most effectively. Table 4.1 presents a list of these periods for males and females.

The basic premise of this theory is that a person's inherent creativity can best blossom during a period of crisis and change (Esquivel, 1995; Freeman, 1993; Hennessey, 1995; Litterst & Eyo, 1993; Moukwa, 1995; Tavalin, 1995; Zerbe, 1992). The six periods displayed in Table 4.1 are ages at which most people experience stress because of life changes. The theory includes the concept that major gains in creative performance are less likely with each succeeding period. That is, what happens to the person in the early years is far more influential than what happens in the later years, because younger people are more susceptible to the influences of the social environment than older people are. In addition, the older

---

Table 4.1. Peak Periods for Creativity.

Males' Ages	Females' Ages
1. 0–5	0–5
2. 11–14	10–13
3. 18–20	18–20
4. 29–31	29–31
5. 40–45	(37?) 40–45
6. 60–65	60–65

Source: *Dacey, 1989b.*

people become, the less likely they are to have a sudden burst of highly creative production.

Albert (1996b) stated that the majority of children who show creative potential do not develop "substantial creativity after puberty into adolescence or adulthood" (p. 44). He proposed that true creativity begins around the age of ten, when the cognitive processes begin to operate on a more mature level, but he noted that a "dead period" may appear around the time of puberty, as social and educational influences at this time stress clarity in thinking and conventionality in behavior, making creative efforts less likely. Stressing how important it is to creative development for adolescents to mature socially and to continue working throughout adolescence, he noted "the remarkably consistent timetable for first major creative products and exceptional sports performances, almost all of which appear in the early to middle twenties in a variety of domains and across cultures" (p. 49).

Mentor and apprentice relationships are particularly influential in young adulthood. Mentors not only recognize and encourage the creative achievements of young adults but also informally teach professional values, ethics, and work habits that become crucial aspects of the younger person's drive and productivity (Mockros, 1996). Creative accomplishment in young and middle adulthood is often heavily influenced, especially for women, by a spouse's capacity and willingness to support the partner's efforts to maintain productivity (Helson, Roberts, & Agronick, 1995; Mockros, 1996; Ochse, 1991). Although it is incontestable that women have historically been far less productive in the arts and sciences than men, this is at least partially due to the social obligations and child-rearing duties that fall upon them (Abra, 1989). "Freedom from interruption by children is a luxury that relatively few women are afforded. . . . Women are constantly held up by people who demand their attention and interrupt their work. They have no wives to insulate them from outside intrusions" (Ochse, 1991, p. 340).

Changes in creativity during later adulthood are now receiving more research attention, and researchers are taking a more optimistic outlook on creativity and aging (Runco, 1996a). In the past, declines in creativity with age have often been attributed to biological deterioration, but as early as 1968, Neugarten suggested that supposed declines in creativity in midlife and beyond are caused by sociocultural stereotypes about aging, rather than by aging itself (Neugarten as cited in Sasser-Coen, 1993).

In another recent study, social influences have also been shown to have an impact on older adults' creativity. Mockros (1996) interviewed ninety-two highly creative men and women over the age of sixty to learn how interpersonal relationships influenced their development as exceptional individuals. She found that social conditions were important to the development of these creators' potential. The work habits, work ethics, and philosophies that continued to sustain their creative efforts originated and were elaborated through interactions with others. Evidence from life-span psychological research combined with scholarship in art history led Cohen-Shalev (1989) to conclude that the number of successfully aging artists has been routinely underestimated and that elderly artists often suffer from discrimination by critics and the public, which is more likely to limit their production than any actual decrements of old age.

Culture's Role in Genius and Creativity

In this section, we move to a consideration of an even broader aspect of the social environment—culture. Of particular interest is something that has been noted since antiquity—great geniuses do not appear at regular intervals in history. During some periods, clusters of brilliant people, often interacting with each other, have flourished. Other periods have been devoid of such eminence.

Why? Do the circumstances in a particular historical era make it possible to fulfill creative potential? For example, was a thirst for philosophical drama during Greece's golden age responsible for its abundance of illustrious playwrights? Were political conditions in late eighteenth-century America responsible for inspiring the writers of the Constitution? Were economic conditions in the Western Hemisphere responsible for the inventions in the late nineteenth and early twentieth centuries?

Or does genius result from genetics, which cannot be predicted, aside from the expectation that there will always be some people who are extremely creative? If so, then the great creative historical epochs have come about because geniuses happened to have been born in them.

One of the first to study the question scientifically was the anthropologist Kroeber (1944). He noted that not only have clusters of geniuses appeared irregularly, but when they do, it is almost always in one particular field of endeavor. Solitary contributions such as those of Copernicus and Kepler have been rare. Kroeber also suggested that cultural improvement tends to start in one small area and then sweep through the culture. Thus, he concluded that cultural conditions are the crucial factor. He argued, "Genetics leaves only an infinitesimal possibility for the racial stock occupying England to have given birth to no geniuses at all between 1450 and 1550 and a whole series of geniuses in literature, music, science, philosophy, and politics between 1550 and 1650" (p. 10).

To argue, however, that the state of the times is the crucial variable begs the question, What is there about a certain period that causes potential genius to come forward and be fulfilled? Another anthropologist, Gray (1966), has offered a theory.

Calling it an "epicyclical theory," Gray suggested that three types of periods are repeated throughout history: social, economic, and political. In each type of cycle, things go from good to bad to good again. The cycles are relatively independent of each other, but when more than one peaks at the same time (when they become highly developed), the odds that creative potential will be realized are greatly increased. When all three cycles peak at once, genius becomes certain. Of course, Gray's theory is much more complicated than this, but these are its essentials. In a marvelously cocksure statement, Kroeber (1944) summarized this point of view: "If we are interested primarily in culture and how it works, we can disregard *personalities* except as *inevitable mechanisms* or *measures of cultural expression*" (italics ours, p. 10).

The great American psychologist William James (1880) took issue with the cultural position, believing that the interaction of highly creative individuals was causative. Whenever such people get together, the community starts "vibrating": "Blow must follow blow so fast that no cooling can occur in the intervals. Then the mass of the nation grows incandescent, and may continue to glow by pure inertia long after the originators of its internal movement have passed away. We often hear surprise that in these high tides of human affairs . . . individual geniuses should seem so exceptionally abundant" (p. 455).

Well-known psychiatrist Silvano Arieti (1976) also rejected the emphasis on cultural factors. He asked, "Can we see Shakespeare only as an inevitable mechanism of Elizabethan culture? Had he not been born, could another Englishman of his time have expressed the culture of his period, as well, or achieved such heights" (p. 299)? Arieti held that people become "geniuses" because of the juxtaposition of three factors:

1. The culture is right. The airplane would not have been invented if the gasoline engine had not been invented. That engine propelled the Wrights' plane, as well sparking the public's interest in travel.

2. The genes are right. The person's intelligence, which is known to be genetic, must be high. Creativity, which may or may not be genetic, must also be high.

3. The interactions are right. Arieti offers the examples of Freud, Jung, and Adler (see Chapter Two). If Jung and Adler had not had Freud to compete over—and against—it is questionable whether either

Jung or Adler would hold such a high position in psychology to-day. Freud, too, worked hard to refute his own mentors, as well as his own students' new ideas. From his letters, we know that he was highly antagonistic to those who revised his theories, although these exchanges undoubtedly fertilized many new discoveries (Webster, 1995).

This is not to say that all creative achievement is born of competition, although much surely has been. In the final analysis, there is always something mysterious about high creativity. Arieti summarized it well: "Actually, the significant synthesis is the creative process itself. It is so significant and unpredictable as to appear magic. Even when a culture is propitious, the significant synthesis occurs in a very small percentage of its people" (1976, p. 302).

Still, cultures may be positive or negative toward genius. Arieti labeled cultures that facilitate creativity "creativogenic" societies. Such a society should, of course, be based on fair and just laws. He pointed to Franklin D. Roosevelt's concept of a society that fosters the "four freedoms": freedom from fear and want, freedom of speech and worship. A society that does not offer such freedoms would stifle creativity. But the availability of these four freedoms would not in themselves guarantee the emergence of genius either.

Nine Features of the "Creativogenic" Society

What characteristics would provide such impetus? Arieti (1976) proposed nine features that seem essential to the "creativogenic" society.

1. The availability of cultural (and certain physical) means. Mozart would not have been successful had he been born in Africa, nor Michelangelo in Alaska.

2. Openness to cultural stimuli. Not only must the means be available to the creative person, but the population (or at least some significant part of it) must also desire the results. Eighth-century Europe was not a very hospitable place in which to be a genius.

3. An emphasis on becoming, not just being. "A culture that puts emphasis only on immediate gratification, sensuousness, comfort, and immediate pleasure does not promote creativity" (p. 314).

4. Free access to cultural media for all citizens without discrimination. In the past, essential information has been made available only to a

privileged class—the clergy, the wealthy, the religious or ethnic majority, and, most often, members of the male sex. This, Arieti said, is the major reason for women's underrepresentation on the lists of great historical achievements. A number of authors have suggested that the woman's role as childbearer "sublimates"—that is, assuages her need—to be creative. Arieti claimed that this is a false explanation, in that society has cast the female role on women, leaving them little choice in the matter.

5. Freedom, or even moderate discrimination, after severe oppression or absolute exclusion. Of course, Arieti does not recommend this incentive, but he predicted that women and minorities would make more creative contributions in the near future.

6. Exposure to different and even contrasting cultural stimuli. Although cultures are strongly reinforced not to change (people usually believe that time has proved the value of cultures), incorporating new stimuli from other cultures makes creativity more likely. American multiculturalism and tolerance have obviously benefited here.

7. Tolerance for and interest in unusual viewpoints and ideas. This concept will be described at length in Chapter Five.

8. The opportunity for interaction between significant persons. As we concluded from the study of creative people's families in Chapter Three, crucial influences on young people's lives can come from many quarters, but only if they live in a society that permits and encourages interaction with others who have different views. For instance, the Warsaw Ghetto of World War II made contact between Christians and Jews virtually impossible, cutting off the chance for the exchange of imaginative ideas.

9. The promotion of incentives and awards. When Arieti wrote this, the possible negative effects of reinforcements had not yet been identified or studied. However, he did seem to have anticipated the importance of what came to be called intrinsic motivation, for he said, "The greatest award to creativity is creativity itself" (p. 324).

How can we discover whether these nine factors are really "creativogenic"? Arieti suggests we look at a group of individuals who have been creative far beyond what would have been expected of a group their size—the Jews. In the next section, we do so.

Modern Societal Effects on Jews' Creativity

The long history of persecution of the Jews has often been cited, and Arieti (1976) stated that not until Napoleon Bonaparte rose to power at the beginning of the nineteenth century (following the incorporation of the Declaration of the Rights of Man and the Citizen into the French Constitution) did Jews find a champion of their human rights. With certain well-known exceptions, the wave of liberation that began in Europe in 1848 with revolutions in Paris, Vienna, Venice, Berlin, and Milan has continued to the present.

Have these more positive conditions been reflected in the creativity of Jewish people? As Arieti documented extensively, the answer is a resounding yes. He cited many examples, such as the following: "Of the four people who have revolutionized the sociocultural world since [1848], two (Freud and Einstein) have been Jews, and one (Marx) was the son of Jewish parents converted to Christianity" (p. 326). The fourth was Darwin. In addition, from 1901 to 1970, the Nobel Prize went to twenty-eight times as many Jews as Gentiles. Second place went to French non-Jews, who won the prize six times as often as Gentiles in the rest of the world.

Arieti found that most of the time, the nine features he suggested have been present in Jewish life. When they have not been present, Jewish creative production has suffered severely. Five characteristics of modern Jews have been especially important.

- A well-established love of education, the pursuit of which made the Jews' liberation into the mainstream of society possible. "When the love of education is well established, it is relatively easy to make the transition from exclusive study of religious books to studies including other disciplines as well" (p. 334).

- Jews have had little prejudice against women who have wished to pursue careers. Consequently, the list of female Jewish innovators is long.

- Centuries of oppression have caused a universal desire in Jews to excel, in part as a means to safety.

- "Sensitized as they were to society's unfairness, they were always in favor of social innovations and reforms" (p. 335).

- Their interactions with persons of different backgrounds have been facilitated by their migrations to avoid persecution and achieve better lives. As a result, many have international relationships, which serve to broaden their perspectives.

Thus in the case of Jewish creativity, Arieti's theory seems to stand up well. He urges that if we were to cultivate eight of his "creativogenic" features (number 5—freedom after severe persecution—is excluded for obvious reasons), they might benefit all of humankind.

In light of the material presented in this chapter and in Chapter Three, one can see that many questions about the social influences on creativity remain to be answered.

PART THREE

PSYCHOLOGICAL FACTORS

5

TEN TRAITS THAT CONTRIBUTE TO THE CREATIVE PERSONALITY

How Kuriosity Killed the Kat

THIS IS THE STORY about a very curious cat named Kat. One day Kat was wandering in the woods where he came upon a big house made of fish. Without thinking he ate much of that house. The next morning when he woke up he had grown considerably larger. Even as he walked down the street he was getting bigger. Finally he got bigger than any building ever made. He walked up to the Empire State building in N.Y.C. and accidentally crushed it. The people had to think of a way to stop him, so they made this great iron box which made the cat curious. He finally got inside it but it was too heavy to get him out of again. There he lived for the rest of his life. But he was still curious until his death, which was 6,820,000 years later. They buried him in the state of Rhode Island, and I mean the whole state.

○

Some people reading this little story by a seventh-grade student might consider it merely cute. Others would notice the restless imagination darting from place to place, the bold exaggeration, the disdain for the trite. These are early signs that this boy's mind has great creative possibilities. He has developed differently from his less imaginative peers.

This chapter examines ten essential personal qualities that are often found to characterize creative individuals. A list of other traits that have also sometimes been found to be involved in creative production appears at the end of the chapter.

Ten Traits

Creativity scholars have not been able to discern whether personal qualities can be direct causes of creativity (Csikszentmihalyi, 1996; Winner,
1996). It seems clear, however, that these personal qualities are intimately
involved in the creative process (Aguilar-Alonso, 1996; Albert, Ed., 1992;
Amabile, Conti, & Collins, 1996; Barron, 1997; Durrheim & Foster,
1997; Eysenck, 1994; Kokot & Colman, 1997; Mellou, 1996; Simonton,
1992, 1995a). In addition, they seem to appear with consistency across
people and time (Albert, Ed., 1992; Dudek & Hall, 1992; Gardner &
Wolf, 1994; Helson, Roberts, & Agronick, 1995; Mellou, 1996; Simonton, 1992).

Winner (1996) stated, "For those who do make it into the roster of creators, a certain set of personality traits proves far more important than
having a high general IQ, or a high domain-specific ability, even one at the
level of prodigy. Creators are hard-driving, focused, dominant, independent risk-takers. . . . High ability children without at least some of these
factors have little hope of becoming major creators as adults" (p. 292).

As an example of how creative personality traits are consistent over
time, Dudek and Hall (1992) conducted a follow-up study of 124 male
architects originally studied by MacKinnon (1964, 1965). Dudek and
Hall concluded that despite life changes, the architects' personality characteristics remained "remarkably stable, and were at least partly responsible for the various degrees of their success" (1992, p. 313).

The best evidence indicates that one of the traits most critical to the creative process is tolerance of ambiguity, and that nine other principal traits
contribute both to the existence of this trait and to its role in promoting
creativity. Those nine traits are stimulus freedom, functional freedom,
flexibility, risk taking, preference for disorder, delay of gratification, freedom from sex-role stereotyping, perseverance, and courage. Another
characteristic, self-control, is partly affective and partly cognitive. We
consider it of such extreme importance to the creative individual's
makeup that we have devoted Chapter Six to this topic.

Tolerance of Ambiguity

An ambiguous situation is one in which no framework exists to help direct one's decisions and actions. Relevant facts are missing, the rules are
unclear, and the right procedures are unavailable (MacKinnon, 1978).
For a five-year-old, the first day of kindergarten would be an example. For
a forty-three-year-old, a high school reunion would be another instance.

People react differently to ambiguous situations. A situation that causes mild concern and heightened interest in some individuals may cause great tension and the desire to flee in others. The ability to remain open-minded in the face of ambiguity (and sometimes to enjoy it a lot) has been shown by both new and older research to be a consistent hallmark of the creative personality (Barron, 1968, 1995; Jay & Perkins, 1997; Sarnoff & Cole, 1983; Torrance, 1979). As Getzels (1975) put it, "From this point of view, the core of creativity is not in the unconscious or 'regression to primary process thought,' even in the service of the ego. It is not in withdrawal from the world; it is in openness to the world" (p. 334).

Imagine that there is a continuum from familiarity to strangeness. At a particular moment, the average person perceives some degree of familiarity or strangeness in a situation. A brother's face, for instance, would seem very familiar, and a flying saucer would seem very strange. Along the same continuum, there are also other emotional reactions to the situation, from boredom to interest, to excitement, fear, and terror. For the creative person, each of the emotional responses will occur at a farther point on this continuum than it would for the average person. Thus for the creative person, it would take a greater degree of strangeness or ambiguity to cause fear or terror. This inclination—to find strangeness interesting or exciting rather than frightening—fosters the ability to react creatively.

Stimulus Freedom

In the Story-Writing Test (Torrance, Peterson, & Davis, 1963), one technique used to assess stimulus freedom, participants are given a very minimal line drawing consisting of a somewhat ambiguous animal facing a blank rectangle. The instructions given with this drawing read, "Make up a story about the picture above. Be as descriptive and imaginative as you can. Think of a story that no one else would. Take up to eight minutes to complete it."

In one of Dacey's studies of creativity (Dacey & Ripple, 1967), twelve hundred junior and senior high school students from three different states took this test. Amazingly, about nine hundred of the stories were almost exactly alike. The typical story went like this:

---
o

Once upon a time there was a cat named Tom. He was very curious. One day he was looking around and spied a suspicious-looking box. He heard a scratching noise coming from it. He lifted up one side and there he saw a mouse named Jerry. Jerry was a fat little mouse and looked delicious. Without thinking, he made a grab for Jerry. The box crashed down on him and broke his head (skull, neck, back, and so forth)! That was how curiosity killed the cat!

○

The other three hundred stories were infinitely more varied. The story by the seventh grader that introduced this chapter was one of them. Here is one more, written by an eighth grader:

○

Joe, the chipmunk, was chasing a butterfly. He was starving. The sky overhead was streaked with clouds, the sun when it shone barely filtered through the trees, the burnt floor of the forest made the day seem completely gloomy. Joe wondered how he was going to get any food. He thought of last night—the men, the monsters. Some had four sharp claws, others had huge round eyes and pointed teeth. Joe was so scared! Suddenly a bear jumped out of the bushes and was after him. He ran to a stream and started swimming. He was safe—only for a little, but . . . [The story stops here because time ran out.]

○

What is the major difference between the first group of common stories and these others, which are so much more flamboyant? The writers of the first group of stories were almost always constrained by the lines that surround the picture.

If you were to reread the instructions for this exercise, you would note that they do not include a rule against going outside the picture's boundaries. Nevertheless, all the writers in the first group acted as though there had been such a rule. Under those circumstances, there isn't much to write about. The picture was purposely made extremely simple in order to see whether the writer's imagination could embellish it.

The writers of the creative stories frequently used the blank rectangle in the picture as a mere departure point from which they could travel to other, more exotic places. Many saw it as a window or a door through which they could exit the picture frame. Others (as in the story that introduced this chapter) stretched their imaginations mightily in describing the rectangle (for example, a house made of fish). And a small number (as in the last story above) simply disregarded it altogether.

The trait illustrated by this activity is known as "stimulus freedom." It has two aspects. When the stated rules of a situation interfere with the creative ideas of people who have stimulus freedom, they are likely to

Figure 5.1. The Nine-Dot Problem.

Source: *Dacey, 1989b.*

bend the rules to meet their needs. More important, they do not assume that rules exist when the situation is ambiguous (Getzels, 1975; Taylor, 1975; Torrance, 1979). The stimulus-bound person follows rules religiously, and when faced with ambiguity is likely to assume nonexistent directions in order to relieve the fear of being wrong. This fear is undoubtedly one of the most effective inhibitors of creativity.

An ability to solve the familiar Nine-Dot Problem presented in Figure 5.1 illustrates stimulus freedom. In this problem, all nine dots must be connected with four straight lines, and the pen or pencil is not allowed to leave the paper.

Torrance (1979) described the relevance of this problem to stimulus freedom:

> This is symbolic of the problem of first- and second-order changes. Most people assume that the nine dots contain a square and that the solution must be found within the square, a self-imposed condition. One's failure does not lie in the impossibility of the task, but in the attempted solutions. A person will continue to fail as long as he attempts only first-order change possibilities. Solutions become easy once one breaks away from the image of the square and looks outside of the nine dots. The solution is a second-order change which involves leaving the "field" [the square]. The analogy between this and many real life family, business, and educational situations is obvious [pp. 178–179].

The solution appears in Figure 5.2.

Breaking free from assumptions about a specific situation is only half the challenge. Sometimes it is also necessary to disengage from the mindset of one's surroundings. Famous creators have been known to go to extremes to achieve this. Levey (cited in Parnes & Harding, 1962) described some of their methods:

> In order to produce a state of inspiration, Schiller kept rotten apples in his desk; Shelley and Rousseau remained bareheaded in the sunshine; Bossuet worked in a cold room with his head wrapped in furs;

Milton, Descartes, Leibniz and Rossini lay stretched out; Tycho Brahe and Leibniz secluded themselves for very long periods. Thoreau built his hermitage, Proust worked in a cork-lined room, Carlyle in a noise-proof chamber, and Balzac wore a monkish working garb; Gretry and Schiller immersed their feet in ice-cold water; Guido Reni could paint, and de Musset could write poetry, only when dressed in magnificent style; Mozart, following exercise; Lamennais, in a room of shadowy darkness, and D'Annunzio, Farnol and Frost only at night. The aesthetician, Baumgarten, advised poets seeking inspiration to ride on horseback, to drink wine in moderation, and, provided they were chaste, to look at beautiful women [p. 87].

Functional Freedom

One way of identifying functional freedom is the Two-String Test (Dacey, 1989b; Ripple & Dacey, 1969; Maier, 1970). In this test, a participant stands between two strings hanging from a ceiling. Each string is almost nine feet long and is permanently attached to the ceiling. The strings are fourteen feet apart. The participant must figure out how to tie the two strings together. Two items are offered for use in finding the solution—a mousetrap and a wooden spring-type clothespin—only one of which may be used. Neither of them is long enough so that a person could use it to reach the second string.

The solution can involve either the clothespin or the mousetrap. Either one can be easily attached to one of the strings, then swung away from the other. The other string is grasped by the person, and the first string is caught as it swings back. Now they may be tied together readily.

Many people are unable to reach this solution because they cannot imagine using clothespins or mousetraps for anything other than their usual purposes (Dacey, 1989b; Duncker, 1945; MacKinnon, 1978; Torrance, 1979). This inability is called functional fixity, and it frequently blocks creative ideas. Its opposite is functional freedom.

Figure 5.2. Solution to the Nine-Dot Problem.

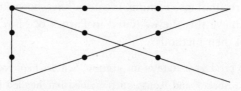

Source: *Dacey, 1989b.*

A case in point. A graduate student in psychology studied the problem and said, "I've got it! The answer is the rattrap. You catch a bunch of rats until you get one that isn't seriously hurt. You make a pet of it, then train it to be a 'trapeze' rat. It will then jump up on one of the strings and swing until it is able to swing over to you while you are holding the other string" (Dacey, 1989b, p. 24)! This is a good example of functional fixity; a rattrap can only be used to capture rats. His solution might work, but it is much more complicated than simply using the trap as a weight.

One young nun who was trying to solve the problem decided that the mousetrap and clothespin were being used as ruses. Lifting the apron of her religious habit (the long formal dress nuns used to wear), she seized the oversized rosary beads hanging from her belt and swung them over her head while holding one of the strings. The beads caught the other string and, beaming with self-satisfaction, she tied the strings together while those watching applauded. Although this is a creative method for solving the problem if you happen to be a nun, it would not be practical for most of us.

Researchers have used the Two-String Test as one technique to explore the functionally free thinking of thousands of people (Maier, 1970). Dacey and his colleagues (Dacey, Madaus, & Crellin, 1968; Dacey & Ripple, 1967; Ripple & Dacey, 1969) looked at the effects of education on functional fixity as seen in the Two-String Test. This ability was demonstrated to be inversely related to years of formal education. Although about 90 percent of sixth graders could solve the problem within the fifteen minutes allowed, only 80 percent of ninth graders could find a solution, just 50 percent of college students were successful, and only about 20 percent of graduate students achieved a solution.

Dacey and his colleagues concluded that education itself interferes with the required ability, which is to redefine the clothespin and the rattrap as weights. The more education a person has, the more rigid her or his perception of function is likely to become. In addition, education itself encourages complexity of thought. Thus, advanced education is more likely to produce a convoluted problem-solving style. This works against producing simple ideas, which comprise many of the world's greatest solutions.

It is necessary to distinguish here between problem solving and creativity. Problem solving may range all the way from the second grader's solution of a simple arithmetic problem to Einstein's theory of relativity. Only at the highly imaginative and original levels can problem solving be considered creative. Nevertheless, it is clear that functional fixity interferes with problem solving at all levels. As Smith and Amner (1997) pointed out, the creative individual is not bound by the stimulus situation.

Flexibility

One of the most interesting findings of the study of creative development has to do with the aspect of flexibility. Smith and Amner (1997) stated that the creative person is flexible in being open to the world, open to change, and prepared to bring about such change.

One instrument that offers an operational definition of flexibility is the Asking Questions Test. In this test, participants are given a simple drawing of a clown who is observing his reflection in water. They are then requested to list all the questions they can think to ask about the drawing. They are further instructed to refrain from using questions that might be answered just by looking at the picture and encouraged to come up with questions that would not occur to anyone else.

To score this test of flexibility, one must count the number of questions that fall into separate categories (Torrance & Templeton, 1963). An analysis of several thousand responses to this test indicate that there are twenty-one categories, such as the clown's clothing, his or her family and home, magical powers, characters not in the picture, whatever is beneath the water's surface, and so on.

Flexibility is the capacity to see the whole of a situation, rather than just a group of uncoordinated details. Many studies have shown that this trait is a critical element in the creative act (Gedo, 1997; MacKinnon, 1975, 1978; Torrance, 1979). Seeing all of the components in a problem, instead of just fixating on one of the parts, is much more likely to produce a creative solution. In high-pressure situations, such as taking a test, most people seem to latch on to the first plausible idea they get and push it as far as they can. For example, a common response to the test above is to ask six or seven questions about the clown's hat or shoes. This is in accordance with the directions, but it is not nearly as imaginative as the same number of divergent questions. Interestingly, flexibility is also closely tied to psychological health (Runco & Charles, 1997).

Risk Taking

A child's game of ringtoss can be used as a simple illustration of risk taking, the fourth outstanding characteristic of creative people (Atkinson, 1964; Cropley, 1997; Perkins, 1981; Shekerjian, 1991; Sternberg & Lubart, 1995). In this game, ten pegs are set up in a line vertical to the player. The farther the peg is from the tosser, the more difficult it is to hit. Therefore, more points are scored for hitting a peg that is farther away from the tossing line. People who aim at the number one position take a very limited risk. Even if they ring the pin all ten times, their maximum possible score is 10 (1 point per pin). Those who aim at the tenth pin have only one-tenth of the likelihood of scoring, so even though the tenth pin is worth 10 points, their most likely score will also be 10 (one success worth 10 points). Those willing to take a moderate risk would probably aim at the fifth pin. Here, the likely score would be 25 (five successes worth 5 points apiece). These figures obviously hold only for this particular game, but they are probably pretty representative of the real world. Those who take tiny or huge risks are less likely to be successful in their endeavors than those who take moderate risks. Unfortunately, as we discussed in Chapter Four, we socialize our children in ways that discourage sensible risk taking and that may even cause them to be risk averse (Sternberg & Lubart, 1995).

Failing to take sensible risks may lead to a sense of security but not to creativity. Sternberg and Lubart told of a well-known psychologist who bragged that she had never had an article rejected by a journal and had never been turned down for a grant. They stated, "If you have never had one of your ideas turned down . . . then the one thing you can be sure of is that you are not taking risks. People who play a very safe game may feel content that they never receive rejections. But you can be quite certain they are not the people who are making the most creative contributions" (1995, p. 214).

In a study examining adults' willingness to take higher risks for greater possible rewards (Sternberg & Lubart, 1996), forty-four participants completed creativity tasks. These involved expanding a title into an actual product (requiring both artwork and writing) and three risk-taking measures (contests, hypothetical scenarios, and a self-report questionnaire).

In the contest portion of the study, participants were invited to enter their artwork in one contest and their writing in another or both in the same contest. Two "pools" were established for each contest, one with a high risk and high payoff (one entrant could win $25) and one with a lower risk and lower payoffs (five entrants could win $10). The hypothetical scenarios included twelve situations in which participants were asked to imagine themselves. In each situation, there were two possible alternatives, one with a high risk and high reward and another with a low risk and low reward. A biographical questionnaire used a seven-point scale to assess risk-taking tendencies, including asking participants if they considered themselves high or low risk takers in drawing and writing.

The results showed that these adults tended to be risk avoidant. In the drawing contest, 73 percent chose the low-risk condition, and in the writing contest, 66 percent selected the low-risk condition. Those who took the low-risk option were given an average creativity score of 2.86 on a seven-point scale by judges with art expertise, whereas those who took the high-risk option received an average creativity score of 4.36. The hypothetical scenarios yielded similar results, supporting a connection between risk taking and creativity. In contrast to the contest and scenario measures, the self-reports showed little relationship to creative performance. The only item in the self-report that correlated (.34) with creative performance was overall risk taking in drawing.

Preference for Disorder

An instrument that is often used to measure this trait is the Barron-Welsh Figure Preference Test (Barron, 1968, 1995; Barron & Welsh, 1952; Welsh, 1959). In this test, participants are shown several pairs of simple, nonrepresentational line drawings and are asked to choose the one they prefer in each pair. The drawings vary in both composition and complexity. Some are extremely sparse and usually centrally balanced, whereas others are more intricate and off-center. Those who choose the largest number of this second kind of drawing are considered more creative.

Creative people regularly prefer complexity and asymmetry and choose these kinds of pictures over those that are simple and symmetrical. The underlying variable, says psychologist Frank Barron, is a preference for disorder, because it is ultimately more interesting to creative people than order. That is not to say that all artists live in disorderly garrets or that all scientists have poor personal grooming habits but rather that highly creative people enjoy the challenge of bringing order out of disorder with their own order (Barron, 1968, 1995; Barron & Welsh, 1952; Eysenck, 1997; MacKinnon, 1975, 1978; Welsh, 1959). They are particularly fascinated by unusual perspectives (Smith & Amner, 1997). "Creative individuals favor disorder and complexity, but only because they wish to integrate it into a higher order—yet simple—synthesis. . . . Creative persons create order in disorder and disorder in order" (Montuori, 1996, pp. 154–155).

MacKinnon (1978) gave an apt description of this preference on the part of creative people, which also suggests its close alliance to tolerance of ambiguity: "It is clear that creative persons are especially disposed to admit complexity and even disorder into their perceptions without being made anxious by the resulting chaos. It is not so much that they like disorder per se, but that they prefer the richness of the disordered to the stark barrenness of the simple. They appear to be challenged by disordered multiplicity, which arouses in them a strong need which in them is serviced by a superior capacity to achieve the most difficult and far-reaching ordering of the richness that they are willing to experience" (p. 62).

Delay of Gratification

The willingness to endure the stress of prolonged effort so as to reap higher pleasures in the long run contributes greatly to creative production. The ability to delay gratification is what makes some people save money in order to make a major purchase. It is also what makes some creative people spend years on a project without recognition or reward (Shekerjian, 1991; Sternberg & Lubart, 1995). As Sternberg and Lubart pointed out, the rewards of creative work are often minimal, especially in the beginning. "The short-term payoffs are for going with the crowd; this is especially so if you are young and if to advance you need to be in the good graces of whoever is managing the crowd. As a result, there is a terrific temptation just to follow what everyone else is doing" (p. 212).

Thomas Edison demonstrated his faith in his statement that creativity is "ninety-nine parts perspiration" by inventing the lightbulb. Early in his work, he had the idea of passing electricity through a filament placed in a vacuum in a glass sphere. Nevertheless, he had to conduct 2,004 experiments, using different materials for the filament, before he discovered that carbonized thread would not burn out quickly. It is quite common for creators to work for years on the same problem before they are able to create their final product.

Freedom from Sex-Role Stereotyping

Unfortunately, history has recognized a marked difference between the achievements of males and females. Until the second half of this century, this was routinely explained as a result of the difference between male and female brains. For the most part, people said, female brains simply lack the "creative gene." Bem (1993) stated that up until very recently, both psychological and psychiatric discourses on masculinity and femininity favored gender traditionalism and pathologized gender deviance by "naturalizing what is essentially just conformity to the cultural requirement that the sex of the body match the gender of the psyche" (p. 115). Only in recent decades have social scientists suggested that the apparent lack of female creative productivity over the centuries may result less from biological differences than from the female role.

It is complicated to separate genetic sex differences from less permanent gender differences, which are learned. Furthermore, it is increasingly clear that gender-role identification, which is first learned in families and then reinforced by school and work experiences, plays a large part in people's beliefs about their own creative potential.

A study done with first graders provides an excellent early but still relevant example of this (Torrance, 1963, 1979). The researchers measured the children's creative abilities by asking them to suggest how three toys could be improved so that they would be more fun to play with. The toys were a fire truck (considered a boy's toy), a nurse's kit (considered a girl's toy), and a stuffed dog (considered neutral at this age). The responses were scored according to fluency (total number of ideas), flexibility (the number of ideas that were qualitatively different from each other), and originality (the number of ideas that no one else in the group had thought of). The average scores broke down as would be expected: boys' scores in each of the category types were higher than girls' scores for the fire truck, girls' scores were similarly superior to those of boys on the nurse's kit, and the two sexes did about equally well with the stuffed dog.

Torrance administered the same test two years later to the same children when they were about to enter third grade. The change was striking; boys were superior to girls on all of the toys, including the nurse's kit. A number of explanations are possible. Perhaps girls simply become less creative with age. This seems unlikely, however, especially over such a short period of time. Torrance concluded that gender-role identification was the cause. He suggested that elementary school teachers (most of whom are female) teach young girls that they should behave according to the status quo. He stated that one often hears teachers ask for "some strong boys to help me," whereas girls are more likely to be praised for being "lady-like."

This study suggests that even if parents do not discourage creative imagination in girls, their elementary school teachers may do so. Recent studies of boys and girls making collages in competitive and noncompetitive situations suggested that being competitive is still more associated with success in boys than in girls (Amabile, 1996).

There is other evidence that gender-role identification is a significant factor in creative ability. A major study of the relationship between gender-role identification and creativity used a questionnaire. Participants were asked to choose from a list of behaviors that might be classified as stereotypically feminine or masculine, such as, "A windstorm usually scares me" or "I like to hunt." The statements were supposed to describe the participants' self-perceived characteristics (Roe, 1946, 1975). It was found that people with an ordinary level of creative ability tended to agree with the "masculine" statements if they were male and with the "feminine" statements if they were female. Highly creative males were found, however, to agree with more of both kinds of statements. This was also true of highly creative females. These highly creative people did not reverse their gender roles; they were just more likely to choose behaviors that were acceptable to them.

Why should this be so? Roe's conclusion was that high creativity requires that individuals have some of the qualities usually ascribed to the opposite sex. Creative males need to have that stereotypically female characteristic—sensitivity to the feelings of others—in order to get in touch with their own creative urges. On the other hand, females need assertiveness, a stereotypically male attribute, in order to champion their ideas courageously in a critical world. To use Ghiselin's phrase (1952), there is a "purity of motive" in these individuals that transcends the more ordinary gender roles.

In his extensive study of highly creative male architects, MacKinnon (1978) also reached this conclusion:

> The evidence is clear. The more creative a person is the more he reveals an openness to his own feelings and emotions, a sensitive intellect and understanding self-awareness, and wide-ranging interests including many which in the American culture are thought of as feminine. In the realm of sexual identification and interest, our creative subjects appear to give more expression to the feminine side of their nature than do less creative persons. In the language of the Swiss psychologist, Carl G. Jung (1956), creative persons are not so completely identified with their masculine persona roles as to blind themselves to or to deny expression to the more feminine traits of the anima [p. 61].

As mentioned earlier in this chapter, Dudek and Hall (1992) found that the architects they studied had retained much of the personalities they exhibited when originally tested twenty-five years later.

In their study of creative women mathematicians, Helson and Crutchfield (1970) did not find that the women had measures of masculine "orientation and interests" that were as high as the men's scores, but the researchers did discover that the women were like the creative men in most other personality traits. Helson asked "how a woman could so suppress her feminine nature to be a mathematician without suppressing her originality also" (p. 248). Helson concluded, "Part of the answer seems to be that the women mathematicians are introverts, whose 'natures' are not the modal American type" (p. 248). More recent work by Helson (1996) and Wink (1991) has suggested that creative people of both sexes are self-directed, as opposed to other-directed, and that they are more successful in work than in relationships. Both of these qualities are more likely to produce creative work and have traditionally been far more acceptable in men than in women.

In the 1970s, a new aspect of gender-role identification was defined. Known as androgyny, it too had ramifications for creative thinking. The word is made up of the Greek words for male, *andro,* and female, *gyne.* It refers to people who are found to have higher than the average number of male and female elements in their personalities. More specifically, they are more likely to behave in a way that is appropriate to a situation, regardless of their gender. For example, when someone forces his way into a line at the movies, the traditional female role calls for a woman to look disapproving but to say nothing. The androgynous female would tell the offender in no uncertain terms to go to the end of the line. When a baby left unattended in a carriage starts to cry, the traditional male response is to look for some woman to take care of its needs. The androgynous male would most likely attempt to comfort the infant.

Androgyny was not seen as the mere midpoint between the two poles of masculinity and femininity. Rather, it represented a higher level of gender-role identification than either of the more traditional roles. Researcher Sandra Bem (1975) conducted an experiment that illustrated the relationship between androgyny and creativity. First, she measured the subjects' level of androgyny with a sex-role test she devised, the Bem Sex-Role Inventory. Then she administered a test that offered choices of pairs of activities; one of the paired activities was usually performed by a male, the other by a female. A pay level was listed next to each activity. In some cases the male activity (for example, oiling hinges in a door factory) paid more, and sometimes the female activity (preparing baby bottles in a hospital) was more highly paid.

It came as no surprise that those rated low in androgyny were much more likely to choose the activities traditionally related to their own sex, even though these were lower paying half the time. In a second phase of the experiment, each subject was asked to perform three "male" tasks, three "female" tasks, and three neutral tasks. Those who identified highly with their own gender felt much worse than the androgynous people about doing a task that was traditionally done by members of the opposite sex. The low-androgyny individuals reported that they did not feel as attractive and likable as they ordinarily did, felt more nervous and peculiar, felt less masculine or feminine, and in general did not enjoy the experience.

Bem concluded that a rigidly stereotypical gender role is costly to the personality (it is, after all, actually a form of functional fixity). Such rigidity frequently causes conflict and necessitates a great expenditure of energy to deal with the stress brought about by the conflicts. Often defense mechanisms (see Chapter Seven) are called into play to avoid awareness of the conflicts. Bem suggested that the androgynous role is far more functional because it fosters the search for the truly appropriate course of action. In addition, an androgynous outlook is obviously more likely to cultivate creativity.

Bem stated more recently (1993) that although the concept of androgyny was not without its problems (the name itself suggests that some characteristics are naturally male and that others are naturally female), this earlier work did challenge ingrained psychological assumptions about masculinity and femininity in a new way. Today, however, the ideal goal is gender neutrality, which is sometimes referred to as freedom from gender-role stereotyping. In reaching this goal, we would "view our sex as so completely given by nature, so capable of exerting its influence automatically, and so limited in its sphere of influence to those domains where it really does matter biologically, that it could be safely tucked away in the back of our minds and left to its own devices" (Bem, 1993, p. 196). Even though creativity has not been encouraged in women historically, many women have made significant creative contributions, especially in the arts and humanities, but also in medicine and science, as well as producing many ingenious inventions of a more mundane nature (Vare & Ptacek, 1987).

Perseverance

Many researchers have noted that successful creators are very strong in their perseverance in the face of frustration and even obstacles that might ordinarily be thought overwhelming. Csikszentmihalyi (1996) stated that those he had studied were almost obsessive in their perseverance. He has also recently defined what he calls the "autotelic" personality, which is usually found in creative individuals. The word is derived from two Greek roots: *auto* (self) and *telos* (goal). Because creative people direct themselves toward a goal, they have great amounts of energy to invest intensely in their work with great perseverance (Csikszentmihalyi, 1997). Torrance (1995a, 1995b) found that the successful creators he has worked with and studied for many years have always been driven to continue with their work and have retained a clear sense of purpose to complete the work they have set for themselves, no matter what obstacles they have had to overcome. Creatively gifted children studied by Winner (1996) were found to have great drive and great willingness to work hard over long periods in order to accomplish their goals. The same kind of commitment to work was found by Gardner (1988a) and by Weber and Perkins (1992).

Sooner or later, all creative people encounter obstacles to the realization of their objectives. By definition, they typically go against what everyone else is doing and must have great powers of perseverance to continue on the path they believe to be correct. As Sternberg and Lubart (1995) observed, Paul Klee did not stop painting in his own way just because gallery owners who were displaying his work told him that customers did not like his work and were not buying it. According to Sternberg and Lubart, one must also be persevering to continue to develop an idea that goes against established ways of looking at something. For example, the very best grant proposals often fail to get funded because the evaluators are unable to see outside the existing paradigms of the field. There may also be obstacles to overcome within the work itself. The problem one is working on may be really difficult, and one may face many failures before reaching any success.

Courage

Paul Torrance (1995c) stated that after all the years he has studied creativity and creative people, he found that courage was the most essential quality for a creator's success. The love of one's work is credited as the source of this: "Having a passionate love for something is probably the key to being courageous" (Torrance, 1995d, p. 129).

Sternberg and Lubart stated that the person who comes up with an original idea must have the courage to be a minority of one, at least in the early stages. Stanford Ovshinsky, an inventor who devised uses for amorphous semiconductor material, described how one must be willing to be this kind of minority: "You must not be afraid of being alone. A lot of people may have good ideas and see different pathways and never have the courage to go against the crowd. Maybe they can't fight in defense of something that they believe in or persevere against great odds. A lot of people don't want to do that. Why should they go through that? I can't speak for other inventors, but I know that what has been important for me has been the ability to stand on my own and not cave in because others don't agree with me" (Sternberg & Lubart, 1995, pp. 226–227).

There are few who can endure the psychological pain of this position for very long, so they prematurely discard ideas that, if followed up and worked with, might prove to be of great value. This is true even in situations that are intentionally organized to bring out all possible ideas, such as a brainstorming session, in which members are told that all ideas, especially those that may seem wild, are solicited and encouraged. Even when such ideas are expressed in this context, they often go unnoticed by participants or observers. For example, in an experiment in which two people taped a brainstorming session separately, most of the truly original ideas were not the ones they recorded (Torrance, 1995d).

One of the most common occurrences in many kinds of creative work is that new ideas are rejected out of hand simply because they threaten the status quo (Sternberg & Lubart, 1995). Many of the established members of certain fields may be unwilling or unable to recognize and put aside for the moment the prejudices inherent in the current state of knowledge in their fields. Common attitudes are maintained by both scientific and social taboos, rather than by rational argument. Social psychologist Kurt Lewin recognized this barrier against creativity as early as 1947. He warned that "any member of the scientific guild who does not adhere strictly to the taboo is looked upon as queer; he is suspected of not adhering to the scientific standards of critical thinking" (cited in Torrance, 1995d, p. 122).

An outstanding example of this may be seen in the life's work of the Australian nurse Sister Elizabeth Kenny, whose method of treating polio's crippling effects saved countless children from permanent paralysis. She performed this work in the decades before the development of effective vaccines against this devastating epidemic. In 1911, Kenny was working as a "bush nurse," providing the only medical care available to far-flung homesteaders in the Australian outback, when she saw a child who lay twisted and in terrible pain. She telegraphed a doctor for advice. The message she received back was, "Infantile paralysis. No known treatment. Do the best you can with the symptoms presenting themselves" (Cohn, 1975, p. 41). She came up with the idea of applying hot, wet towels and blankets and gently moving the child's legs back into normal positions. "The sight would have chilled eminent infantile paralysis authorities thousands of miles away" (p. 42). Within less than a week, Kenny treated five more afflicted children in the same way, and all of them recovered fully. A year passed before she was able to discuss with doctors what she had done. They would not believe her results, as the accepted treatment for polio at that time was to immobilize patients in casts and splints, sometimes for months, and then fit them with braces or wheelchairs, which they would need for the rest of their lives. Kenny was horrified at the fates of these children and courageously fought for more than thirty years to have her treatment method finally accepted by orthodox medicine.

As Montuori (1997) observed, taking one's creative product out of the shelter of the studio or laboratory is in itself an act of courage on the creator's part. Each time, the creator must overcome the fear that the brainchild may be ridiculed or rejected. The creator balances this fear against the need to present the idea for public consideration and possibly harsh criticism. "As we present our creative product to others, perhaps we also need the knowledge that we are pushing our own boundaries along with those of our audience. We are naked to ourselves as well as to others" (p. 205).

A study of forty innovators who were given the MacArthur Award convinced Shekerjian (1991) that all these winners had the courage to continue with their work in the face of opposition. She stated that they were not quitters, even in the face of insult, defeat, humiliation, despondency, hostility, boredom, or indifference. They continued, believing in their work and themselves and learning from their failures. As Sternberg and Lubart (1995) stressed, it is important to remember that we often only see or hear of creative people after they have become successful. In almost every case, however, they have had to sustain courage over long periods of time when no one believed in them in order to reach such a high level of achievement. It is not unusual for creative work to remain unappreciated until after the creator's death.

Other Creative Personal Qualities

As reported at the beginning of this chapter, research indicates that these ten personal qualities are strongly involved in creativity. Numerous other traits may also play a relevant role, however (Amabile, 1996; Csikszentmihalyi, 1990, 1993b, 1996, 1997; Dacey & Packer, 1992; Mellou, 1996; Roy, 1996; Sheldon, 1995; Torrance, 1995d; Winner, 1996). What follows is a summary of these traits. Creative persons

- Are more sensitive to the existence of problems.

- Have a somewhat greater tendency toward emotional disturbance but also have more self-control to deal with this tendency.

- Are able to be both analytical and intuitive in their thinking.

- Are able to think both convergently (the ability to solve problems that have only one correct answer) and divergently (the ability to solve problems that have many possible answers).

- Have higher-than-average intelligence but do not often measure in the "genius" range.
- Are more open to experience and less defensive about accepting new information.
- See themselves as responsible for most of what happens to them.
- Enjoy being playful and childlike.
- Engage more frequently in solitary activities, especially as children.
- Are more likely to question the status quo.
- Are more independent of others' judgments.
- Are less afraid of their own impulses and hidden emotions.
- Like to do their own planning, make their own decisions, and need the least training and experience in self-guidance.
- Do not like to work with others and prefer their own judgment of their work to the judgment of others. They therefore seldom ask others for opinions.
- Take a hopeful outlook when presented with complex difficult tasks.
- Have the most ideas when given a chance to express individual opinions. These ideas frequently invoke the ridicule of others.
- Are most likely to stand their ground in the face of criticism.
- Are the most resourceful when unusual circumstances arise.
- Are not necessarily the "best" students.
- Show an imaginative use of their extensive vocabularies.
- Are more original. Their ideas are qualitatively different from everyone else's.

Of course, not all creative people exhibit all of these qualities, but all demonstrate a significant number of them. In the next chapter, we will discuss self-control, an important aspect of successful and productive creators.

6

THE SPECIAL CONTRIBUTION
OF SELF-CONTROL

IT IS A COMMON STEREOTYPE that creative people are wild, uninhibited, and impulsive. Perhaps this stereotype is related to the media portrayal of artists and scientists as slovenly or eccentric. This description may in fact fit some highly creative people. It is important to realize, however, that this stereotype is quite inaccurate more often than not (Dacey & Packer, 1992). It is hard to imagine Beethoven as being indolent and impulsive when composing his fifth symphony. In order to accomplish something of such magnitude, it is necessary to have great discipline. The quality that motivates such creative production and processes may be referred to as "self-control."

An almost symbiotic relationship exists between creativity and self-control, in that one needs creativity in order to envision a plan or visualize a desired outcome, two elements that are essential to self-control. One also needs self-control in order to use time wisely, work diligently, and have the perseverance to develop creative products fully. Research on the lifestyles of highly productive adolescents provided insight in this area (Dacey, 1989a, 1989c; Dacey & Packer, 1992) and supported the idea that, contrary to the stereotype of the unrestrained creative person, most creative people manifest high levels of self-control.

In order to relate the importance of self-control to creativity, we will provide a working definition of this concept. *Self-control* may be defined as a set of cognitive and attitudinal skills that may be learned throughout the lifetime. These skills permit people to do (or not do) what they wish, when that is not easy.

Achieving self-control is not simple. It requires effort and determination. This process is not beyond the capabilities of most people, however.

Dacey and his associates have developed the CCOPE Program, a model (see Figure 6.1) and a process that encourage the acquisition of self-control (Connelly, Harris, Dacey, & King, 1995; Dacey, Amara, & Seavey, 1993; Dacey, deSalvatore, & Robinson, 1997). This model and procedure will be discussed in detail later in the chapter.

Role of Parenting in Self-Control

Much of the research on self-control conducted by Dacey and associates reinforced the notion that self-control contributes to creativity. In a study that examined highly creative individuals and their families (Dacey, 1989c), biological, psychological, and social factors were found to interact in ways that affect creativity. For example, the most important finding in this study is that parenting style interacts with genetic inheritance in fostering creative children. Drawing from a subject pool of fifty-six families in which at least one parent or one child was identified as being highly creative, Dacey found that an unusual parenting style emerged.

Baumrind (1989) has identified the most common styles of parenting: authoritarian, permissive (either indulgent or neglectful), and authoritative. Authoritarian parents tend to be strict without much discussion about why rules and regulations are enforced in the home. Such parents typically place excessive demands on their children and do not incorporate a democratic system of behavior. Permissive parents, on the other hand, lean toward the opposite extreme in their childrearing. They tend to incorporate a laissez-faire approach, leaving children to their own instincts in terms of behavior. They are either indulgently permissive because they believe in giving their children maximum freedom, or they are neglectfully permissive because they just don't care. The authoritative parenting style combines structure and discipline with reasoning and rationale. Authoritative parents provide an environment in which decisions are made more democratically.

In Dacey and Packer's study, described in their book, *The Nurturing Parent* (1992), another style of parenting was revealed, which they termed the "nurturing" style. This technique was strikingly common among almost all of the families in which high creativity was fostered. Parents in these households were keenly interested in their children's behavior, but they seldom prescribed rules to govern it. These parents relied on modeling and family discussions to convey a well-defined set of values to their children, and they expected their children to make their own personal decisions based on these values. Only after a child had made his or her

Figure 6.1. Dacey's Model of the Self-Control Process.

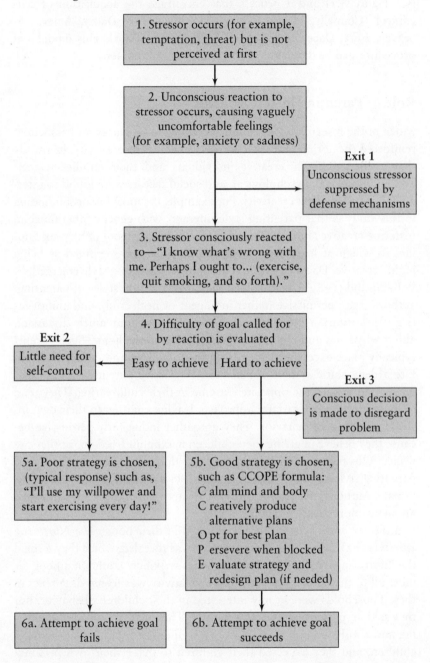

decision about an issue and carried it out would these parents let the child know how they felt about it. In other words, these children were provided with control of a given situation, and they considered their parents' disappointment sufficient motivation to influence their behavior.

Another aspect of parenting shared in these creative families was that the parents recognized their children's creative potential at an early age. Parents revealed that they recognized abilities, such as distinctive thought patterns and great problem-solving skills, in their children when the children were very young. Although parents did not necessarily set out to foster such abilities, once these skills were recognized, the parents became excited and encouraged them. These parents provided a wide range of opportunities (for example, lessons, equipment) that cultivated these traits.

Furthermore, all of the creative subjects in this study agreed that they tended to work harder than their peers or schoolmates. These individuals applied their strong commitment and dedication in numerous areas, such as school, jobs, and chores. It appears that instead of leading an impulsive, haphazard life, these creative people possessed a sense of organization and planning that allowed them to succeed in their endeavors. This strength may otherwise be known as self-control.

Further examination of the effects of parenting on creativity revealed that creative children are able to practice and exercise self-control in an environment that fosters this growth. Every time parents encourage their children to anticipate the consequences of their actions, to assume responsibility, and to make decisions, they are building skills that strengthen their mental focus. Continued experience with this process allows nurtured children to develop confidence in their abilities and increases their motivation to stick to a plan or alter their behavior. In *The Nurturing Parent*, Dacey and Packer explore ways in which parents can contribute to this growth in their children's minds.

Dacey and Packer also provide exercises that promote such development. For example, an activity called "Create Your Own World" suggests that parents read *The Little Prince* by Antoine de Saint-Exupéry to their children. The child in the story is in charge of his own planet, and the activity is for the child to imagine what his or her own planet might look like. Once the child has an image in mind, he or she can construct it using a beach ball as a base. This type of interaction is an important part of Dacey's model of self-control, specifically with regard to one's ability to plan a course of action or inaction creatively. Another useful resource of this type is provided in an article by Begley entitled *How to Build a Baby's Brain* (1997).

Self-Control in Schools

Can self-control skills be taught by regular teachers in a variety of settings, such as classrooms? As part of a conflict prevention program, Dacey, deSalvatore, and Robinson (1997) undertook to provide middle school students with the skills necessary to circumvent the so-called fight-or-flight response. This refers to the two instinctual human reactions to danger: fighting the enemy or fleeing to safer surroundings. For several years, researchers involved with the Boston College Conflict Prevention Program (BCCPP) have sought to examine this phenomenon (Connelly, Harris, Dacey, & King, 1995; Dacey, Amara, & Seavey, 1993; Dacey, deSalvatore, & Robinson, 1997). The project has proceeded from the premise that individuals' ability to manage conflicts derives from their ability to regulate behavior.

Whereas self-control skills can be learned in adulthood, the basis for becoming a self-controlled adult appears to be formed throughout childhood and adolescence (Mischel, Shoda, & Rodriguez, 1989). With regard to the fight-or-flight response, a middle school–aged individual would exercise self-control by doing something neither aggressive nor overtly evasive in the face of danger or conflict. The self-controlled individual is motivated by the anticipated outcomes and recognizes that these will not occur immediately. This lag in achieving the desired outcome is also termed "delay of gratification," which will be expanded on later.

The BCCPP trained teachers to teach their students (1) how to recognize when they were feeling stress and (2) how to calm down once they achieved this recognition. Students were taught to recognize symptoms of high stress, such as increased heart rate, labored breathing, and perspiration. They were supposed to learn to control their internal body processes during conflict situations and thereby to improve the situations' outcomes. The study's results supported the BCCPP researchers' hypothesis that students would feel empowered by their ability to control their physiological responses. In turn, they were able to take proactive measures to avoid conflict, which ultimately affected their retention rate in the middle school.

This type of self-control is one of two types that Dacey and Packer discussed in The Nurturing Parent (1992). The first type is the immediate control that we use in our everyday lives at any given moment, such as conforming to appropriate forms of behavior, sticking to a routine, or following a schedule to meet a deadline. The second type of self-control is the type exemplified by the study discussed above. It requires insight, faith, and a vision of the future. This type of self-control is not easy for people to achieve, and it is motivated by passion, self-confidence, and a sense of self-worth. Dacey and Packer elaborate as follows:

> These two types of self-control are mutually inclusive: where we will be one year from now is going to be influenced by our impulse control in the moment; how we control ourselves in the moment is going to be influenced by where we want to be one year from now. Keeping these two forces in balance is one of the most difficult things a human being can do. . . . When they are in balance, the person is a powerful, virtually unstoppable force, capable of going almost anywhere and doing almost anything. One can think of maturity as the increasing ability to use long-term goals to govern short-term behavior. Most people learn enough self-control to conform to society's laws, to hold down a job, and to fulfill their important responsibilities to others. Yet many of these people still trudge through life with the feeling that they are *not* in control. They feel plagued by bad habits and a lack of willpower. Long-term goals remain elusive or unidentified. Self-esteem is weakened by an inability to do the things their mind tells them they should want to do [1992, p. 132].

Therefore, self-control affects individuals' creativity. According to Dacey (1989b), creativity may blossom at any age, but certain peak periods provide the best opportunities for creative growth. During these peak periods, self-control may contribute most powerfully to creative success (see Chapter Four). These peak periods suggest times in one's life when the opportunities for creative growth are present. This is not to say that creative growth is restricted to these peak periods. On the contrary, people may experience creative growth at different times across the life span. Moreover, the ability to be creative does not necessarily decline with age.

Biopsychosocial Model of Self-Control

Following from this research and other findings, Dacey decided to examine self-control in relation to creativity, because the connections seemed both obvious and intriguing (see Figure 6.1). Through further study, Dacey developed CCOPE, a biopsychosocial model of self-control. The letters in this acronym refer to steps in the process of achieving self-control:

○ Calming the nervous system

○ Creatively planning coping techniques

○ Opting for the best plan

○ Persisting when motivation flags

○ Evaluating the plan's efficacy

The model is biopsychosocial by nature, in that biological, psychological, and social influences interact at each of the steps. These five steps ultimately create the sense of self-control that fosters creative growth. An explanation of each step in the process follows.

Calming the Nervous System

The first step, calming the nervous system, is perhaps the most important one. From a biological standpoint, there are obvious differences in temperament that cause some people to react more calmly to stressors than others. However, when one's body is in a state of stress, everyone's self-control is threatened, because strain causes tension and distraction, impairing all efforts, both physiological and other. In today's society, the pressures of everyday life have increased the stress we feel, and the results of such stress initially cause what is known as the "alarm reaction." This is akin to the fight-or-flight reaction discussed earlier.

The alarm reaction begins when the brain perceives danger (either through a thought in the cortex or a feeling in the subcortex) and sends a message to the adrenal glands, stimulating them for fight-or-flight action. The adrenal glands consist of two parts, an inner portion called the adrenal medulla and an outer portion called the adrenal cortex. The medulla emits adrenaline and noradrenaline, two hormones that regulate automatic functions such as blood vessel constriction, heart rate, gastrointestinal movements, pupil dilation, and glucose metabolism. The adrenal cortex secretes a variety of hormones called corticosteroids. These hormones regulate many important body functions, including salt and water metabolism, carbohydrate fat, and resistance to infection and other stresses.

During states of alarm, adrenal hormones pour into the bloodstream where they are carried to all parts of the body, like soldiers going to their battle stations. Until further orders from the brain arrive, their presence increases muscle strength, dilates pupils to let in more light, and contracts peripheral blood vessels to increase blood pressure. In states of alarm, many people become overanxious, and their brains send out too many hormones, making them all the more stressed. This overload of hormones happens because of the brain, but also because of other aspects of body physiology. Common complications include hyperventilating and hypoglycemia.

Canadian scientist Hans Selye (1956, 1974, 1975, 1982) conducted a series of studies that led to the discovery of the "general adaptation syndrome." This is basically an alarm reaction, a generalized marshaling of the body's defensive forces when a foreign substance enters the body. Wanting to gain a better understanding of this syndrome, Selye examined what occurred when stress is present in animals for long periods. He found that if the animal survives the initial alarm response set off against the foreign substance, its body enters a state of resistance. In this second stage, an almost complete reversal of the alarm reaction occurs, and the animal appears to gain strength and completely adapt to the stressor.

If the stressful injections of the foreign substance continue for a long time, however, the animal's adaptational energy begins to deplete (Selye, 1982). This eventually leads to a state of exhaustion in which physiological responses revert to their condition during the initial state of alarm. The ability to handle stress decreases, the level of resistance is lost, and the animal ultimately dies.

Selye suggested that all resistance to stress inevitably causes irreversible chemical scars that build up in the system. These scars are signs of aging. As a person grows older, the ability to remain in the resistance stage decreases. Eventually, people succumb to some stressor such as a disease, because their ability to resist it has weakened through aging.

The capacity to calm the nervous system enhances resistance. How can we learn to calm our nervous system? From a biological standpoint, several methods can calm the body, such as muscle control or yoga, controlled breathing, and soothing music or sounds. Yoga is a scientifically proven relaxation method that reduces the level of nervous arousal. When a person has induced this response, which occurs largely in the brain's subcortex, he or she will find it easier to perform the cortex's creative ideas. Thus, in this relaxed state, people are likely to make better plans and achieve their goals.

Another method, sensory awareness, allows people to become aware of their inner environment, including their heart rate; breathing; tension in their muscles, ligaments, tendons, colon, and vessels; and pain in their joints. Sensory awareness is a formula for discovering what these inner stimuli are and what effects they are having. As people become aware of these stimuli, they can adapt procedures to alleviate strain and can be better equipped to deal with problems presented by the outer world.

Humor is a simple and often overlooked aid in stress relief. A good laugh actually produces a surge of endorphins, which are hormones that cause a sense of pleasure and well-being. Endorphins (which are also produced when alcohol enters the body) have a calming effect for an average of thirty-six hours.

From a psychological perspective, visualization and self-hypnosis are two methods of calming the nervous system. The ability to visualize, which may include mental representations of taste and touch in addition to sight, is truly vital to self-control.

An example of a visualization technique would be for a person to picture seven scenes that he or she finds particularly tranquil. Next, the person should write a phrase describing each scene on an index card and should arrange the cards in descending order in terms of their degree of tranquillity. Once the list has been produced and arranged in order, the person can memorize the list and practice visualizing each scene, starting with number seven and ending with number one. Eventually, merely counting backward from seven to one and visualizing one of the scenes works well. Self-hypnosis is a method in which individuals are able to go to an imaginary place where they come to feel that they are "under." Then, they can deal with their conflicts with more tranquillity.

One of the simplest techniques available is what Benson (1975, 1984) called the "relaxation response." Benson was the first to do medical evaluations on the supposed benefits of meditation. He defined the relaxation response as "the inborn capacity of the body to enter a special state characterized by lowered heart rate, decreased rate of breathing, lowered blood pressure, slower brain waves, and an overall reduction of the speed of metabolism. In addition, the changes produced by this response counteract the harmful effects and uncomfortable feelings of stress" (1984, pp. 4–5). This method works by interfering with what Benson calls "worry cycles," which are "unproductive grooves or circuits that cause the mind to 'play' over and over again, almost involuntarily, the same anxieties or uncreative, health-impairing thought" (p. 5).

In his first book, *The Relaxation Response* (1975), he recommended four steps to achieve a state of relaxation and to interrupt worry cycles:

1. Find a quiet environment.
2. Consciously relax the body's muscles.
3. Focus for ten to twenty minutes on a mental device, such as the word *one* or a brief prayer.
4. Assume a passive attitude toward intrusive thoughts, such as the question, "Why am I doing this silly exercise?"

Benson's studies found solid evidence that meditation has many benefits, such as relieving headaches, enhancing creativity, reducing blood pressure, overcoming insomnia, and alleviating the symptoms of anxiety that include nausea, vomiting, diarrhea, constipation, short temper, and the inability to get along with others.

In his second book, *Beyond the Relaxation Response* (1984), Benson reported on the importance of spiritual belief in bringing about a response. In other words, by using a prayer or mantra that is in some way powerful to the individual, the person will attain even better results with the method. He expanded the number of steps to eight:

1. Pick a brief phrase or word that reflects your basic belief system.
2. Choose a comfortable position.
3. Close your eyes.
4. Relax your muscles.
5. Become aware of your breathing, and start using your focus word.
6. Maintain a passive attitude.
7. Continue for a set period of time.
8. Practice the technique twice daily.

Creatively Planning Coping Techniques

The capacity to plan creatively depends on general intellectual ability, which in turn relies on complex macro- and microneuronal systems (see Chapter Ten), extensive hemispheric interactions (see Chapter Eleven), the absence of mental derangement, and rich learning experiences (Dacey & Packer, 1992).

Creative ability involves the capacity to integrate a situation's components and to develop the plans necessary to initiate action and to work toward a desired end (Restak, 1984). Numerous publications have offered curricula for facilitating creative thinking (one of the best is by Kimball, 1993). Because this whole book is about creativity, nothing further about creative planning will be added here.

Opting for the Best Plan

Motivation is important in the next phase of Dacey's model of self-control. By the time one reaches the stage of opting for the best plan, one has already generated a number of alternate plans. Choosing the most efficacious approach involves all three of the biopsychosocial factors. The main biological influence is temperament. A patient and contemplative person will be more likely to weigh several options than one who is impulsive or has a short attention span.

The psychological factors that contribute to opting for the best plan are more complex and will require an extensive examination. The ability to visualize, which was discussed in terms of calming the nervous system, is also paramount here. The ability to anticipate possible outcomes is a skill that allows individuals to choose the best course of action.

Likewise, the absence of defense mechanisms (Chapter Seven) makes it easier to opt for the best plan. When one is comfortable with one's sense of self, few internal obstacles can diminish self-control. It is this sense of self, or self-image, that is so insightfully explored in Albert Bandura's latest book, *Self-Efficacy* (1997). Bandura views self-efficacy as the degree to which people believe in their ability to carry out plans or tasks. He considers this sense of confidence or security to be the key component of human functioning.

Self-efficacy is not a one-dimensional concept but in fact consists of "a host of microsensory, perceptual, and information processing activities" (1997, p. 4). The beliefs that result from self-efficacy govern aspirations, the choice of behaviors, the coordination of efforts directed at a goal, and emotional reactions. In terms of opting for the best plan, self-efficacy permits one to imagine the plan or goal and to take action to achieve that goal. For Bandura, self-efficacy is an interactive process between the cognitive act of generating the objectives and the intentional process of executing the plan necessary to reach one's goals.

The role of the self is important to Bandura's explanation of self-efficacy. Individuals have self-influence if they are able to analyze a situation and consider different ways of acting. When they have considered the likelihood of being able to carry out the desired actions and the consequences of the proposed action, they are then able to act, based on that decision. In Bandura's theory, people act as both agent (by acting on the environment) and object (by acting on themselves). The person who plans a strategy is the same person who evaluates the plan, as well as evaluating the person's knowledge and abilities. Bandura refers to his view as a "social cognitive theory," and it supports the notion of a person's being simultaneously agent and object. This resolves the perennial self-control theory question, What does it mean to say, "I control me"?

Human beings operate in a reciprocal cause-and-effect manner, in which internal factors, behavior, and the environment interact and influence each other bidirectionally. Social structures (the family and the workplace, for example) are developed through the individual's active participation. Social structures both foster and impede personal development on a daily basis, depending on the roles individuals play in a given situation. The efficacious individual is able to seize opportunities and, if necessary, find ways to overcome or alter societal restraints. Inefficacious people, on the other hand, are easily frustrated by obstacles and are less likely to take advantage of opportunities that would help them reach their goals.

The idea that the results of everyday situations are inevitable is known as "determinism." Whereas some theorists may consider freedom to be the opposite of determinism, Bandura has disagreed with this idea. According to him, the efficacious individual is able to choose freely, in that freedom "is the exercise of self-influence to bring about desired results" (p. 7). The more that people are able to exercise numerous options and evaluate their own behavior, the more freedom they will have to make things happen. Therefore, the ability to make things happen is the ultimate form of freedom.

The sense of accomplishment that accompanies repeated achievement greatly improves one's self-esteem. Experience with actions that provide satisfaction and self-worth are much preferred and are more likely to be repeated than actions that contradict one's personal standards. The greater a person's "foresight, proficiency, and self-influence, all of which are acquirable skills, the more successful they are in achieving what they seek" (p. 8), and thus the more likely the person is to opt for appropriate goals and plans that will meet them.

The bidirectional effects of accomplishment and self-esteem undermine the notion that human beings are merely pawns in a larger scheme controlled by other, greater forces. This contradicts behavioral theories such as Skinner's (1971), which propose that the environment controls human behavior. Humans indeed possess, or may acquire, the skills necessary to reflect on their own actions and experiences, which influences the actions they take in the future. Behavioral theorists disregard the fact that humans are capable of choosing actions based on forethought and on a consideration of outcomes, rather than solely responding to environmental reinforcements and punishments. In this, Bandura has provided an excellent example of the contextual approach defined in Chapter One.

Because of the hard work involved in accomplishing things, the exercise of self-control is accompanied by numerous responsibilities. Bandura noted that "it is usually the most self-efficacious individuals who assume leadership positions of high potential stress and strain" (p. 16). He suggested that incentives and other rewards are necessary to convince people to take charge of activities that involve heavy risks, serious responsibilities, and complicated skills.

One alternative to the personal investment required in order to control desired outcomes is to let some other individual exert control over the situation (also called "yielding"). The other individual therefore assumes the risks and responsibilities, whereas the first person continues to reap the benefits of this arrangement. An example would be entrusting one's life to a pilot or surgeon when one is afraid to do so. As U.S. citizens, people relinquish control of major issues when they elect government officials, yet by working through numerous political channels, people may continue striving for the recognition of their own personal interests. The "codependent" marriage is another example.

Bandura cited several conditions under which people are prone to relinquish control simply because it is easier than assuming control. One example is when the effort required to master an activity seems to outweigh the benefits. Another example is when people have performed poorly in previous situations and therefore come to expect that they will not succeed in future performances in similar situations. The presence of an opponent who appears extremely confident or of a rigid mind-set can undermine one's use of knowledge or skills. Also, gender and racial stereotyping negatively affect the use of cognitive skills. All of these environmental conditions may influence one's performance in a given situation if one is not able to visualize or anticipate desired outcomes. Obviously, this inability would seriously interfere with opting for the best plan.

As to the social influences included in the opting stage of Dacey's self-control model, role models and medial influences are noteworthy. Role models may exist in the form of parents, teachers, or other individuals who exhibit self-control or self-efficacy. By studying situations in which admired models acted based on experience in order to affect a desired outcome, children and youth may develop the skills necessary to enact similar successes in their own lives.

For this very reason, the media can exert a powerful influence over the development of self-control in terms of opting for the best plan. All too often, people in today's society are instructed to get everything done more and more quickly to produce outcomes that are not necessarily desirable but that meet some deadline. Television commercials present services and products that make life easier and quicker. As mentioned, self-efficacy and self-control require a good deal of hard work. The media have the tools to alter the perceptions of people who are all too eager to rely on a cleaning product or alcoholic beverage that promises to take control in a certain situation. People who hope to attain long-term goals need to build the self-confidence that fosters self-control.

Shapiro (Shapiro, Potkin, Jin, & Brown, 1993; Shapiro, Sandman, Grossman, & Grossman, 1995) has developed a model of self-control that examines how opting for a certain plan may result in one of four outcomes. The four quadrants in Shapiro's model are determined by the amount of assertiveness and yielding on the horizontal axis and by their positive and negative consequences on the vertical axis (see Table 6.1).

The first possible outcome is the result of active control and positive assertion. An example of this would be planning to run two miles a day to improve one's cardiovascular fitness and then sticking to the plan. The second outcome Shapiro describes is the result of relinquishing control and positively yielding to another. The person in this situation accepts another person's control. An example of this would be when a person allows a surgeon to perform surgery on her. The third quadrant specifies too much control (overcontrol) combined with negative assertiveness. This is the case in which a person attempts to exercise an extreme amount of control, such as the perfectionist who can never experience satisfaction. The final possible outcome consists of too little control and negative yielding. This is the case with drug addicts who may be unable to yield to an outside source for assistance.

Persisting When Motivation Flags

It is difficult to maintain motivation throughout the self-control process, as evidenced by the increase in violence in today's society. The fourth step in Dacey's self-control model is to persist even when motivation decreases. The concept of faith is a major component in terms of both biological and psychological influences on the ability to persist. E. O. Wilson suggested that a person is either born with or without a "faith gene" (Dacey & Travers, 1996; Wilson, 1978). It is hypothesized that this gene directly influences one's capacity to have faith in oneself, a plan, or a higher power. The existence of such a gene has not been scientifically demonstrated, however. What some researchers consider to be more

Table 6.1. Shapiro's Model of Self-Control.

	Assertiveness	Yielding
Positive	Active control, positive assertiveness	Relinquishing control, positive yielding
Negative	Overcontrol, negative assertiveness	Too little control, negative yielding

likely is the idea of inherited ego strength, which may manifest itself in terms of temperament or, more specifically, self-confidence.

Faith gives the individual the motivation to continue at times when all other indications suggest giving up. People need not have faith in themselves in order to persevere, but faith in a higher power is often enough to affect the decision to persist or throw in the towel. Those individuals with a sense of spirituality seem to display more self-control. For example, the majority of active alcoholics do not believe in a Supreme Being, whereas the majority of recovering alcoholics say they do hold such beliefs. Recovering alcoholics furthermore testify that reliance on a "higher power" is central to their recovery (King, 1995). Spirituality has to do with one's relationship to life's universal wholeness, as opposed to everyday earthly matters, and it involves one's search for meaning and purpose in existence. Being spiritual also means striving to enlarge one's connection to that force lying within, a force that can make it possible to transcend the ordinary self and reach one's fullest potential.

The traditional view of God is that of the all-knowing, all-powerful, ever-caring Father whose will we should strive to know and fulfill. Faith in the help we can receive from God develops in six stages, according to theologian James Fowler (1991). His theory has implications for the degree of faith individuals can have in their plans. The major ramification of Fowler's work is that as we get older, we may develop a deeper faith in our plans, ourselves, and in God's help, but this will not necessarily happen.

Fowler believes strongly that cognitive and emotional needs are inseparable in the development of a spiritual faith in God. Spirituality cannot develop faster than intellectual ability, and it also depends on the development of personality. Thus, Fowler's theory of faith development integrates the role of the unconscious, needs, personal strivings, and cognitive growth.

According to Fowler, faith develops in six steps. He has said that the stages in faith development can be delayed indefinitely, but a person must have reached at least a certain minimal age at each stage in order to move on to a succeeding stage. His six stages are as follows.

1. Intuitive-projective faith. For intuitive-projective faith, the minimal age is four years. In this stage, the individual focuses on surface qualities, as portrayed by adult models. This stage depends to a great extent on fantasy. Conceptions of God or a Supreme Being reflect a belief in magic.

2. Mythical-literal faith. For mythical-literal faith, the minimal age is five to six years. Fantasy ceases to be a primary source of knowledge at this stage, and verification of facts becomes necessary. Verification of truth comes not from actual experience but from such authorities as

teachers, parents, books, and traditions. Faith in this stage is mainly concrete and depends heavily on stories told by highly credible storytellers. For example, the traditional story of Adam and Eve is taken quite literally in this stage.

3. Poetic-conventional faith. For poetic-conventional faith, the minimal age is twelve to thirteen years. Faith is still conventional and depends on the opinions of other, more authoritative persons. Now, the individual moves away from family influence and into new relationships. Faith begins to provide a coherent and meaningful synthesis of these relationships.

There is an awareness of symbolism and a realization that there is more than one way of knowing truth. Learned facts are still taken as the main source of information, but individuals in stage 3 begin to trust their own judgment and the quality of selected authorities. Nevertheless, they do not yet place full confidence in their own judgment.

4. Individuating-reflective faith. For individuating-reflective faith, the minimal age is eighteen to nineteen years. Youths in stage 3 are unable to synthesize new areas of experience, because depending on others in the community does not always solve problems. Individuals in stage 4 begin to assume responsibility for their own beliefs, attitudes, commitments, and lifestyles. The faith learned in earlier stages is now disregarded, and greater attention is paid to one's own experience. For individuals who still need authority figures, there is a tendency to join and become completely devoted to clubs organized around dogmatic philosophies (for example, the 700 Club and the NRA) and cults.

5. Paradoxical-consolidation faith. For paradoxical-consolidation faith, the minimal age is thirty. In this stage such elements of faith as symbols, rituals, and beliefs start to become understood and consolidated. The person begins to realize that other approaches to dealing with such complex questions as the supernatural and Supreme Being can be as valid as her or his own. The individual at this stage considers all people to belong to the same universal community and has a true regard for the kinship of all people.

6. Universalizing faith. For universalizing faith, the minimal age is forty years. Few people ever reach this level. Here the individual lives in the real world but is not of it. Such persons do not merely recognize the mutuality of existence; they act on the basis of it. People at this stage appear to be truly genuine and lack the need to "save face" that exists at the lower stages. Thus, they are most likely to persevere with their plans in the face of adversity.

The development and nurturing of faith enable what theorists call "delay of gratification." This concept generally refers to the act of postponing immediate results or rewards for the more desirable rewards that

will take a longer amount of time to acquire. The delay of gratification obviously requires a good amount of patience, but it is also a fundamental
component of self-control.

A. W. Logue discussed the concept of delay of gratification in great detail in her 1995 book *Self-Control: Waiting Until Tomorrow for What
You Want Today*. Logue argued that delay of gratification is essentially the
same as self-control and that immediate gratification equates to impulsiveness. Her operational definition of delay of gratification is choosing
a larger, more delayed outcome over a smaller, less delayed one. An example of this would be opting to study for an important test scheduled for
the next morning, rather than going to the movies with friends. The long-
range benefits of a good grade on the test (a better GPA, college, or job)
would seem to outweigh the short-term satisfaction of seeing a movie.
Time is an important element in her definition, for without time, there is
no delay that distinguishes the value of one gain from another.

Logue mentioned, however, that from an evolutionary perspective,
humans have developed a tendency to discount delayed outcomes. This
newer attitude leads to impulsive behavior. Logue emphasized the benefits
of acting impulsively in certain situations, which renders context an important factor in the larger picture of delay of gratification. For example,
when humans live in an unpredictable environment (a war or natural dis-
aster) and are not expected to live past their reproductive years, it is not
necessarily wise for them to delay gratification, because procreation is imperative for the group's survival. In fact, genes that may have contributed
to humans' ancestors' lives may well have increased an individual's suitability for that particular environment.

Situation-specific differences therefore exist in terms of self-control, depending on the immediate value of rewards. A person who is extremely
thirsty would most likely prefer water over money as a reward. In our society, the notion has also evolved that self-control is good or desired,
whereas impulsiveness is bad or discouraged. Rather than jumping to the
conclusion that impulsiveness indicates a lack of character or moral fiber,
Logue stressed that it is important to note the environment within which
certain behavior occurs.

Children progress through two stages in the development of delay of
gratification (Sonuga-Barke, Lea, and Webley, 1989). In the first stage,
children learn to wait for an outcome because it can be to their advantage
to wait instead of choosing an immediate outcome. In the second stage,
children learn that it is not always advantageous to wait for the long-term
outcome. They figure out that there are certain situations in which impulsiveness is the better response. The two factors that contribute significantly to the development of self-control choices are the ability to

estimate time and the ability to direct attention away from immediate stimuli by, for example, singing a song or playing a game. As people grow and mature, Logue has suggested that positive experiences that result from longer delays will increase their willingness to delay gratification.

Another factor that affects choices is the amount of effort necessary to achieve a desired result. Logue stated, "Experience with rewards following a substantial expended effort for delivery can result in a generalized increased tendency to choose such rewards" (1995, p. 43). Although the amount of effort may seem intimidating at the onset, there is often a strong sense of satisfaction derived from hard work and persistence when the desired rewards are achieved. For some individuals, identification with an admired figure or hero may provide sufficient motivation for self-control.

Children may admire their parents for various reasons, which makes them ideal role models for self-control. A family that not only espouses certain values but also puts them into practice has a better chance of transmitting self-control and persistence to its children. If parents encourage children's efforts and teach children that hard work results in significant payoffs, children will be motivated to persist in the face of daunting circumstances. Once a child has learned through social reinforcement that goals can be realized, he or she can proceed to the last stage, evaluating a plan's efficacy.

Evaluating the Plan's Efficacy

Evaluation is crucial for self-control, and ultimately for creativity, for if a plan is not achieving the desired results, then it is best for the individual to initiate a new course of action. The work of Getzels and Csikszentmihalyi (1975) is noteworthy in this regard. The authors were interested with learning more about the role of problem finding (being sensitive to the existence of problems) in the creative process. They studied a group of artists in order to observe problem finding in the process of creative achievement, such as drawing a picture.

> Drawing a picture may be seen as a process of solution to a problem. Although this problem is often not consciously formulated by the artist, it may be assumed that without some source of problematic feelings the artist would have nothing to do. It may be assumed further that if the artist begins a painting as a process of personal discovery of an aesthetic problem, his work will be relatively more original than if he begins a painting to fit a standard aesthetic problem. . . . In the first case he is working with what we have called a "discovered problem," in the second with a "presented problem" [p. 108].

The researchers observed each artist from start to finish from the time he or she composed a group of objects for a still life through completion of the actual drawing. They were able to note differences in the way artists proceeded, even prior to the actual drawing. For instance, some artists explored one or two objects, whereas some handled close to twenty. Some simply picked up the objects, but others smelled them, bit them, held them up to the light, and felt their texture. Many chose the same objects as their peers, whereas some chose unique or original objects for their drawing.

Even during the actual drawing, or problem-solving stage, some artists changed their position, materials, or the structure of their drawings, which indicated to the authors that these artists were still problem finding while involved with the process of problem solving (drawing). The authors investigated the artists' progress several years later and discovered that those who had achieved greater success were, in fact, those who had scored highest in terms of many problem-finding variables.

The results of the study of artists show how important open-mindedness is to the evaluation stage of the self-control process. The successful artists were able to explore their environments without superimposing their own needs. They wanted to experience their task fully, not just do an adequate job. This attitude is vital in the evaluation phase.

This ability is further enhanced by feedback or monitoring by another individual, a "buddy." In some situations, a person may benefit from the perspective of an outside observer who is able to provide less biased insight. In the case of a parent-child relationship, a parent may assist a child in evaluating a plan by suggesting different tactics to try and by providing encouragement for the progress the child has already made. This recognition can bolster the child's enthusiasm and is a way of modeling behavior that the child can incorporate into his or her own repertoire of self-control skills.

Dacey's model of self-control outlines five steps on the path to self-control. Studies have indicated that self-control is an important ingredient in the creative process, as it provides an individual with disciplinary and analytical tools. Contrary to the idea of a creative individual as unrestrained and impulsive, the person who is able to exert self-control is more likely to achieve distinction in a creative realm.

The CCOPE model incorporates biological, psychological, and social influences with the steps to self-control. In order to gain a more complete understanding of this process, it is important to recognize the factors that contribute to success in this area. The elements in this model are not mu-

tually exclusive and may occur during various steps in the process. The interaction between the environment and the individual's biological and psychological makeup fosters an exciting and ongoing development that can ultimately lead to a more creative human being. Table 6.2 summarizes some of the elements that play vital roles in the process.

Table 6.2. The CCOPE Model.

	Biological	Psychological	Social
C (Calming the nervous system)	Muscle control, breathing, listening to music or sounds (mantras), temperament	Visualizing	Spending time alone or with a trusted other person
C (Creatively planning coping techniques)	Genetic ability, inherited IQ, complex microneuronal systems, absence of mental illness	Encouragement of early experiences, fathers' encouragement (especially with girls), little use of defense mechanisms	Being with creative peers or in an environment that fosters creativity, having nurturing parents
O (Opting for the best plan)	Genetic ability, inherited IQ, complex microneuronal systems, absence of mental illness, temperament	Self-esteem, visualization, delay of gratification, ability to anticipate outcomes, absence of defense mechanisms	Having role models, being influenced by media
P (Persisting when motivation flags)	Faith gene (the ability to have faith is genetic), ego strength (inherited), temperament	Identification with admired figure, delay of gratification, religious training or spirituality, early positive experiences, self-confidence	Having family belief system, modeling and encouragement from significant others
E (Evaluating the plan's efficacy)	IQ	Absence of mental illness, self-awareness	Modeling and encouragement from significant others

7

THE FORMATION OF CREATIVE PERSONALITY TRAITS

THE TEN QUALITIES examined in Chapter Five give us one perspective on the creative personality, but not on how it comes about. This chapter describes both early and current theories that seek to explain the formation of creative personality traits. In Chapter Two, we discussed several theories that have attempted to explain the creative personality over the years. Most of them fall rather decisively into one of two schools of thought: psychoanalytic or humanistic.

Early Theories

Psychoanalytic Views

Here is a quick summary of the most salient points of psychoanalytic theories. Sigmund Freud, the originator of psychoanalysis, postulated defense mechanisms, especially sublimation, as the origin of the creative impulse. Carl Jung, once a member of Freud's inner circle of colleagues, believed that creativity arose through an individual's ability to link his or her personal unconscious with the collective unconscious (1933, 1956). Ernst Kris argued that the Freudian concept of primary process thinking, accessed through the defense mechanism of regression, formed the basis of creativity (1952, 1965a, 1965b). Otto Rank believed that as children grew and attempted to form their own wills, only those whose parents supported this development could become innovators who were possessed of a creative personality. The others would become "acquiescors." Alfred Adler (1917) proposed yet another defense mechanism—compensation for feelings of inferiority—as the basis for creativity. Emanuel

Hammer offered an updated version of Adler's view (1984), based on his work with college art students. Those he categorized as highly creative were most often emotionally reserved; suffered from feelings of rejection by others; were more likely to resort to fantasy in their daily lives; were much more in touch with their own deep, personal, intimate regions; and were self-directed, independent, individual, and willing to expend great effort to accomplish their aims. Hammer also addressed the age-old question of whether creativity is next to madness. He found that his young artists definitely manifested emotional disturbance but were also endowed with a superior ability to deal with their problems. He cited numerous famous persons for whom this was true, including W. H. Auden and Edmund Wilson.

In general, psychoanalytic theorists see creativity as the result of overcoming some problem, usually one that began in childhood. The creative person is viewed as someone who has had a traumatic experience or psychopathology, which he or she dealt with by allowing conscious and unconscious ideas to mingle into an innovative resolution of the trauma. The creative act is seen as transforming an unhealthy psychic state into a healthy one. Psychoanalytically oriented theorists basically view a person as fairly passive, as a reactor to his or her life circumstances rather than an active agent. Closely allied with the psychoanalytic view is the contention that some kinds of mental illness and drug and alcohol use contribute to creativity, particularly in its artistic and literary manifestations.

Humanistic Views

In contrast to the psychoanalytic view of the person as largely acted on by unconscious drives, the humanist view stresses that people are able to make active choices as they construct their lives. The most important of the early humanistic thinkers are Abraham Maslow, Carl Rogers, and Erich Fromm. Maslow, who founded humanistic or "third force" psychology, contended that humans have a six-level hierarchy of needs. The highest two needs, self-actualization and aesthetic needs, are the basis of creativity, in his view. "The concept of creativeness and the concept of the healthy, self-actualizing, fully human person seem to be coming closer and closer together, and may perhaps turn out to be the same thing" (Maslow, 1971, p. 57). Building on Maslow's ideas, Carl Rogers believed that openness to experience, faith in self-evaluations, and the ability to experiment and explore the possibilities of ambiguous situations were the primary characteristics of creative persons. Fromm maintained that self-transcendence was the principal source of creativity, as it allows the person to have an objective self-knowledge, to be puzzled or surprised, to concentrate deeply, and to tolerate ambiguous situations.

Behaviorism, which was a potent force in American psychology for much of the earlier half of the twentieth century, did not contribute to the study of creative personality. Its adherents considered creative production to be strictly a product of appropriate reinforcers provided by society. B. F. Skinner believed that creativity itself was a result of random "mutations." He compared creating a work of art to having a child and argued that in both cases the creator is no more than a "locus" through which environmental variables act and that the creator "adds nothing to the creation" (Epstein, 1996, p. 214).

Current Theories

In this section we examine contemporary thought in both the psychoanalytic and humanistic schools. Although psychoanalytic theories have come under severe criticism in recent years (Eisenman, 1997, Eysenck, 1992a; Masson, 1984, 1990; Webster, 1995), some interesting ideas may still be gleaned from their works. Humanists view creativity as resulting from a high degree of psychological health. This view contradicts psychoanalytic theories. Humanist theories are often influenced by existential philosophy, which emphasized that individuals are free to make choices that establish their own futures.

Psychoanalytic Theories

Some psychoanalytically oriented theorists continue to subscribe to the Freudian hypothesis that all creative activity originates in such instinctual drives as the need to overcome "narcissistic" injuries (anything that damages the self-concept) suffered in childhood or to redirect unacceptable energies (sublimation), but most no longer believe that this is universally true. In some instances, creativity may be stimulated by an attempt to make reparations for destructiveness, to mourn a loss, or even for "the tendentious motives Freud believed to be central for creativity—money, prestige, or sexual rewards" (Gedo, 1997, p. 33). Gedo believed, however, that all of these motives are ancillary and that none is sufficient in itself to sustain a commitment to the creative life. Emphasizing the joy of exercising one's competence, he referred to the way in which "self-esteem born of great accomplishments irresistibly pulls persons with major talent into ceaseless exercise of their gifts" (Gedo, 1996, p. 9). Diamond (1996) countered orthodox Freudian doctrine by concluding that although creative activities can provide a healthy and constructive outlet for negative feelings, creativity should never be seen as only a by-product of personal conflicts. He stated that if this were the case, "All neurotics and psychotics would be very creative—which they are not" (p. 257).

Two other investigators (Ehrenzweig, 1975; Noy, 1969) have updated the psychoanalytic notion of primary process thinking (fantasizing, wishful, dreamlike) and secondary process thinking (logical, orderly, realistic). In their more modern view, secondary process thinking is not a development from a primitive to a higher level. Instead, both are independent processes that should remain accessible to the individual throughout life. Suggesting several modifications to Kris's theory, Martindale and Dailey (1996) proposed that we first "strip the theory of its psychoanalytic baggage" (p. 409) and only consider the continuum from primary process to secondary process thinking in a descriptive manner. They stated that this continuum is a type of conscious thought, not "something that occurs in the Freudian unconscious" (p. 409). Bucci (1993) has proposed that beyond the availability of both primary and secondary thought processes, there can develop an integration of the two, which she refers to as "referential activity." Bucci believes that the quality of creativity depends on the creator's access to as much of this referential activity as possible.

Oremland (1997) used an influential branch of psychoanalytic thought known as object relations, which was developed by such Freudians as Melanie Klein and D. W. Winnicott, to explain the origins of creative personality. Oremland stated that "creativity is a form of object relatedness" (p. 93). As used in this context, *object* is a technical word in psychoanalytic theory that refers more often to a person than to a thing. The child's first object is usually the mother. *Object relatedness* refers to the child's or subject's involvement with such an actual person. The theory also specifies an internal object, which is the subject's mental representation of people, including oneself. Finally, there is the concept of a transitional object, which is neither a subjective object nor an internal object but an early possession, such as the common "security blanket."

In Oremland's view, Freud's original conception of sublimation as the source of creativity cannot be useful because the idea of social acceptability is essential to it; the originality necessary for creativity is not often likely to be socially acceptable. Oremland reinterpreted sublimation by distinguishing the social acceptability of "contents" from that of "mode." In this, Oremland is in accord with Whitebook (1994), who stated that sublimation is a "process through which genetic material, with all its contingency, privacy, and particularity, is transformed into cultural objects such as paintings, political constitutions, mathematical proofs, musical compositions, scientific theories ... which can claim public validity in their respective domains" (p. 327). These authors considered sublimation to be a psychical process of transforming an object that is both internal and external, giving it an externalizing capacity, thereby allowing for the creation of external objects. In this way, sublimation is defined as being of a different and higher order than other defense mechanisms such as reaction formation and denial.

Eisenman (1997) proposed that one of the problems with the psychoanalytic viewpoint is that its language is highly abstract and often very difficult to understand. He believed that although some of the insights gained from psychoanalytic interpretation may be helpful, the application of this intrapsychic approach is limited, especially because it fails to look at humans as biological and social beings. It either overemphasizes personality or fails to realize how personality interacts with these other important aspects of the individual. Gillette (1992) admitted that the psychoanalytic field is resistant to new ideas. Although Kernberg (1993) was a staunch believer in psychoanalysis, he was forced to acknowledge that the contributions of this kind of research have been limited.

Gedo (1996) stated that psychoanalysis can make the greatest contribution to the study of the creative personality's origins by continuing to make comparative studies of the personality types best suited to particular kinds of creativity. These new investigations should give priority "to the fact that, whatever the sources of creative behavior may be, ultimately every human action must necessarily reflect those structured psychological dispositions called *character*" (Gedo, 1997, p. 36).

Mental Illness Theories

The question of the relationship between creativity and mental illness is ancient and still produces controversy. Many present-day psychologists and psychiatrists have demonstrated that such a link does appear to exist (for example, Briggs, 1988; Eisenman, 1997; Goodwin & Jamison, 1990; Jamison, 1993, 1995; Panter, Panter, Virshup, & Virshup, 1995; Richards, 1993). Sometimes, an investigator who previously doubted that there is a connection has become convinced through study and observation that the milder manifestations of some mental illnesses may contribute to creativity (Eisenman, 1997). Others maintain that no form of mental illness facilitates creativity. In fact, they argue that psychopathology actively interferes with it (Rothenberg, 1990, 1993).

By far the most common condition found in creative individuals is manic-depressive or bipolar disorder (see also Chapter Ten). Many biographical studies of prominent creators have found that although milder manifestations of bipolar mood swings may enhance creativity in high-ability individuals, severe episodes are not only unproductive in terms of creative achievement but may even end in suicide. For example, Vincent van Gogh is known to have suffered mental problems severe enough to require hospitalization (Panter, 1995). Edvard Munch underwent psychiatric treatment, after which the nature of his paintings became different (Warick & Warick, 1995). Poet Sylvia Plath was subject to manic-depressive episodes (Robertson, 1995), as was Virginia Woolf (Bond, 1995). Of these four, three committed suicide.

Colin Martindale (1990) examined the lives of twenty-one English and twenty-one French poets born between 1670 and 1909 and found that between 40 and 55 percent of them had significant psychopathology. An excellent study by Arnold Ludwig (1992) of persons whose biographies had been reviewed by the *New York Times Book Review* between 1960 and 1990 revealed that poets had the highest rates of mania, psychosis, and psychiatric hospitalizations and that 18 percent of them committed suicide. He also found, in his comparison of those in the creative arts to those in professions such as science and business, that members of the arts group were at least twice as likely to suffer from some form of mental disorder and were six times as likely to have been hospitalized for psychiatric reasons. Similarly high rates of mental disturbances of some description were found by Jamison (1993).

Kay Redfield Jamison, who is considered the foremost American authority on bipolar disorder and who herself suffers from the illness, has provided extensive evidence that this disorder is far more common in creative populations than probability would indicate (Jamison, 1993, 1995). She gave a well-reasoned explanation for the controversy surrounding the issue of the "'mad genius' versus 'healthy artist' debate" (1993, p. 95). Observing that the debate arises from confusion about the meaning of the term *madness* and a lack of understanding about the actual character of bipolar disorder, she stated

> Any attempt to arbitrarily polarize thought, behavior, and emotion into clear-cut "sanity" or "insanity" is destined to fail: it defies common sense and it is contrary to what we know about the infinite varieties and gradations of disease in general and psychiatric illness in particular. "Madness," in fact, occurs only in the extreme forms of

mania and depression: most people who have manic-depressive illness never become psychotic. Those who do lose their reason—are deluded, hallucinate, or act in particularly strange and bizarre ways—are irrational for limited periods of time only, and are otherwise well able to think clearly and act rationally. Manic-depressive illness, unlike schizophrenia or Alzheimer's disease, is not a dementing illness. It may on occasion result in episodes of acute psychosis and flagrant irrationality, but these bouts of madness are almost always temporary and seldom progress to chronic insanity. Yet the assumption that psychosis is an all-or-nothing sort of phenomenon, and that it is stable in its instability, leads to tremendous confusion: Van Gogh, it is said, could not have been mad, as his paintings reflect lucidity of the highest order. Lucidity, however, is not incompatible with occasional bouts of madness, just as extended periods of normal physical health are not incompatible with occasional bouts of hypertension, diabetic crisis, hyperthyroidism, or any other kind of acute exacerbation of underlying metabolic disease [1993, p. 96].

Richards's (1994) inclusive description of five bipolar "spectrum" conditions (bipolar I, II, and III, cyclothymia, and hyperthymia) gives a clearer understanding of mental conditions that may be classified as some form of manic depression. Bipolar I, which is the condition most commonly known as manic-depressive illness, has both strong manic mood elevations and severe depressions. Bipolar II is milder, with hypomanic (less intense) mood elevations as well as severe depressions. Bipolar III manifests itself first with depression; hypomania only reveals itself in the wake of treatment with antidepressant medication. Some people diagnosed with bipolar II or bipolar III disorder consider themselves only depressives. The two conditions at the milder end of the spectrum, cyclothymia, with milder mood elevations and depressions, and hyperthymia, which is characterized by hypomanic moods but no depression, round out the picture of the range of severity these conditions encompass. Variations in the frequency and amplitude of bipolar mood swings are extensive, and some people can function normally for many years between manic or depressive episodes. Schuldberg (1990) also agreed that bipolar disorder occurred along a continuum and believed that schizophrenia had this characteristic, as well.

Several studies by Richards and her colleagues have empirically demonstrated that both everyday creativity (such as creating a new recipe) and eminent creativity (such as inventing the lightbulb) may be linked with some form of bipolar mood swings, but this is more likely in the case of eminent creativity (Richards, 1993, 1994, 1996; Richards & Kinney, 1990). It was found that for everyday and eminent creators alike, many cognitive, affective, and behavioral factors were linked with mood elevation—for example, an increased mental capacity for unusual associations and creative problem solving. Mood swings were considered a possible spur to higher creativity through many possible effects, such as greater motivation for creative risk taking, given that elevated moods include high degrees of self-confidence and courage. Richards concluded that the "overall result is an active, courageous, and affectively integrated cognitive style" (1994, p. 67). She noted, however, "It is also a pattern to which not only persons at risk for bipolar disorder are privy" (1994, p. 67). Jamison (1993) agreed, pointing out that those like Rothenberg (1990, 1993) who question the validity of studies maintaining that there can be a link between creativity and psychopathology are at odds with a great deal of evidence from history, biography, and scientific studies. She suggested that the reason for this is that the symptom patterns of manic-depressive illness, which are subtle, complex, and fluctuating, may be poorly understood. In addition, there may be an insufficient appreciation for the cyclic nature of this class of disorder.

There is at least one documented case of a person whose long affliction with this illness was greatly ameliorated by the discovery and growth of her own creativity. Elizabeth Layton (1909–1993), a journalist who suffered for thirty years from manic depression, lost a son to liver disease when she was sixty-seven years old, which precipitated a prolonged depression. At her sister's suggestion, she enrolled in a contour-drawing class to distract herself from this pain. The contour-drawing technique involves drawing while looking only at the subject, not the paper, in order to avoid criticizing one's work and to draw only what one feels about the subject. Doing this kind of drawing gave Layton "an explosive catharsis and possible exorcism" (Epstein, 1995, p. 244). She began to work up to ten hours a day on her drawings, often writing commentaries about their meaning.

In less than a year, this creative production led to a complete and permanent remission of her depression. After some of her work had been exhibited in a student show, a reporter who admired it brought it to the attention of the resident art therapist at the Menninger Foundation, Robert Ault. He recognized its superior quality and arranged for an exhibition of her work. Many more shows and prizes followed, culminating in a one-artist show by the Smithsonian in 1992, the year before she died

(Rogers, 1995). In contrast to the many people who feel that some degree of hypomania fuels their creative ideas and productivity, this artist was able to use her work to overcome the disorder's effects.

Eysenck's Theory of Psychoticism

Hans Eysenck has developed a concept that he calls "psychoticism." He believes that psychoticism is biologically based and underlies the creative personality (1992b, 1993a, 1993b, 1995, 1996, 1997). This trait was originally considered to be present in those who had high scores in all measures of psychopathology included in the Minnesota Multiphasic Personality Inventory (MMPI). Eysenck later developed his own instrument, the Eysenck Personality Questionnaire, to ferret out these psychotic qualities. He defined psychoticism as "a dispositional trait underlying susceptibility to the development of psychotic symptoms" (1993b, p. 151), but stated that one must carefully distinguish between psychoticism and actual psychosis. "Psychosis as a clinical state adds something to a high degree of psychoticism, which transforms it into a proper mental illness irreconcilable with genuine creativity" (1993b, p. 157). He further explained that some traits often found in psychotics and their relatives "are correlated to form a continuum ranging from psychotic through average to highly socialized, conventional, and altruistic" (1997, p. 46). Although some empirical work has found psychoticism to be highly correlated with the production of more ideas and more unique ideas (Stavridou & Furnham, 1996), many investigators have criticized this concept.

Rothenberg (1993) pointed out that Eysenck's theory is overreliant on "one alleged finding that he believes supports this theory directly: 'The choice of unique responses on the word association test is a good measure of psychosis, of psychoticism, and of creativity'" (p. 217). Rothenberg's own empirical work with 165 artists and scientists yielded evidence that when emotional or mental illness was present in these subjects, it interfered with their work, rather than facilitating it.

In her commentary on Eysenck's theory, Richards (1993) emphasized that the state (temporary) as well as the trait (permanent) phenomena of psychopathology must both be considered in evaluating the worth of the psychoticism hypothesis, whether the focus is on eminent or everyday creativity, creative ability, or motivation. Claridge (1993) offered a number of criticisms. For instance, the majority of laboratory studies cited by Eysenck in support of his psychoticism-creativity connection used clinically based scales, which Claridge believed to be invalid for this construct. He suggested that the traits measured by Eysenck's scales relate more to the success aspect of creative achievement, in that those who possess them may be more able to persuade others of the worth of their ideas, whether or not they are truly creative.

Perhaps Stephanie Dudek offered the best summary criticism of Eysenck's position:

> In short, Eysenck has offered a personality trait theory of creativity (i.e., psychoticism), for which he attempts to show a genetic base. He has developed a test to measure its presence or, rather, to infer its presence. He has admitted that, without high intelligence, the trait of psychoticism (overinclusive thinking) will not result in effective creative achievement. However, he has not presented any evidence whatsoever to show that creative persons scoring high on the Psychoticism scale would also score high on some objective measure of overinclusive thinking. Moreover, neither he nor any of his collaborators have even attempted to independently measure presence of overinclusive thinking in any of the creative artists, architects, writers, or scientists to whom psychoticism (overinclusive thinking) as an essential trait of creativity has been attributed [1993, p. 192].

Addiction Theories

Another ordinarily disabling condition that has sometimes been linked to artistic and particularly literary creativity is the use of or addiction to alcohol or other psychoactive drugs. Many literary figures and some artists have believed that they were most able to contact their unconscious and produce their best work while under the influence of a psychoactive drug. By and large, this belief is not supported by research (Kerr, Schaffer, Chambers, & Hallowell, 1991). Well-known examples of those who claimed sometimes to be able to use alcohol as a spur to their ideas include Tennessee Williams, F. Scott Fitzgerald, Carson McCullers, and Jean Rhys. Many others, however, found that the work they produced while using alcohol was inferior to their standards, and they ceased drinking specifically to improve the quality of their work (Leonard, 1990). Still others, such as Jackson Pollock (known as the originator of the drip-and-splatter technique of painting, with which he is usually identified) died young because of their addictions. Pollock, who had gone through many years of treatment for alcohol abuse, actually produced the works considered to be his best during three years when he was sober. He ultimately returned to destructive drinking and died while driving drunk at the age of forty-four (Virshup, 1995).

A 1994 study employing a balanced placebo design conducted by Lapp, Collins, and Izzo noted the difficulty of differentiating drug effects from other influences in the creative person's milieu. This difficulty confounds other life circumstances with the predilection for drug use. Their main hypothesis was that alcohol or expectations about alcohol affect creativity.

They did their experiment with 116 men who were moderate to heavy social drinkers. Participants were first given a battery of questionnaires to assess their drinking habits and expectations about alcohol's effects, and they were then given an alcoholic or nonalcoholic beverage. They were told that what they had been given was either plain tonic water or vodka and tonic. The drink's actual alcohol content ranged from none to 2.2 milliliters of 80-proof vodka per kilogram of body weight. After drinking, participants' measured blood alcohol concentrations ranged from 0.00 to 0.02. They were then given sixty-four cards made from Audubon wildflower illustrations and asked to sort them into natural groups and aesthetically pleasing groups. Subsequently, they self-rated the perceived goodness of each group. At the end of the experiment, each was asked whether he had received an alcoholic or nonalcoholic beverage. Responses were assessed for the effects of the actual dose, the expected dose, and the combined effects of the actual dose and the expected dose. It was concluded that there was no true pharmacological effect that enhanced the creativity of the card arrangements, but that there was a probable enhancement of creativity as operationally defined in this experiment because of the expected effects of alcohol. The investigators argued that alcohol's expected effects might be enough to produce dependence in those who believed that the drug allowed them to be more creative, which may explain the prevalence of alcohol use by some creative individuals.

Norlander and Gustafson performed a series of empirical studies of the effects of alcohol intake on creativity. These studies indicated that there was a discernible pattern to the effects in different phases of the creative process based on the model developed by Wallas (preparation, incubation, illumination, verification), with an additional final stage of restitution or rest. They found that a moderate amount of alcohol made the incubation phase easier (Norlander & Gustafson, 1996) but that it also made the preparation phase more difficult (Gustafson & Norlander, 1994). The illumination phase, in which participants were asked to give as many ideas as possible about a stimulus object, also produced fewer solutions when alcohol was present (Gustafson, 1991), but the restitution phase was facilitated by alcohol (Gustafson & Norlander, 1995). From these results, the researchers suggested tentatively that the phases of creativity that are based on secondary processes (preparation, illumination, and verification) may be obstructed by the use of alcohol but that phases based largely on primary processes (incubation and restitution) may be facilitated by such use (Norlander & Gustafson, 1996).

It would appear that both anecdotal and empirical evidence fail to support the belief that alcohol aids in creative production.

Humanistic Theories

Health, growth, and the uniqueness of each individual are three major themes in the work of humanistic psychologists. They give a much smaller role to unconscious drives and compensation for deficits in the personality and much more credit to positive, self-fulfilling tendencies. As Rothenberg (1993) stressed, creativity is both complex and healthy. The individual is seen as an active agent in the formation of his or her own life and work, rather than being a largely passive victim of circumstances. The humanists also see the development of creativity as occurring throughout life, rather than developing mainly in the first five years.

The idea that creativity can be cultivated throughout the life span has had its strongest proponent in psychologist Abraham Maslow, who was well known for his opposition to the psychoanalytic point of view. Maslow considered creativity to be "multimotivated," springing from a person's wish to communicate with others, to surmount interpersonal barriers, and to bring ideas into concrete existence (Abra, 1989).

Rhodes (1990) discussed growth in creativity in Maslovian terms of "deficiency" creativity and "being" creativity. As mentioned in Chapter Two, Maslow (1962) identified a hierarchy of needs, progressing from deficiency needs, which are largely physiological and psychological survival needs, to such growth or being needs as knowledge, self-expression, integration, and creativity. A person who has met all these needs is said to be self-actualized. Rhodes extended Maslow's ideas to describe a range of growth in creativity. Although some individuals may use their creative expression to meet "deficiency" needs, as is suggested in psychoanalytic and mental illness theories, the intrinsic and extrinsic rewards of such expression may propel them further to the "being" levels of creativity. When deficiency needs have been transcended, creative work brings a higher level of satisfaction to both the creator and the audience. This view was also expressed by Arieti (1976): "Although creativity is by no means the only way in which the human being can grow, it is one of the most important. The growth occurs not only in the creative person but in all those who are affected by the innovation" (p. 413).

Maslow himself did not make the distinction between deficiency creativity and being creativity and therefore did not discuss how deficiency needs might be met through the use of creativity. Rhodes proposed to correct what she considered Maslow's oversight of this issue, pointing out that individuals with potential creative talent with no everyday means of meeting their deficiency needs because of an emotionally repressive or deprived environment might use their creativity in the service of self-healing. This view was also supported by Storr (1988), who noted that there are times when "partial deprivation of interpersonal relationships encourages imagination to flourish" (p. 106). Imagination can be used not only as a way of retreating from the world but also as a way of acting upon it and making one's mark. This perspective is clearly congruent with Rhodes's view that creative expression can be motivated by deficiency needs and that its use can lead to greater development of creative skills, so that a rewarding way of life results from what began as compensation for emotional or physical impoverishment. Even if deficiency needs are considered extrinsic motivation for creative expression, the creative experience itself can result in increasingly intrinsic motives to continue one's work.

An example of progress from deficiency creativity to being creativity may be seen in the life of the well-known writer John Cheever, whose parents were alcoholics: "Cheever as a child felt helpless and unable to communicate with them. His turning to writing seemed to serve as a way to bring order into a chaotic, disorganized experience and, in a sense, as a way to get his parents to hear him. The writing may also have become a means of compensating for his own feelings of weakness and loss" (Rothenberg, 1990, pp. 199–200).

Rhodes suggested that others do future research evolving from this theory using qualitative case studies. Those could offer sufficient detail to elaborate further how creativity arising out of deficiency needs can be a vehicle for growth and the passage to being creativity.

Psychologist Frank Barron emphasized that one must choose to endeavor to make meaning in one's life and work, and he noted that one's creative works can also stimulate others' creativity, as those works have a capacity to create new conditions (1988, 1997). He stated that in its deeper philosophical implications, "Creativity is a quest for meaning . . . an attempt to penetrate the mystery of the self, and perhaps the even greater mystery of Being" (1997, p. 2).

In much of his work, he also pinpointed ego strength as a salient feature of the health and resilience of the creative personality:

We associate the ego with order; the unconscious with disorder. . . . The creative individual, in a generalized preference for apparent disorder, turns to the dimly realized life of the unconscious and is likely to have more than the usual amount of respect for the forces of the irrational in himself and in others. . . . I believe that the creative individual not only respects the irrational in himself, but courts it as the most promising source of novelty in his own thought. Creative individuals reject the demand of society that they should shun in themselves the primitive, the uncultured, the naive, the magical, the nonsensical. . . . When individuals think in ways which are customarily tabooed, their fellows may regard them as mentally unbalanced. In my view, this kind of imbalance is more likely to be healthy than unhealthy [Barron, 1995, p. 66].

This concept demonstrates a view of creative persons as those with enough inner security to be open and unthreatened by the questioning of their beliefs and identity, people who are "fundamentally organized enough to become temporarily disorganized" (Montuori, 1996, p. 153). The healthy creative person has the flexibility to allow for a relaxation of ego controls and to continue feeling intact, confident that control can always be reestablished (Schuldberg, 1996).

Barron also saw something of the divine in human creators. Defining creativity as "the ability and propensity (or will) to bring something new into existence," (1995, p. 313) he stated that although what humans create is less than light, or the world, or new beings, the human act of creation is nevertheless on the same model. In creating, we participate in a mystery: "The call to create has been built deep inside the creatures" (1995, p. 313). Seeing creativity very broadly—including in its manifestations ways of breaking out of stultifying patterns in personal relationships and new ways of doing ordinary work, as well as the creation of products—Barron considered that all humans are potentially and actively creative all our lives, becoming "transformed transformers" (1995, p. 313).

After taking into consideration the numberless encounters he has had with creative people and his study of creativity over more than forty years, Barron (1997) identified the overriding, prevailing theme as that of freedom. He asked whether we are "free to create" and expanded on the several meanings condensed in that phrase. For one thing, there should be an inward balance of constraint and abandon, an openness to the movements and actions of the mind, spirit, and emotion. Emotional space and work space must be also available: "You must be free to go, free to stay;

free to speak, free to be silent. Spinoza says somewhere that 'freedom of thought is an indefeasible natural right,' and that leaves lots of room for silence" (p. 20). Freedom to create also implies a society that is not invested in controlling creative outcomes, unlike that of medieval Europe, where painters, for example, were restricted to the depiction of religious themes (see Chapter Two). Freedom to create further implies an ability to communicate unpopular ideas without fear of reprisal. The phrase can have an existential meaning, too, in that we as human beings are free to create because we have free will.

There is also an existential flavor to the nascent theory of Kokot and Colman (1997). They stated that when they interviewed creative adults, these creators shared some common feelings and experiences that were scarcely mentioned in the literature. Although they found it difficult to verbalize the feeling in any precise way, these creative people all had a sense of being different, not only in the sense of being unlike other adults, but especially in being different from themselves as they were as children. Many described themselves as striving to reclaim what they called their "original creativity," over which they suffered a sense of loss, and a feeling of being "irretrievably 'programmed.'" Some have accepted that they probably will never experience the fulfillment they had as children again, whereas others continue to investigate how they came to be the way they are now, as opposed to how they began their creative lives.

Kokot and Coleman hypothesized that creativity is a mode of being that is more than the aspects of personality it incorporates and more than a gift that one may use. They attempted to explain how a false sense of self arises from the inherent conditioning in our process of socializing children and how this is inimical to the growth and development of creativity, possibly stifling it entirely. Their personal experience with highly creative children led them to believe that these children live closer to the essence of being than most, an idea that they closely compared to Maslow's concept of self-actualization. They called this mode of being that they observed in creative children "living in essence."

This state of existence can be studied before the socialization process has caused the child to develop a full social ego, or false self. The false self is a veneer that initially serves to protect the natural being underlying it but that ultimately causes the natural being to be forgotten and to become inaccessible to the person. A highly creative child is likely to remain, at least for a longer time than the average child, in the natural state of "essence." Kokot and Coleman speculated that "the fact that they may represent pure, original human potential is more crucial than their ability to create" (p. 219). With an eye toward preserving as much as possible of this living in essence, Kokot and Coleman suggested that teaching creativity should not be geared toward "prompting creative products or artificially stimulating creative thinking. If educationalists study and acknowledge the essence of being creative, the products and thoughts will come naturally" (p. 225).

The unconscious mind and compensation for a problematic childhood certainly appear to be catalytic in the lives of many highly productive people, as the psychoanalytic position would suggest. In their excellent study called *Three Hundred Eminent Personalities* (1978), Mildred, Victor, and Ted Goertzel found this point of view to be especially descriptive of writers, most of whom had had a difficult childhood. In his study of children who had suffered the loss of one or both of their parents, Eisenstadt (1994) learned that once the pain and stress of bereavement had been mastered, a strong motivation to excel developed. He believed that creative striving was a deeply restorative act. MacKinnon (1978) verified that creative people often remember having an unhappy childhood, but he pointed out that individuals who are known to be especially sensitive and open to experience may have exaggerated at least some of their memories. The ability to overcome adversity has surely motivated numerous creative efforts throughout history. This finding, by the way, appears to contradict Rank's position that the "neurotic" personality never results in creativity (Chapter Two).

Virtually all psychoanalytic writers also emphasize the first years of life as a critical period, at the end of which creative ability becomes fixed. Most agree, however, that intense psychoanalysis is sometimes able to overcome this early fixation. A distinct undertone of the psychoanalytic viewpoint (with the exception of Carl Jung) is that creative people tend to suffer from emotional disturbance; in fact, some have gone so far as to assert that "creativity is next to madness." In his study of a hundred eminent American architects, Donald MacKinnon (1978) found that indeed they did have a higher-than-average level of what Eysenck calls psychoticism but that they also had an unusually great capacity for dealing effectively with it. Although no psychoanalytic theorist would suggest that creative people necessarily tend to be mentally ill, we have seen that with some creators there appears to be some such relationship.

On the other hand, an emphasis on a healthy ability to handle life's dilemmas is representative of the humanistic school of thought. This school draws its name from its belief that, ultimately, humans determine their own fates, rather than having them shaped by theological, cosmic, or other forces. This is not to say that humanism is atheistic but that it sees self-reliance as a natural human trait. Humanists view creativity as being more conscious, cognitive, and intentional than psychoanalysts do. The humanistic concept is that creativity is born through a striving for the highest possibilities in life, rather than as a defense against neurosis.

Psychiatrist R. D. Laing (1970) suggested that creative people may seem strange, not because they are unbalanced but because they see the truth so clearly. They lack the ordinary defense mechanisms so common in the rest of us and thus are often deeply pained by the many injustices in the world. Their noble attempts to right these wrongs frequently drive their efforts.

It is our opinion, therefore, that although psychoanalysis extends a number of theoretically rich paths, the positive, active, self-fulfilling concepts of the humanists are more likely to produce fruitful insights into the infinitely complex creative process.

8

CREATIVE COGNITIVE
PROCESSES

EARLY MODELS of the mental processes involved in creativity include the associationist, Gestalt, and cognitive-developmental approaches. Whereas associationism and Gestaltism involve relationships among ideas, the cognitive-developmental approach focuses on developmental changes that occur with age. More recently, new theories of the cognitive process embellish these early theories through concepts of combination and expansion and through metaphors, analogies, and mental models. Before we present the current cognitive theories, we will briefly review the theories that gave rise to these new hypotheses (associationism, the Gestalt position, and early cognitive-developmental approaches).

Associationism

Associationism was the dominant model of the mind for many years, dating back to the Greek philosophers. This model postulated that ideas in our minds are associated with other ideas and that thinking is simply a process of moving from one idea to another by way of a chain of associations. In the late nineteenth century, Sir Francis Galton promulgated the concept that ideas in the unconscious mind can be brought into consciousness through association of thoughts, especially by means of "free association," and that creative ideas are thus born.

Other theorists also subscribed to associationist ideas. James, a contemporary of Galton, emphasized an individual's ability to extract "right" ideas rather than "wrong" ones in a particular environment. In the 1920s, Wallas proposed four stages by which associations among ideas develop

Exhibit 8.1. Remote Associates Test.

Instructions: In this test you are presented with three words and are asked to find a fourth word that is related to the other three. Write this word in the space to the right. For example, what word do you think is related to these three?

cookies   sixteen   heart   _____

The answer in this case is *sweet*. Cookies are sweet; sweet is part of the phrase *sweet sixteen,* and it is part of the word *sweetheart.*

Here is another example:

poke   go   molasses   _____

You should have written "slow" in the space provided. Slow poke, go slow, slow as molasses. As you can see, the fourth word may be related to the other three for various reasons. Now try these.

1. flap   tire   beanstalk   _____

2. mountain   up   school   _____

3. package   cardboard   fist   _____

4. surprise   line   birthday   _____

5. madman   acorn   bolt   _____

6. telephone   high   electric   _____

7. hair   income   fish   _____

8. cream   bulb   heavy   _____

9. up   knife   Band-Aid   _____

10. snow   wash   black   _____

11. out   home   jail   _____

12. slugger   belfry   ball   _____

13. stage   game   actor   _____

14. Roman   arithmetic   one   _____

15. cat   color   holes   _____

16. belle   snow   beach   _____

in the creative process—preparation, incubation, illumination, and verification. More recently, Sarnoff Mednick (1962) proposed a theory based
on associationism, which has generated some current research into
associationism.

Before reading an explanation of this popular theory, you may want to
try your hand at the facsimile of the Remote Associates Test, which Mednick designed to test his theory. The test appears in Exhibit 8.1.

Mednick believed that creativity is the process by which ideas that are
already in the mind are associated in unusual, original, and useful combinations. Every image or concept we have is associated with other images and concepts. All the associations linked to a particular idea are
arranged in a list. Those associations at the top of the list are most closely
linked to the idea. As we move down the list, the strength of association
becomes weaker, and the associated ideas come to mind less quickly.
Table 8.1 gives an example of an idea and the strength of some possible
associations. The highest rating is 10, indicating that the word *ride* is
most closely associated with *bike*.

When people think about solving a problem, they mentally cast about
for an association that might serve as a solution. Most of us accept the
first idea that seems to solve the problem. Mednick argued that creative
people are those who go further down the list, searching for more unusual
but higher-quality associations to solve their problems. It is these remote
associations that produce creative products. The poet Marianne Moore
put together remote associations in a pleasing new way when she wrote,
"the lion's ferocious chrysanthemum head." Although this billowy flower

---

Table 8.1. Sample Associations with the Word *Bike*.

Strength	Association
10	Ride
9	Run
8	Transportation, red
7	Ten-speed
6	Fast
5	
4	The hill on County Road
3	Mary and Jake
2	
1	Athletic supporter

is seldom associated with ferocity, the apparent contradiction is appealing—it makes us see lions in a new and startling fashion.

Some people have very short lists of ideas that are strongly associated with each other; they can produce only a few associations. These people are often rigid and dogmatic in their beliefs and tend to produce little that is creative. Others have longer lists of less tightly associated ideas and are not so threatened by being wrong. They have the flexibility that encourages the mental search for remote associations. Some of their freely associated ideas may be silly, but some produce really creative combinations. Most people fall somewhere between these extremes.

A facsimile of Mednick's Remote Associates Test appeared earlier in this chapter. This test was designed to measure the ability to associate ideas flexibly and freely. Here are the correct answers.

ANSWERS TO THE REMOTE ASSOCIATES TEST FACSIMILE

1. jack	9. cut
2. grade, high	10. white
3. box	11. house
4. party	12. bat
5. nut	13. play
6. wire	14. numeral
7. net	15. black
8. light	16. ball

Another aspect of Mednick's theory has to do with cognitive style. Some people tend to think of the world in visual images—he calls such people "visualizers." Others tend to use words to symbolize objects—he calls those people "verbalizers." Since some problems are primarily visual and others are primarily verbal, we can expect to find a strong relationship between the type of problem and the cognitive style used to solve it.

A final part of Mednick's theory has to do with the way in which a problem is defined. If the definition is narrow, a person will rule out many kinds of associations, some of which might well offer good solutions. Yet there remains the question of how the mind puts mutually remote elements together in a way that is creatively useful. Mednick suggested three explanations:

○ Serendipity. Elements that rarely occur together in the environment nevertheless occasionally do. The creative person can recognize a link between elements that meets some previously unmet need. The invention of the X ray and the discoveries of penicillin and radium are familiar examples.

○ Similarity. Sometimes, the creative person recognizes a connection between two otherwise remote elements—a link that others have failed to notice. Marianne Moore's flower-headed lion typifies this type of association.

○ Mediation. Ideas that have nothing in common with each other may have some significant association with a third element. Again, the mediation may only be spotted by a person whose mind is open to such a possibility. The Remote Associates Test is an especially good example of this third approach.

Coney and Serna (1995) pointed out that a common thread runs through all of the speculations about the nature of creativity. Each of the associationist theorists we have mentioned agreed that, as a cognitive process, the essence of creative thought lies in one's ability to bring together various mental elements to form new and effective combinations. Another group of theorists known as Gestalt psychologists argued, however, that the whole of any idea always amounts to more than merely the sum of its parts.

Gestalt Position

Gestaltists have always been opposed to the associationist position. Developed by Max Wertheimer and his colleagues Wolfgang Köhler and Kurt Koffka, the gestalt position asserted that "gestalts," or configurations in the mind, are at the root of the insights that inform creative thought. These configurations are intricately related to one another, as well as to the contexts in which they occur. In the tradition of Gestalt psychology, there are five interrelated views of insight: completing a schema or outline, suddenly reorganizing visual information, reformulating a problem, removing mental blocks, and finding an analogue to a problem. Howard Gruber has proposed a theory that provides a neo-Gestalt point of view.

A student of Piaget's and a coauthor of Wertheimer's (Gruber, Terrell, & Wertheimer, 1964), Gruber and his students pioneered a case study approach in an effort to describe the creative mental process. He laboriously studied the notebooks of the great biologist Charles Darwin to find clues to the pathways of thought taken by a genius. After reconstructing

Darwin's thinking, Gruber suggested five characteristics of the scientific creative mental process:

○ The person views problems as a whole and deals with them by analyzing their various interacting subsystems.

○ There is a distinct view of the ultimate goal, which guides and motivates the work.

○ Each problem is represented by a number of themes or dominant metaphors. In Darwin's case, some of these were survival, heredity, and natural selection.

○ There is a strong empathy for the subject or subjects under study.

○ A distinct sense of loneliness and a sense that failure is always possible are often present, and the fight against discouragement is constant.

It is apparent that both the associationist and Gestalt schools of thought have a clear-cut theoretical orientation. The body of research known as the cognitive-developmental approach is relatively new and not as organized yet.

Early Cognitive-Developmental Approaches

The cognitive-developmental approach, which has sprung in a very general way from the theory of cognitive-developmentalist Jean Piaget, emphasizes cognitive changes that occur with age. Within this context, theorists in this camp look at creativity from the standpoint of such concepts as cognitive style, cognitive mobility, and the use of metaphor.

Cognitive Style

Cognitive style might be described as a unique style of one's mental functioning. It pertains not to how well individuals think but to the particular way they go about it. A primary aspect of cognitive style has become known as field independence and field dependence. Herman Witken and his associates (Witken & others, 1954, 1962), as well as numerous other researchers, have studied the phenomenon for decades. *Field independence* refers to the ability to look at a whole picture or problem, break it up into parts, and then attend to the more relevant parts while blocking out the less relevant parts.

The two principle measures of field independence are the Rod and Frame Test and the Embedded Figures Test. In the former task, a person

Figure 8.1. Rod and Frame Test.

Source: *Dacey, 1989b.*

is placed in a completely dark room and is then confronted with a luminous rod within a tilted luminous frame. The subject must place the rod in an upright position while disregarding the context of the tilted frame (see Figure 8.1). Likewise, the Embedded Figures Test involves recognizing a small but relevant form within a larger field of meaningless forms (see Figure 8.2). The solution to the Embedded Figures Test appears in Figure 8.3.

Although Witken's early efforts in this area did not attempt to link the concept of field independence to creativity, more and more creativity researchers have turned to this aspect of cognitive style. Gestaltists such as Wertheimer (1945) proposed that a major task of creativity involved the ability to break up a problem-solving task into parts that are not immediately recognizable and then to reorganize them in new, meaningful ways that solve the problem creatively.

Cognitive Mobility

Another aspect of cognitive style, mobility, comes from Heinz Werner's comparative developmental theory. He argued (1957) that development progresses in distinct areas. An infant begins life with a singular, global system, which includes physical movement, emotions, and the senses, all rolled into one process. As the individual develops, the processes begin to separate from one another, new processes such as cognition appear, and

Figure 8.2. Embedded Figures Test.

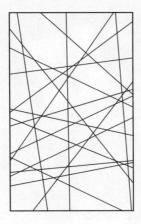

Source: *Dacey, 1989b.*

more complex and efficient processes emerge that dominate the previous ones. The earlier, primitive processes are still available to the individual, however.

For most problem solving, it would be most efficient to have a highly developed, complex system, along with the ability to call on the previously developed, more primitive systems. Although he believed in this principle for all psychological processes, Werner felt that psychological "mobility" was especially useful in creativity. Individuals who are able to move readily between complex and primitive cognitions are more likely to produce valuable ideas.

The early work on field independence and creativity was inconclusive. Spotts and Mackler (1967) used the Embedded Figures Test to assess field independence, and Torrance (1974a, 1974b) and Guilford (1967) developed tests to assess creativity. These researchers all found that college males who possess greater field independence also test higher for creativity. Although this relationship was not particularly strong, it was stronger than the relationship between measured field independence and measured intelligence. Other researchers at the time (Bieri, Bradburn, & Galinski, 1958; McWhinnie, 1967) also found that field-independent individuals showed only slightly more creativity than their field-dependent counterparts.

Researchers began to suspect that field independence alone did not adequately account for creative performance and started to look at how field independence was influenced by Werner's concept of cognitive mobility

(Bloomberg, 1971). According to this view, a creative person has achieved a high degree of field independence but can also flexibly operate at a field-dependent level when the problem calls for it. Cognitive mobility is the ability to move from one mental process to another. This notion recalls some of the research done on brain lateralization (see Chapter Eleven); high creativity might be attributable less to right-brain dominance and more to an ability to use both hemispheres in an efficient, integrated manner.

Gamble and Kellner (1968) looked at cognitive mobility with a measure called the Stroop Color-Word Test. In this test, a subject must quickly and accurately identify ink colors that are spelled out incongruently (for example, the word *red* is printed in green ink, and the right answer is *green*). The authors assumed that recognizing a color is a more primitive process than reading and that creative people would be able to call on that process more readily than less creative people. In their study, they found that subjects who scored high on the Remote Associates Test also did well on the Stroop Color-Word Test. More recently, Golden (1975) assessed subjects with divergent-thinking tasks, teacher ratings of creativity, and a new group version of the Stroop Color-Word Test and found that highly creative individuals scored significantly higher on the mobility task.

In an interesting study of cognitive mobility that used a projective psychoanalytic technique, Hersch (1962) compared the responses of creative

Figure 8.3. Solution to the Embedded Figures Test.

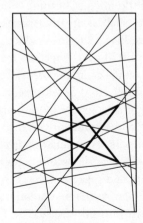

Source: *Dacey, 1989b.*

subjects on the Rorschach Test to the responses of less creative subjects and schizophrenics. The researcher speculated that the subjects who were creative (as determined by their actual achievements) not only would have more mature responses available than the less creative subjects but would also be more able to use primitive responses, similar to schizophrenics' responses. Hersch used a method of categorizing the Rorschach responses into mature or primitive responses on the basis of Werner's theory. The results showed that the creative subjects did have greater access to both mature and primitive responses than less creative subjects. The creative subjects also used more mature responses than the schizophrenics, and although their primitive responses were similar in some ways, they were also distinctly different. These results confirmed Werner's theory.

Piagetian Theory

Briefly, Piaget's theory of cognitive development states that the child grows through four general stages. In the sensorimotor stage, from birth to two years, babies organize their physical actions. In the preoperational stage, from two to seven years, children learn to think using symbols and internal images, but their thinking is not yet systematic or logical. From seven to eleven years, children reach the stage of concrete operations wherein they can think systematically but only in reference to concrete objects or activities. Piaget's fourth and last stage is called formal operations, which may develop in children around twelve years or older. In formal operations, children attain the ability to think abstractly and hypothetically (Crain, 1980).

Unfortunately, Jean Piaget himself did not have much to say about creativity, because he had little interest in topics concerning individual differences. A unique ability such as creativity does not fit in well with his theory of universal stages. Piaget's followers have, however, attempted to speculate about creativity within a Piagetian framework. Much of this speculation has centered on the creative potential of formal thought. (This is Piaget's final stage of intellectual development, in which children who are twelve and older begin to consider hypothetical questions based not on reality but on fanciful and abstract possibilities. Children are also able to consider many more factors in combination in order to solve problems.)

Gruber (1981) discussed several possible aspects of a link between formal thought and creativity and suggested that Darwin's great creative discovery of evolution is similar to the first creative processes that children discover when they move into adolescence and the formal operations stage. Feldman (1980) proposed that creativity be viewed as a Piagetian transition into a new thought structure. Arlin (1975) suggested a fifth stage beyond formal operations. She viewed formal operations as a largely convergent, problem-solving stage, whereas the new stage is viewed as a divergent, problem-finding stage (similar to Getzels and Csikszentmihalyi's 1975 conclusion that problem-finding skills differentiated between successful and unsuccessful artists).

A number of studies over the years have shown that field-independent subjects perform better than field-dependent subjects on some of Piaget's formal operational tasks (Lawson, 1976; Neimark, 1975; Stone & Day, 1980). Noppe (1985) examined formal thought and field independence along with cognitive mobility to see how the combination of these variables affects creativity. The idea is that cognitive mobility allows a person to use different kinds of perception in order to extract all the relevant parts of a problem, both big and small. The person then uses convergent formal thought processes to arrive at appropriate solutions. In support of this view, Noppe found that field independence or dependence and formal thought are good predictors of creative ability.

Use of Metaphor

A rather new concept that has received considerable attention is the ability to use and understand metaphors. Common sense suggests a relationship between efficient metaphor use and creativity. Using a metaphor in speech involves calling attention to a similarity between two seemingly dissimilar things. This suggests a process similar to divergent thinking (wherein the person comes up with an original idea rather than the expected "right" answer), and there is a growing body of research support for this relationship between divergent thinking and metaphor use (for example, Kogan, 1983).

Kogan believed that the use of metaphor can explain the difference between ordinary divergent thinking and high-quality divergent thinking. A creative person must be able not only to think of many different things from various categories but also to compare them in unique, qualitatively different ways. Although metaphors are typically first used by older children and adolescents, an outgrowth from this research has looked at the symbolic play of very young children and how it relates to creativity (see Kogan, 1983, for a review). Children's early imaginative play may be viewed as a precursor of later metaphor use and creativity.

Block and Block (1980) provided an interesting attempt to integrate the work on cognitive styles with the personality characteristics associated with creativity. These researchers had proposed earlier that such diverse areas of psychology as learning, perception, interpersonal behaviors, attitudes, and problem solving could be viewed within the constructs of "ego control" and "ego resiliency." As the use of the term *ego* suggests, their work could be broadly viewed as an effort to reconcile some aspects of psychoanalytic theory with the more recent behavioral and cognitive research that tends to ignore personality and social context.

Ego control refers to the extent to which a person can express or contain impulses, feelings, and desires. Within this construct, ego overcontrol refers to the ability to control impulse, delay gratification, suppress emotions, and avoid distractions. Ego undercontrol is the opposite. The other construct, ego resiliency, refers to a person's ability to modify his or her level of ego control to meet a situation's demands. Ego-resilient individuals can resourcefully adapt to changing circumstances, carefully size up a situation, and make good use of all the problem-solving strategies available to them. On the other hand, ego-brittle individuals have little flexibility or awareness of the demands of changing situations. When faced with an ambiguous situation or increasing stress, such people tend to perseverate or become disorganized.

Block and Block have examined these two constructs in a longitudinal study of 130 children who have been periodically assessed from age three with a combination of experimental tasks, observer descriptions, and self-report instruments. The aim of this research goes well beyond our concern with creativity, and the Blocks have directly discussed the issue of creativity infrequently (Harrington, Block, & Block, 1983). Yet their results have disclosed interesting links between the cognitive styles discussed earlier and the personality characteristics associated with ego control and ego resiliency. In addition to the relationship between ego control and delay of gratification, they have found that ego resiliency relates to field independence or dependence and tolerance of ambiguity, as well as the ability to handle anxiety under stress.

One of the best sources on the study of the role of metaphor has been the work done by Howard Gardner and his associates at Harvard University's Project Zero. His seminal 1982 book, *Art, Mind, and Brain: A Cognitive Approach to Creativity,* offered many insights into the process. Gardner based his research on the theories of three eminent structuralists: Jean Piaget, Noam Chomsky, and Claude Lévi-Strauss. He stated, "These thinkers share a belief that the mind operates according to specifiable rules—often unconscious ones—and that these can be ferreted out and made explicit by the systematic examination of human language, action, and problem-solving" (p. 4).

Gardner's main efforts focused on the relationship between children's art and their understanding of metaphor, specifically with normal and brain-damaged children. He describes the experience of telling youngsters at a seder how, after a plague, Pharaoh's "heart was turned to stone." The children interpreted the metaphor variously, but only the older ones could understand the link between the physical universe (hard rocks) and psychological traits (a stubborn lack of feeling). Younger children are more apt to apply magical interpretations (God or a witch did it). Gardner argued that the development of the understanding of metaphoric language is as sequential as the stages proposed by Piaget and Erikson and is closely related to the types of development treated in those theories.

Examining such children's metaphors as a bald man's having a "barefoot head" and an elephant's being seen as wearing a "gas mask," Gardner and Winner (1982) found that the level of sophistication clearly changed with age. Interestingly, there appear to be two opposing features:

1. When children are asked to explain figures of speech, they get steadily better at it as they get older.

2. Very young children seem to be the best at making up their own metaphors, however. Furthermore, their own metaphors tend to be one of two types: "Children who make their metaphors on visual resemblances may approach experience largely in terms of the physical qualities of objects. On the other hand, children who base their metaphors on action sequences may view the world in terms of the way events unfold over time. We believe that the difference may continue into adulthood, underlying diverse styles in the creation and appreciation of artistic forms" (Gardner & Winner, 1982, p. 164).

These researchers believe that the spontaneous production of metaphors declines somewhat during the school years. This is probably because the child, having mastered a basic vocabulary, has less of a need to "stretch the resources of language to express new meanings" (p. 165). In addition, there is greater pressure from teachers and parents to get the right answers, so children take fewer risks with their language.

It is exciting to think that Gardner and Winner may be offering us an explanation as to why some people become scientists and why others become writers. This may be an important key to fostering such talent. Of course, this is not to say that they have explained why children develop one of the two forms of "metaphorizing" (or neither), but their work appears to be a giant step in the right direction.

Summary of Traditional Cognitive Theories

An analysis of cognitive aspects of creativity can be grouped into three schools of thought, each one significantly different from the other two. Which is right, or perhaps more right? The classic disparity between associationist and Gestalt conceptions of cognitive processes is still evident in current cognitive theories, although the difference is not structured in the same terms. As Mayer (1995) stated

> The resurgence of interest in analogical reasoning and expert problem solving provides a modern battleground for the conflict. On one side, the associationist view seems to be vindicated by the finding that analogical transfer—solving a new problem by using a previously solved problem—depends on experience in solving specifically related problems. However, remnants of the Gestalt view can be found in the proposal that analogical problem solving is not an automatic process in which trial-and-error application of past experience results in creative solutions; instead . . . the problem solver must strategically control processes such as abstracting a general principle or structure from specific problems or recognizing . . . the same underlying structure [pp. 27–28].

The current emphasis on the importance of domain-specific knowledge is consistent with the associationist approach, whereas the need to understand the process that leads to understanding a problem's underlying structure is the same as the gestaltists' search for *insight*.

Current Cognitive Theories

Research in cognitive psychology has studied cognition's logical aspects more systematically than it has studied the creative side of the cognitive process, but work in this second area is increasing. For example, Pesut (1990) proposed a model of creative thinking as a "self-regulatory metacognitive process" (p. 105), which he believed to be rich in heuristic possibilities. Metacognition, or "thinking about thinking," refers to one's knowledge of and attention to one's own thinking processes, including monitoring and regulating these processes actively. Pesut linked the concepts of self-regulation—in which he included self-monitoring, self-evaluation, and self-reinforcement—with metacognition to describe creative thinking. He hypothesized that an individual can consciously implement methods of thinking that generate creative associations, thus helping him or her to achieve a creative goal. By practicing these methods, the person develops greater metacognitive knowledge and is able to use such strategies as self-instruction, brainstorming, and synectics, in which people make familiar things strange and strange things familiar through the use of different kinds of analogies (Gordon, 1961, cited in Dacey, 1989b) to enhance creative thought.

The early theories of creative cognition—associationist, Gestaltist, and cognitive-developmental—have been revisited and revised according to the results of recent research and investigative efforts. Current theories tend to fall into two categories: (1) creative metaphors, analogies, and mental models and (2) combination and expansion theories. Each of these categories embellishes on the earlier positions and provides new insight into the cognitive aspects of creativity.

Metaphors, Analogies, and Mental Models

Theories that have taken a new look at the role of metaphor in creativity have focused on the ways in which an individual can shift from one understanding of a concept or meaning to a new and different perspective. Chi (1997) argued that creative individuals possess the ability to cross ontological boundaries, with *ontology* defined as the nature of being. Chi described the "Aha" experience of creativity as an ontological shift, because "once a concept has been re-represented on a different ontological tree, the concept immediately inherits the attributes of that tree. This immediate experience can produce the 'Aha' phenomenon" (p. 230).

For example, the common phrases, "You make my blood boil" or "Let him stew awhile" are metaphors about the heating of fluid. The emotion—anger—is usually on the ontological tree of mental states, but these metaphors place the emotion on the ontological tree of substance (heated fluid). The emotion therefore inherits the substance's characteristics and crosses the ontological boundary of mental states to material substances. Chi suggested that the use of metaphors that require this kind of shifting across ontological categories may be a common form of creativity.

Shifts across ontological trees must be considered major shifts. It is into this class that major scientific discoveries are likely to fall. Minor ontological shifts occur more frequently and may be experienced by a larger number of people. These minor shifts may be thought of as crossing ontological branches, rather than entire trees.

Everyday experiences that may seem ordinary form the basis of Gibbs's (1997) theory of creativity, specifically with regard to a creative person's understanding of linguistic meaning. Gibbs stated that human beings learn to recognize common metaphoric concepts because of everyday bodily experiences. Both linguistic and psychological studies of embodied meaning bear out the notion that many creative ideas are derived from familiar experiences. The fact that creative artists have been found to talk about abstract concepts in embodied metaphorical ways is additional evidence of the "embodied nature of categorization processes in general" (p. 371).

In accord with the creative cognition approach of Smith, Ward, and Finke (1995b), Gibbs suggested that no single process can be identified as the only mechanism for creative cognition. Ward (1995) further stated that "when people use their imagination to develop their ideas, those ideas are heavily structured in predictable ways" (p. 157) based on prior experience. Gibbs did not intend to imply that the study of creativity must be restricted to underlying patterns of bodily experience, but he noted that "much of the motivation for why people think about concepts in the way they do, including many creative forms, is grounded in the mind and the body" (p. 371).

Analogy is related to the concept of metaphor in creative cognition. As Bruner (1973) phrased it in his book's title, people go "beyond the information given" when they use analogies and metaphors. Perkins (1997) developed a theory of creative systems and stated that a good analogy can help tame what he calls "Klondike spaces" by reducing the number of possibilities considered, crossing "canyon boundaries" by relating one domain to another, and transporting thinking beyond an "oasis" (p. 527).

The *Klondike space* was defined as a "problem space" by Perkins. "The image is one of searching for gold in the Klondike" (p. 527) and is defined using metaphors of wilderness (suitable solutions scattered over a large space), plateau (no clear gradient of promise), canyon (limiting boundaries that are often unrecognized), and oasis (the difficulty of leaving an area of partial promise). He contrasted Klondike spaces with *homing spaces,* which are spaces of possibility "with a clear gradient of promise that an iterative search process can track to a solution" (p. 527).

Perkins placed these two spaces on the extreme ends of a continuum and noted that most search spaces (the areas explored in the search for a solution) fall somewhere in between. Exceptional creativity, according to Perkins, is indicative of a search in a Klondike space, whereas more mundane creativity is carried out in homing spaces. The difference lies in a person's ability to go beyond the information presented and to apply it to a new, yet similar, problem that has a less certain solution.

Markman, Yamauchi, and Makin (1997) proposed that "even mundane concepts can establish a foundation for great scientific advances" (p. 202). They speculated that what they described as "category learning" may give insight into creative processes on a larger scale, because many examples of creative invention have involved extending existing categories to new functions. The central assumption in this concept is that category representations result from what we learn as we manipulate, perceive, think about, and reason with objects in the world. "What people learn about an item or category in a given situation depends on how they use it" (p. 181).

Based on their empirical findings, the authors suggested that category acquisition does not necessarily require extreme effort of the sort attributed to large-scale creativity. They concluded that although concept acquisition is creative, "It may not be creative in the same way that scientific discovery and invention are creative" (p. 202). Some tasks may require classification (for example, deciding where an item belongs), whereas other tasks may require inference (for example, inferring what features an item has based on features given). Markman and colleagues advocated their multifaceted approach to category learning because it pinpoints the ways in which the tasks used to learn categories can affect the structure of the representations developed. This approach is important for the study of creativity in that an understanding of how we go beyond existing categories must be based on a knowledge of how categories are constructed. This understanding must also depend on an understanding of which operations work best to extend categories that may lead to the creation of new categories.

Combination and Expansion Theories

Another way of examining categories or associations among categories is by way of the combinations an individual may make that relate to creativity. Combination and expansion theories differ from associationist theories in positing that concepts are not merely associated but combined to produce new concepts or creative ideas. Various aspects of conceptual combination of ideas and categories may be unified when they are considered to be parts of a coherence mechanism, which is a mental construct people use to make sense of what they see and hear. Thagard (1997) argued that every concept has a "network of associated concepts" (p. 131).

These concepts may be coherence-driven or incoherence-driven. Coherence-driven combinations are those concepts already available to an individual that are adequate for making sense of a situation. Incoherence-driven combinations result when failures of conceptual coherence lead to more creative combinations. Incoherence-driven combinations can invoke a wider search for interpretations, which may use high-level cognitive processes, such as analogy.

An example of coherence-driven combination is the word *lawyer*. Most people associate that concept with such words as *intelligent, professional,* and *educated*. Negative constraints between concepts are based on contradictions or negative combinations, such as *lawyer* and *poor*. The principal author recently encountered an example of incoherence-driven combination in a headline that read, "How to Keep Your Employees from Becoming Web Potatoes." Whereas he could not find a coherent interpretation of the phrase "Web potato" at first, he then recalled the expression "couch potato" and realized that just as a couch potato describes one who watches too much television, a Web potato must describe someone who spends too much time on the Internet.

The theory posited by Shoben and Gagne (1997) also considers the fact that we are able to produce and understand combinations of words that we have not heard before or heard in combination before. They suggested that "conceptual combination involves finding the relation that is appropriate based on the modifier or head noun" (p. 31). Creating new concepts involves a complicated selection of one relationship from several possible alternatives. Two approaches to the study of conceptual combinations are the "schema modification model" and the "taxonomic approach."

In the schema modification model, the head noun is represented by a schema of various dimensions, and conceptual combination involves having the modifier fill one of those dimensions. For example, in the phrase "red apple," *apple* is the head noun, and *red* fills the color dimension of the schema for apple. The taxonomic approach is based on the notion that there is a classification system of thematic relations into which all concepts can fit. Many researchers who use this approach assume that only a small number of relations must be specified, but others believe in an almost infinite number of possible relationships, largely determined by context.

The empirical work of Shoben and Gagne brought them to two main conclusions. First, people usually generate word combinations in familiar ways. Using modifiers in uncommon ways requires some amount of creativity. Thus, people tend to engage in mundane creativity rather than extraordinary creativity. Shoben and Gagne also concluded that the creation of new concepts is most often "a highly constrained application of an old and frequent relation to a new domain" (pp. 48–49).

The work of Runco (1993; 1994; Ed., 1994) suggested that the construction of any combination reflects the desire to create such combinations. Specifically, Runco stated that a person cannot be interested in solving a problem or working productively without recognizing that there is a problem. The person must first cognitively appraise the situation as a problem that deserves attention and effort. "Simply put, cognitive appraisal is necessary for the affective interest" (1993, p. 222).

Runco argued that creativity is not simply a cognitive characteristic or a personality characteristic but an interplay between cognitive and extracognitive factors that may be inextricable. Creative cognition is more than problem solving, according to Runco, who also stressed that selective and evaluative processes are necessary parts of the creative process that deserve consideration in future research. Runco's assertions have implications for education in light of the fact that many researchers have stopped using the Guilford (1967) and Torrance (1974a,b) tests. The concept of divergent thinking should not be dismissed, in Runco's opinion, because such tests are now administered, scored, and interpreted differently as a result of research from the late 1980s or early 1990s.

The cognitive aspects of creativity presented by the early schools of thought—associationist, Gestalt, and cognitive-developmental—are being examined in new and exciting perspectives in current research. The more recent theories present interpretations of the older theories in light of the decades of empirical research findings and hypotheses. Which is right, or at least more correct? The next generation of researchers in this area will indeed have a rich base from which to challenge old ideas and build bridges to new interpretations.

9

CREATIVE PROBLEM SOLVING

TRUE CREATIVE GENIUS is rare, but there is considerable evidence that almost everyone has at least some creative ability. Normally, we use it in trying to solve problems. Table 9.1 compares seven models of problem solving. No two models agree completely on the "right" sequence of steps in the process. Nevertheless, taken as a whole, they offer a comprehensive picture of what researchers have found when they have tried to recreate how good problem solvers go about solving problems.

There is an inherent weakness in each of these studies' methodologies. For every model, the researchers interviewed a variety of problem solvers and then summarized what they heard. It is possible (and probably likely) that the persons who were interviewed remembered the sequence of the problem-solving efforts as being more orderly than it actually was. They may have "tidied up" the process unconsciously. This was the contention of Guilford (1970, 1975), who saw the process as much less logical and sequential than these other theorists.

Guilford's Theory of Intellectual Functioning

J. P. Guilford was the first to call for a great expansion in research on creativity (see Chapter Two). He and his colleagues then attempted an even more ambitious project—mapping the intellectual operations of the human mind (with a special interest in creative functioning). Through the use of factor analysis, they produced the classic theory Guilford called the "structure of intellect."

The authors wish to acknowledge Christopher Wu's contributions to this chapter.

Table 9.1. Seven Models of the Creative Problem-Solving Process.

Stage	Wallas	Dewey	Rossman	Bransford and Stein	Vaigiu	Osborne	Polya
1	Preparing	Sensing difficulty Defining difficulty	Observing problem Formulating problem Surveying available information	Identifying problems Defining problem	Preparing Creating definition Feeling frustrated	Finding facts Problem Preparing	Understanding the problem
2	Incubating				Incubating		
3	Illuminating	Suggesting possible solutions	Formulating solutions	Exploring approaches	Illumination	Finding idea Producing idea Developing idea	Deciding what to do
4	Verifying	Considering consequences	Critically examining solutions	Looking at effects		Finding solution Evaluating	Carrying out the plan
5			Formulating new ideas				Looking back
6		Accepting a solution	Accepting and testing new ideas accepted			Adopting ideas	

In building this theory, he and his associates gave a wide variety of mental tests to a large number of people. Some were standard IQ tests; others were more unusual, such as tests of spatial relations and social knowledge. He wanted to see how ability on one type of test interrelated with ability on other types of tests. From this, he believed he could identify the basic cognitive abilities.

Guilford's most significant finding was that the intellect consists of five types of mental operations. These mental operations form a central theme in his model of creative problem solving and are described below.

FIVE OPERATIONS OF THE STRUCTURE OF INTELLECT

1. *Cognition,* which means discovery, rediscovery, or recognition of a situation's relevant characteristics

2. *Memory,* which implies retention of what is known

3. *Convergent thinking,* which means thinking that results in the right answer to a question that can have only one right answer ("How much is 2 + 2?")

4. *Divergent thinking,* which means thinking in different directions or searching for a variety of answers to questions that may have many right answers ("What would happen if it rained up?")

5. *Evaluation,* which means reaching decisions about the accuracy, goodness, or suitability of information that has been generated by the previous four operations

Although all five operations are involved in creative thinking to some extent, Guilford believed that the two types of productive thinking—convergent and divergent thinking—are most important. Divergent thinking is essential in generating a wide range of ideas. Convergent thinking is then used to identify the most useful or appropriate of the possible solutions that the thinker has produced.

Guilford's model of creative problem solving (CPS model) is based solidly on his theory of the intellect's structure. A schematic drawing of his model appears in Figure 9.1.

Guilford stated that problem-solving behavior begins with some input, either from the outside environment or from within the body. The latter he referred to as "somatic input." The individual is often not consciously aware that new information is being presented and is sometimes unwilling to let it become conscious. Thus at this first stage, there is a filter, which determines whether the input will have any influence on behavior. Exit I represents an unconscious avoidance of the problem altogether. If

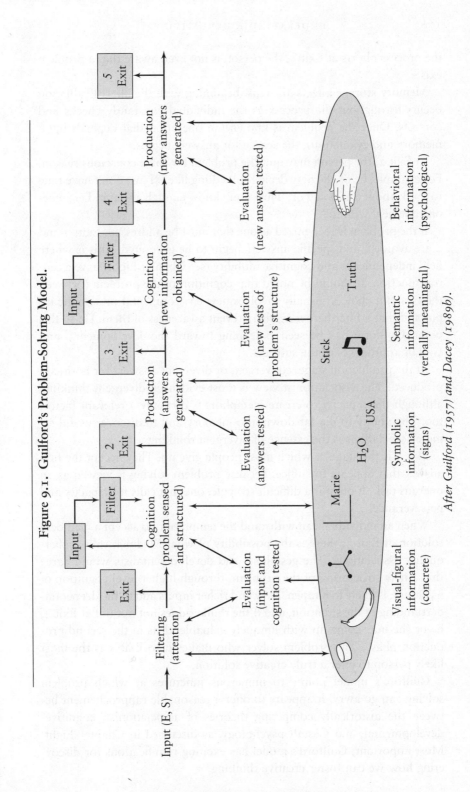

Figure 9.1. Guilford's Problem-Solving Model.

Input (E, S) →

Filtering (attention)

Evaluation (input and cognition tested)

1 Exit

Input → Cognition (problem sensed and structured) → Filter

Evaluation (answers tested)

2 Exit

Production (answers generated)

3 Exit

Evaluation (new tests of problem's structure)

Input → Cognition (new information obtained) → Filter

4 Exit

Evaluation (new answers tested)

Production (new answers generated)

5 Exit →

Visual-figural information (concrete)

Marie

Symbolic information (signs)

H₂O   USA

Stick

♩

Semantic information (verbally meaningful)

Truth

Behavioral information (psychological)

After Guilford (1957) and Dacey (1989b).

the process aborts at Exit 1, the person is not even aware that a problem exists.

Memory storage affects all steps, beginning with the filter. Evaluation occurs throughout the process as the individual constantly checks and corrects. Once the problem is known (an operation that depends upon memory and evaluation), the search for answers begins.

At Exit 2, the person may quit the problem for some conscious reason. For example, he or she may decide something like, "I just don't have time to think about this now" or "I just don't know enough about it. Let someone else deal with it."

If the problem is recognized as one that must be addressed, Exits 1 and 2 are avoided, and specific answers begin to be generated. This is where field independence and cognitive mobility (see Chapter Eight) have a central function. It should be noted that cognition of the problem (between the two exit choices) usually involves new environmental or somatic input and that a filter here may also prevent awareness of them. Up to this point, Guilford may be seen as leaning toward the developmental and Gestalt approaches to the subject.

At the production stage, convergent or divergent answers (or both) are produced. The associationist view is most evident in divergent thinking, although the capacity to create metaphors is certainly a relevant factor, too. The ability to dig far down into memory and to discover useful remote associations is the essence of divergent thinking.

Exit 3 is the stage at which most people give up. They accept the first answer that appears to suffice, because problem solving is viewed as an onerous task. It often *is* a difficult struggle, one that calls for tenacity and perseverance.

When an individual can withstand the temptation to accept a mediocre solution at Exit 3, there is the possibility of what Mednick calls higher-quality associations. The gestaltists and developmentalists would agree that a new structuring of the problem, through higher-level cognition of its nature, is likely to happen. New and richer inputs add to the deeper understanding of the situation, and if the thinker does not opt out at Exit 4, he or she may come up with uniquely valuable ideas in the second production phase. The problem solver who makes it to Exit 5 is the most likely person to offer a truly creative solution.

Guilford's model points to numerous junctures at which problem solving can go awry. It appears to offer a reasonable rapprochement between the historically competing theories of associationist, cognitive-developmental, and Gestalt psychology, as discussed in Chapter Eight. Most important, Guilford's model has exciting ramifications for discovering how we can foster creative thinking.

Other Approaches to Creative Problem Solving

Guilford's model appears to have been a catalyst for new ways of thinking about problem solving. In the remainder of this chapter, we review what we believe are the most creative of these approaches.

Lateral Thinking

In his book *Lateral Thinking* (1970), Edward deBono suggested a distinction between vertical thinking (which means mental operations that move in a straight line back and forth between lower-and higher-level concepts) and lateral thinking (which means looking for alternate ways of defining or interpreting a problem). For instance, lateral thinkers might create a list of synonyms of the concept with which they are dealing to develop useful, related ideas. As he put it, "Vertical thinking digs the same hole deeper; lateral thinking is concerned with digging a hole in another place" (p. 15).

In later publications (1971, 1984), deBono presented additional evidence that lateral thinking plays an essential role in divergent thinking. He has contrasted vertical and lateral thinking in several ways.

○ Vertical thinking is selective, whereas lateral thinking is generative. Vertical thinking is aimed at finding the right solution by following one path, but lateral thinking is more concerned with richness than with rightness and is therefore more likely to generate numerous pathways of thought.

○ Vertical thinking is analytical, whereas lateral thinking is provocative. Lateral thinkers seek information not for its own sake but for its ability to provoke or shock them. It does not even have to be true, as long as it is effective.

○ Lateral thinking welcomes intrusions by "irrelevant" information. New thinking patterns are seldom structured from within; some outside influence is usually necessary. According to deBono, the more irrelevant an idea seems, the greater the possibility is that it will effectively alter the existing thought pattern.

○ Vertical thinking is sequential, whereas lateral thinking can make mental jumps. Vertical thinking proceeds through a series of steps, with each step emerging from the preceding step. Lateral thinkers, on the other hand, feel free to make "psychic leaps." They can jump around, using conscious and unconscious material, and they do not worry about the logic of their thinking, because they know they can come back later to reorganize their ideas and fill in the details.

○ Vertical thinking is "high probability," whereas lateral thinking is "low probability." Vertical thinking is more likely to give you a good answer, but you will need lateral thinking for a great one (though the odds for getting such a superlative idea are also lower).

Langer's concept of "mindfulness" (Benassi, Mahler, & Asdigian, 1993; Langer, 1993, 1996) is similar. She defines mindfulness as having three qualities: implicit multiple perspectives, openness to new information, and alertness to distinction (the ability to create new categories). She calls the last category "sideways learning" and distinguishes it from "top-down" deduction and "bottom-up" induction. What Langer (and deBono) attempt to do is restructure traditional ways of thinking about thinking. The logical model of problem solving is an ordered sequence, a geometric line of thought. Mindfulness requires being able to move "sideways" off the regular line, making a kind of "orthogonal shift."

Componential Approach

If thought is fixed into a one-dimensional linear mode, a sideways move will give more "degrees of freedom." A lateral move may bring a shift in point of view and another degree of freedom, preventing a person from getting stuck in an existing dimension. Such shifts are the components in Sternberg's componential theory (1997).

The three elements of Sternberg's theory are knowledge acquisition; higher-order processes of monitoring, planning, and decision making; and a performance component that processes tasks. Davidson, Deuser, and Sternberg (1994) use the componential approach in a problem-solving model with four processes:

1. Finding and defining the problem
2. Mentally representing the problem
3. Planning how to solve the problem
4. Evaluating performance on the problem

Each process benefits from lateral or sideways thinking. Take for example this problem:

○

A runner heads east from Worcester, running at a steady pace of ten miles per hour. Another runner heads west from Boston, twenty minutes later, running at a steady twelve miles per hour. Who will be closer to Worcester when they meet?

○

The "trick" to the question is to encode the relevance of the question's last part, "when they meet." When the runners meet, they will be equally close to Worcester, because they will be in the exact same spot. Most of us are conditioned to think a certain way when confronted by distance, rate, and time problems. Hence we are functionally fixated to apply a formula, rather than reading the problem with an open mind.

Domain-Individual-Field Interaction Model

Sternberg's componential view of problem solving may be seen as part of a larger system known as the domain-individual-field interaction (DIFI) model. The knowledge-acquisition components are part of an individual's mind (such as a psychologist). The person in turn interacts with a domain of knowledge (such as psychology), as well as a field of expert practitioners, who collectively judge the domain (such as the American Psychological Association). The DIFI model (Feldman, Csikszentmihalyi, & Gardner, 1994a) is a biopsychosocial version of such a system.

Human beings have a limited capacity to deal simultaneously with multiple concepts. Ideally, one would use the DIFI system as a whole to look at the dynamics of a problem to be solved. It is usually easier, however, to begin from the standpoint of the individual or individuals involved in the problem rather than with the abstractions of a domain or field. Then, to be effective, creative problem solving must take into account the rules of the domain and the judgment of the field. Csikszentmihalyi (1996) cited the ideas about problem solving put forth by the distinguished inventor Jacob Rabinow. Rabinow identified three elements of creative thought: energy or persistence to pursue new ideas; a large knowledge base; and good judgment, which means a nose for distinguishing the fruitful ideas from the bad ones. The first criterion resides in the person. The second stems from extended immersion in the domain of knowledge (Gardner, 1997a). The last criterion emerges from the internalization of the domain and reflects the individual's own expertise as a member of the field of practitioners.

When each component of the DIFI system is synchronized with the other two, the result is what Csikszentmihalyi (1990) called "flow." Flow can be variously described as a "peak experience," "losing oneself," "one-pointedness," or "being in the zone." Flow is the intrinsic reward for pursuing a challenging goal. Regardless of the activity, if innovators maintain an optimal match between the challenge of the problem and their own skills, they will experience flow. The heart of the creative dialectic is the tension between challenge and skill. Hegel called it thesis and antithesis. Piaget renamed it assimilation and accommodation. In each case, the "transformational imperative" (Feldman & others, 1994b) requires an ability to stay open to freedom and yet to recognize necessary structure. When people internalize the DIFI system, they create a mental proving ground in which ideas may clash and work against each other to produce useful creations.

Drawing on his previous work (1990), Csikszentmihalyi recently characterized flow as the balancing of boredom and anxiety. Complexity can therefore be examined as the interplay between the two extremes (see Table 9.2). In summary, when these seven opposing dyads are in balance, they characterize the divergent thinker in a state of flow.

Gardner (1997a, 1997b) provided a useful typology of creative exemplars. His typology also represented a person-focused view of the DIFI perspective. He posited four types of innovators: the Maker, the Master, the Introspector, and the Influencer. The first two have particular relevance here. The "Master" exemplifies the existing domain of knowledge (by doing excellent work within the parameters of that domain), whereas the "Maker" creates new domains. The evolution of a domain may be viewed through the eyes of Makers and Masters.

Makers bring forth what has heretofore been unexamined or unrealized. Sigmund Freud represents an example of a Maker. He dove into the sea of possibility to emerge with a new pearl of knowledge—psychoanalysis. Makers' strengths are as problem finders and system builders. Makers instinctively know where to find what they are looking for and how to construct a new conceptual structure for transforming the domain.

By contrast, Masters (for example, Wolfgang Mozart or Henry Ford) focus on the existing domain. Masters take the domain's existing prob-

---

Table 9.2. Csikszentmihalyi's Dyads.

Qualities Used to Escape Boredom	Qualities Used to Overcome Anxiety
Agency	Communion
Passion	Detachment
Divergent thinking	Convergent thinking
Playfulness	Discipline
Extroversion	Introversion
Energy	Quietude
Iconoclasm	Tradition

Source: *Based on Csikszentmihalyi & Rathunde (1993).*

lems and solve them. Rather than choosing their point of entry in the field's periphery, in its obscure topics, Masters focus on the centers of activity, the turbulent vertexes of established interest. Gardner identifies three techniques that creative individuals use in their intellectual enterprises.

The first technique is leveraging their existing intellectual strength. Gardner (1993b) identified seven types of intelligence: logical or mathematical, visual or spatial, bodily or kinesthetic, linguistic, musical, interpersonal, and intrapersonal. Given this framework, none of the exemplars he studied embodied all seven uniformly. Instead, they each exhibited sufficient intrapersonal intelligence to focus on their strengths and ignore their weaknesses. Freud lamented his lack of mathematical ability but focused his formidable intrapersonal intelligence and linguistic skills to create the study of psychoanalysis. The Nobel Prize–winning organic chemist Robert Burns Woodward leveraged his extraordinary visuospatial intelligence on the problems of organic synthesis, neglecting his family and children through two marriages. In the case of T. S. Eliot, the poet endured years of an unhappy marriage to his wife, who was eventually institutionalized. After his divorce and remarriage, his increased happiness was matched with a corresponding decrease in creative productivity.

The second technique that Gardner's creative exemplars used was to reflect on their intellectual enterprise. This practice allowed them to take a global view of their creative endeavor. Their reflection also indicates that they were open to interacting with the field of knowledge, which allowed them to be well informed about the domain's current state. Personal journals, regular meetings with confidants, and daily meditations are all ways of reflecting on one's intellectual pursuit.

Finally, creative persons are able to frame their experience in a positive light. All of them face failures in the course of their careers. Each time, they have taken the experience and reframed it in a useful direction. This constructive viewpoint motivates creators to go further because they can build a more successful life story for themselves. This reframing ability plays an important role in Albert Bandura's concept of self-efficacy, which in turn is vital to creative production.

Self-Efficacy

As discussed in Chapter Six, the self that acts and the self that evaluates those actions are the same. *Agency* is the capacity to act intentionally. When people view their own ability to do something, they assume the freedom to act with intention. Before acting, they must believe in their self-efficacy. Embedded scripts of doubt and inability reduce the possibility of discovering fresh and appropriate new ideas. Self-efficacy allows the maximum initial divergence, because cognitive limits are not set in place prematurely.

The sources of self-efficacy may be interpreted from a biopsychosocial perspective as the interaction between individuals and their environments. Biologically, for instance, individuals are genetically predisposed to have certain arousal levels and affective temperaments. As they master life's challenges, they gain a direct source of psychological feedback for perceived self-efficacy. In addition, self-efficacy derives from the social context through direct imitation or vicarious modeling of inspiring idols. When people address new situations that require adaptation, the capacity to identify with admired models can facilitate that adaptation. We might say such efficacious people serve as metaphors for the idealized goal. In fact, metaphors play a significant role in both self-control and creativity.

Metaphorical Thinking and CPS

As pointed out in Chapter Eight, a *metaphor* is a word or phrase that stands for another word or phrase by forming a comparison or analogy. Using a metaphor involves calling attention to a similarity between two seemingly dissimilar things.

Cicone, Gardner, and Winner (1981) noted that the Shakespeare Parallel Text Series translates the Bard's plays into everyday English. "Stand and unfold yourself" becomes "Stand still and tell me who you are." According to them, offering such a translation is a step in the wrong direction. "If, as we have shown, students of this age have the potential to deal with complex metaphors, there is no necessity to rewrite Shakespeare" (p. 214).

Metaphors help us solve problems. They give fullness of meaning and allow nuances of thought through the imaginative juxtaposition of topic and vehicle. In addition, working with metaphors limbers up the mind in the same way that stretching exercises prepare us for extended physical activity. Finally, by making creative leaps to other domains of thought and imagery, metaphors invite more of the remote associations described in Chapter Eight.

A time-honored technique that has metaphor as its base is known as *synectics* (Gordon, 1972). The word is coined from two Greek words meaning the joining together of different and apparently irrelevant elements. Gordon deemphasized the roles of inspiration and of "genius," believing that everyone can greatly improve their creative abilities if they understand the underlying psychological processes. This assumption is directly counter to the view that if the individual does any analysis of the problem-solving process, it will hinder or even stop the process. Another theoretical assumption of synectics is that the emotional, irrational components of the creative process are more important than the intellectual, rational components and that these emotional, irrational components must be understood in order to increase creative ability. As Gordon put it, "To make the familiar strange is to distort, invert, or transpose the everyday ways of looking and responding which render the world a secure and familiar place. . . . It is the conscious attempt to achieve a new look at the same old world, people, ideas, feelings, and things. In the 'familiar world' objects are always right-side-up; the child who bends and peers at the world from between his legs is experimenting with the familiar made strange" (1972, p. 296).

A synectics problem-solving session uses four primary mechanisms for making the familiar strange. Each is metaphorical in character. They are personal analogy, direct analogy, symbolic analogy, and fantasy analogy.

Personal analogy refers to a personal identification with the elements of a problem. The process is similar to empathy, except that the problem solver can identify with inanimate problems such as the movement of subatomic particles or a piece of music rather than just with other people's feelings.

Direct analogy refers to a direct comparison of parallel facts, knowledge, or technology. A good example of direct analogy is Alexander Graham Bell's first telephone, whose design was based on his observations of the way the human ear worked.

Symbolic analogy uses objective and impersonal images to describe the problem. The image conjured up may not be realistic or technologically possible, but it is aesthetically satisfying. Symbolic analogy captures the essence of a relationship between a problem and a poetic response.

With *fantasy analogy,* synectics takes Freud's view that artistic creativity is the fulfillment of a wish and extends that view to technical invention. This mechanism is typically used with problem-solving groups as the group asks itself, "In our wildest fantasies, how do we want this solution to work?" Possible solutions are then translated into more practical terms and reevaluated.

Sociodrama

Sociodrama is also a group problem-solving process but with a twist. Adapted by Torrance (1975, 1982), sociodrama is a dramatic method used to solve a group or interpersonal problem. Essentially, the problem-solving group is placed in a deliberately contrived, dramatic context. The individuals involved gather and decide on a problem, place it within a dramatic setting, assign roles, and then improvise a play.

The group's leader or "director" must guide the sociodrama session toward possible solutions in an objective way, trying not to influence the outcome. The leader may use a variety of production techniques before, during, and after a sociodrama session. The leader may also provide props, music, lights, decorations, and so forth, all in an effort to create the right atmosphere so that the "actors" will identify with their characters and setting.

Isaksen's Guidelines

Numerous sets of guidelines for effective problem solving have been published (for example, Dacey, 1989a; Hallman, 1967). Scott Isaksen (1983) has offered perhaps the most helpful set for adult problem solvers, which we present here.

- o Recognize some previously unrecognized and unused potential.
- o Respect an individual's need to work alone; encourage self-initiated projects.
- o Allow and encourage an individual to succeed in an area and in a way that is possible for him or her.
- o Permit contributions to the plan to be different for various individuals; express the value of individual differences.
- o Reduce pressure, and provide a nonpunitive environment. That is, create a feeling of psychological safety, whether the setting is the home, classroom, or workplace.
- o Tolerate complexity and disorder, at least for a period.
- o Communicate that you are "for" the individual rather than "against" him or her.
- o Support and reinforce unusual ideas and responses.
- o Use mistakes as positive opportunities to help individuals understand errors and meet acceptable standards in a supportive atmosphere.
- o Adapt to individual interests and ideas whenever possible.
- o Allow time for individuals to think about and develop their creative ideas. Not all creativity occurs immediately and spontaneously.

○ Create a climate of mutual respect and acceptance among individuals so they will share, develop, and learn from one another as well as independently.

○ Be aware that creativity is a multifaceted phenomenon; it enters all curricular areas, not just arts and crafts.

○ Encourage divergent activities by being a resource and a provider rather than a controller.

○ Listen to and laugh with individuals; a warm supportive atmosphere provides freedom and security in exploratory and developmental thinking.

○ Allow individuals to have choices and be part of the decision-making process; let them help control their activities.

○ Let everyone get involved, and demonstrate the value of involvement by supporting individual ideas and solutions to problems and projects.

○ Criticism kills. Use it carefully and in small doses.

○ Encourage and use provocative questions; move away from the sole use of convergent, one-answer questions.

○ Don't be afraid to start something different!

We will end with a true story about problem solving. We think it will serve as an example of many of the principles reviewed in this chapter.

The Reluctantly Creative Student

A professor was about to give a student a zero for his answer to a physics question. The student claimed that he should receive a perfect score and would have if the system were not set up against students. The question was, "Show how it is possible to determine the height of a tall building with the aid of a barometer."

The student's answer was, "Take the barometer to the top of the building, attach a long rope to it, lower the barometer to the street, and then bring it up, measuring the length of the rope. The length of the rope is the height of the building."

Now this is an interesting answer, but should the student get credit for it? The student answered the question completely and correctly. On the other hand, if full credit were given, it would reflect a level of knowledge of physics that the student might not possess. The professor decided to give the student another six minutes to answer the question, warning him that the answer should show some knowledge of physics. At the end of five minutes, he had not written anything. Asked if he wished to give up, he said no. He had many answers to this problem; he was just thinking of the best one. In the next minute, he dashed off his answer: "Take the barometer to the top of the building and lean over the edge of the roof. Drop the barometer, timing its fall with a stopwatch. Then using the appropriate formula, calculate the height of the building."

At this point, the professor asked the student what other answers he had to the problem. "Oh," said the student, "there are many ways of getting the height of a tall building with the aid of a barometer. For example, you could take the barometer out on a sunny day and measure the height of the barometer, the length of its shadow, and the length of the building's shadow. By using simple proportions, you could determine the building's height.

"You could take the barometer and begin to walk up the stairs. As you climbed the stairs, you could mark off the length of the barometer along the wall. If you counted the number of marks, this would give you the height of the building in barometer units. It's a very direct method.

"Of course, if you want a more sophisticated method, you can tie the barometer to the end of a string, swing it as a pendulum, and determining the value of g, you can calculate the height of the building. If you don't limit me to physics solutions to this problem, there are many other answers, such as taking the barometer to the basement and knocking on the superintendent's door. When the superintendent answers, you say, 'Mr. Superintendent, I have a very fine barometer here. If you tell me the height of this building, I will give you the barometer.'"

The student was not as cooperative as he might have been, but he certainly demonstrated a talent for imaginative problem solving. How is it that such talents come about? In the next section of this book, we will examine two other aspects of the biopsychosocial model: biological influences at the cellular and hemispheric levels.

PART FOUR

BIOLOGICAL FACTORS

10

THE BRAIN AT
THE CELLULAR LEVEL

THE FUNDAMENTAL CAPABILITIES of all human beings are fixed at the moment of their conception. This takes place in the brain cells called macroneurons. Nevertheless, neuron growth and hormonal changes are still influenced by the child's early environment, especially for the first one to two years after birth. Thus, even these most basic biological building blocks for creativity are affected by (and affect) a person's psychological and social milieu. In this chapter, we will review research that has looked at the roles of neurons (specifically microneurons), memory (with emphasis on the protein CREB), and neurotransmitters (most particularly ACTH) in the creative process.

Historically, the biological influence on creativity has been examined from the standpoint that it is somehow linked to insanity or mental illness (Jamison, 1997). At one level, case studies of individuals who have been diagnosed with mental disorders such as bipolar disease (or manic depression, as it used to be called) and who have exhibited creative accomplishment seem to support this idea. A closer examination of precisely what structures and chemical activities occur in the brains of these and other creative individuals is warranted, however.

Communication Among Neurons

A neurobiological approach to creativity provides insight into how cognitive skills such as learning or creativity can be encouraged (Gardner, 1993a). It is important to note that the neuron differs from other cells in

The authors wish to acknowledge Holly Malin's contributions to this chapter.

two ways. First, the cell body has long extensions or fibers that branch out in various directions and act as the cables through which signals are sent (via axons) and received (via dendrites). Second, this function is made possible by the membranes enclosing these fibers, which are electrical and which therefore carry electrical impulses throughout the nervous system (Harth, 1993).

The process of transmission within the brain is similar to connections within a computer, in which one cell is linked to another by way of a cablelike network of interconnecting fibers (Restak, 1991). The axon extensions are closely aligned with the dendrites of another neuron. Information is passed along by hormones known as neurotransmitters that the axons exude. These hormones float across the synaptic junction to insert themselves into the dendrites' reception areas, much as keys fit into a keyhole. If enough keys "fit," the electronic "message" is carried on to the next neuron. This is the essence of electrochemical communication in the human body. The more complex the neuronal pathways, the more complex thinking can be. It follows that those individuals with the most complex systems are most likely to generate creative ideas, if only because they have so many more ideas.

The effects of deviation from normal neurotransmitter function may be observed in patients who are diagnosed with mental illness. Studies conducted by neuroscientists support the finding that mental illness is the result of alterations in brain functioning (Restak, 1991). For example, a psychosis often occurs with changes in neurotransmitter balances or shifts in the brain's electrical patterns. These patterns may help to explain why some individuals with mental illnesses manifest few if any creative products.

In every human, the brain's primary pathway, the macroneuronal system, is the major vehicle for thought. The average adult human brain has ten billion neurons (Restak, 1984), each of which has an average of one hundred connections with other neurons. In this system alone, the number of possible combinations of neuronal connections seems almost infinite.

This is only part of the picture, however. Juxtaposed between these billions of macroneuron pathways are tiny switching circuits, composed of microneurons and their axons and dendrites, which make connections between the macroneuronal "highways." These additional highways (see Figure 10.1) provide an incredible increase in the number of variations that creative thought may take.

The critical variable in this process is the microneuron's capacity to continue developing throughout the first one and a half years of one's life

Figure 10.1. Stages in the Early Development of Microneurons.

| Term | 2–4 days | 7–10 days | 15–30 days | 50–70 days |

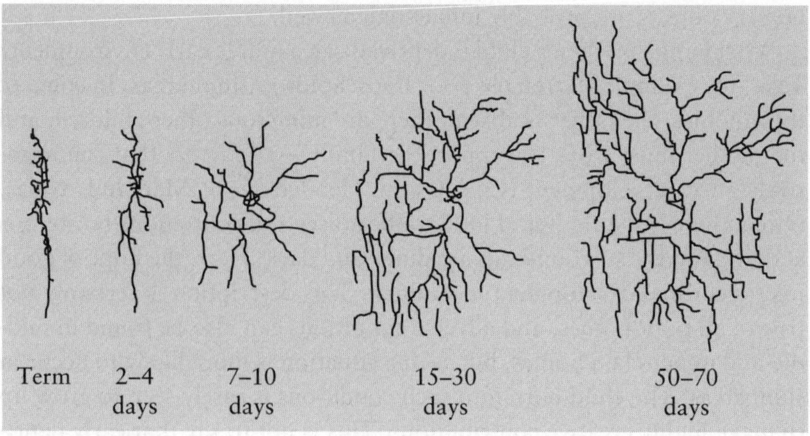

Source: *Dacey, 1989b.*

(Dacey & Gordon, 1971; Dacey & Travers, 1996). The way in which these minuscule neurons develop depends greatly on many factors, such as the conditions present in the environment.

It seems likely that many factors affect intrauterine and postnatal development of microneurons. It has been very difficult to examine these factors in humans. To do so, researchers usually have to obtain permission to examine brain samples from newly deceased infants. They then attempt to discern whether aspects of children's environments, such as diet and social interaction, are related to microneuronal development. Obviously, this is extremely difficult to do because the infants must have died of causes that did not affect normal brain growth, and the parents have to agree to an autopsy. On rare occasions, such studies have been performed on institutionalized children, but these only provided information about the effects of social (and sometimes dietary) deprivation. Most of our knowledge has come from experiments with development in young animals, mostly dogs and monkeys. Although they aren't conclusive, such investigations give us strong reason to speculate on the effects of early experience on human brain growth.

In addition to such obvious environmental forces as diet and social interaction, other more subtle conditions appear to affect the type of brain development on which creativity depends. Noise level appears to be important; either too little or too much sound may be detrimental. Well-modulated sounds, such as gentle music, would be likely to have a positive effect. Other factors such as pastel room colors and gently moving nursery objects are probably influential, as well.

What happens when a child is deprived of a suitable early environment? Take, for example, extremely poor households in slum areas. In some of these homes, the father is absent, there are numerous other children, and the mother must work to support the family—all factors that can negatively affect development (Cox, Owen, Henderson, & Margand, 1992). Often, there is the clamor of loud traffic noises and continuous boisterous activity, and the surroundings are dingy and dark. Here, the hope of good microneuronal development is minimal. This description is certainly not true of all poor homes, and adverse conditions can also be found in middle-and upper-class homes, but such a situation is more likely to occur in slum areas. The child born into such conditions is rarely seen to grow up to make highly creative contributions. This is not to say that early deprivation always causes decreased microneuronal growth or low creative ability, but the relationship is obviously strong.

Two aspects of mental functioning are apparently affected by the environment: the ability to take in information and the ability to process it. Studies indicate that in deprived children, these two abilities contrast sharply with the behaviors of creative children. The contrast is evident in Table 10.1.

Information intake and processing capabilities appear to be quite different. The challenge is to isolate what causes this difference. Does interaction with a rich environment affect the brain's interconnectivity, as the previously discussed data suggest? Researchers have always assumed that a rich environment will lead to greater information intake and therefore to a greater amount of stored knowledge about the environment. Does a rich environment also cause more variation in modes of thinking or information processing? It would seem that variations in the environment alone would not be enough to alter modes of thinking. In addition, human learners need to try out different modes of information processing. They learn these primarily through interpersonal interactions with significant others who encourage them to deal with information in an exploratory manner.

With regard to this topic, Hunt's classic refutation (1969) of Jensen (1969) is of interest. Jensen alleged that early compensatory education of low-income children does not help. Hunt argued that projects such as Head Start and, in fact, early childhood education in Western cultures do not begin until the child is at least three years old, which is too late. He

Table 10.1. Comparison of Two Mental Abilities in Two Types of Children.

Intake Ability	Processing Ability
Deprived children	
Failure to attend selectively to their environment	Lessened ability to imagine the consequences of their actions
Fewer cognitive structures	Lowered problem-solving and planning abilities
Difficulty sustaining attention to tasks	Impulsiveness and failure to inhibit inappropriate responses
Hyperarousal in response to stimulation	Rigid response to problematic situations
Creative children	
Tolerance of ambiguity and inconsistency	Interest in conceptual conflict
Ability to judge stimuli in many ways	Ability to tolerate inconsistent information
Great category breadth	Search for mediating concepts to explain observations
Great perceptual curiosity	Sensitivity to inconsistency in information

Source: *Dacey, 1989b.*

said that "mankind has not yet developed and deployed a form of early childhood education (from birth to age five) to permit him to achieve his full genotypic potential" (p. 279). He argued that even if the genetic factors within a particular racial group do make for lower intelligence (minorities are the typical targets of this charge), there is every reason to believe that appropriate environmental stimulation could alleviate the difference over a relatively short period of time. He cited Western humans' average height increase of more than one foot within two centuries as evidence of genetic structures' responsiveness to the environment.

Changes in neurological factors (specifically microneurons) influencing intelligence and creativity might be brought about not only through educational stimuli (for example, creative toys) but also through neurosurgery and chemical and electronic stimulation (Begley, 1997; Dacey & Travers, 1996). Perhaps we could develop kits of information and materials designed to stimulate microneuronal growth in the neonate and young child. Maybe we could include this type of information in courses on childhood and the family that would be presented on a regular basis in our secondary schools. Of course, neurological factors are likely to be necessary, but most unlikely to be sufficient, to ensure creativity. Further research on this biological factor seems likely to reap valuable societal rewards.

Memory

Because they virtually always have superior knowledge of the domain in which they work (and often other domains as well), there can be little doubt that highly creative persons have superior memory functions. These functions include not only the ability to remember large quantities of information but also the uncanny capacity to recognize what is worth remembering and what to avoid storing in the first place. We will begin explaining this process by looking first at what memory is.

The study of memory has caused considerable excitement in the scientific community in the last few years, as great strides have been made in solving the mystery of how it works (for example, Bito, Tsien, & Deisseroth, 1996; Frankland & others, 1997; Greenberg & Frank, 1994; Kaestner & others, 1996; Kamino & others, 1997; Kiebler & others, 1996; McGaugh & Guzowski, 1997; Moore, Dixon, & Dash, 1995). Although all the microbiological studies conducted on memory thus far have involved animals, human research will occur soon.

Sea Slugs, Fruit Flies, Mice, and CREBs

From the research thus far performed on animals (sea slugs, fruit flies, and mice), it is clear that the memory process is controlled by the flow of a variety of proteins. This flow is governed by a master protein known as CREB. There are four distinct steps in the process (see Figure 10.2).

HOW CREBS WORK. In his essay entitled "A Gene for Nothing," Sapolsky (1997) noted that we are learning that many genes are not coded to perform a specific function but rather work to control the operation of other genes. The gene, he pointed out, "does not produce a behavior, an emotion, or even a fleeting thought. It produces a protein. Proteins include some hormones (which carry messages between cells) and neurotransmitters (which carry messages between nerve cells)" (p. 41).

Thus, CREBs are the central factor in what will and what will not be remembered. To be more specific, there are CREB activator proteins and CREB inhibitor proteins (Del Vecchio, Zhou, Tully, & Yin, 1995; Tully & Yin, 1996). It has been found that animals given a dose of the inhibitor

Figure 10.2. The Memory Process at the Neuronal Level.

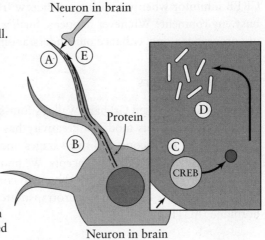

A. A nervous signal arrives triggering production of a chemical inside the nerve cell.

B. The chemical travels to the cell's nucleus, where it activates the CREB protein.

C. The active CREB protein targets a site on the cell's DNA, where it activates a set of nearby genes.

D. & E. The proteins made by the genes trigger growth in the dendrite to strengthen the connection, the presumed structural basis of memory.

Neuron in brain

Protein

Neuron in brain

Source: *Dacey and Travers, 1996.*

protein have an impaired memory and that those given the activator protein have much sharper memory storage ability. For example, fruit flies typically need ten training sessions to associate an odor with an electric shock. Those that were inhibited could form no lasting memories at all. Those given the activator protein dose learned the association in just one trial. Neurobiologist Timothy Tully (Tully & Yin, 1996, p. 265) stated, "This implies these flies have photographic memory. They are just like students who could read a book once, see it in their mind, and tell that the answer is in paragraph 3 on page 274."

Both aspects of CREB proteins are essential to all thought processes, but they are especially important for the remote associations that are so much a part of creativity (see Chapter Eight). We need to remember essential items, while not getting caught up in trivia, which can interfere with the mental search for creative ideas. The CREB inhibitor is also akin to Guilford's filtering mechanism (1975), which he claimed works at the beginning of all problem-solving sequences (see Chapter Nine). It has also been found that short learning periods interspersed with rest or recreation breaks facilitate long-term memory, presumably so that CREB activator proteins can be rejuvenated (Tully & Yin, 1996).

How the CREB process works is not yet known, but it appears to function more effectively in highly creative people than in others. Where this inquiry will lead is an interesting question. Will we someday ingest a synthetic CREB activator when involved in a complex learning task or a CREB inhibitor when we wish to withdraw from the stimulation of our busy environment? Whatever happens, further investigation of the memory process can only enhance our understanding of creativity.

Neurotransmitters

Chapter Two discussed Graham Wallas's four-stage theory of the creative process. Although his model of creativity has been discredited as being too simplistic, his second and third stages, incubation and illumination, are still considered insightful concepts. We find it fascinating to speculate about a neurobiological basis for these two constructs, most particularly in light of recent research on a neurotransmitter, the adrenocorticotropic hormone (ACTH).

ACTH

ACTH is one of several neurotransmitting hormones secreted by the pituitary gland when it is stimulated by the hypothalamus. ACTH secretions increase in response to stress and other external stimuli and in turn stimulate the adrenal cortex (the outer layer of the adrenal gland), which secretes other hormones into the bloodstream. The adrenal cortex, once stimulated by ACTH, directly affects functions that include the metabolizing of salts, carbohydrates, proteins, fats, and water; sexual function; neuromuscular function; resistance to infection and other stressors; and the functions of additional endocrine glands. At low levels of activity or stimulation, lower levels of ACTH are secreted.

These hormonal relationships have suggested a biological model of the creative process to David deWeid (1995). He proposed that ACTH neuropeptides act as vehicles that aid communication between neurons. They also influence the potential for active transmission of impulses between the brain's two hemispheres.

The notion of such interhemispheric communication is not new to the study of creativity. It is similar to the combination of divergent and convergent thinking supported by Guilford (1975). Based on a 1987 study of rats whose damaged nerves were injected with ACTH, deWeid observed that ACTH neuropeptides enhanced the regeneration of nerve fibers. He therefore concluded that ACTH facilitates connections between neurons by affecting plasticity (deWeid, 1995).

These findings may pertain to the popular nineteenth-century notion that "creativity is next to madness." Although mental illness by itself cannot be responsible for creativity, the ACTH hypothesis may have particular relevance for manic-depressive patients (see also Chapter Seven). Jamison (1997) considered the relationship between manic-depressive illness and creativity by examining celebrated artists, musicians, and writers who had been hospitalized because of mania or depression. Depressed episodes consist of "intense melancholic spells, apathy, lethargy, impaired memory and concentration, and loss of pleasure in typically enjoyable events" (Jamison, 1997, p. 44). On the other end of the continuum, manic episodes consist of elevated self-esteem, "abundant energy, sleeplessness, high productivity, rapid speech, and thoughts that move quickly and fluidly from one topic to another" (p. 46).

It is possible that very little ACTH is produced during depressed episodes, which would cause a deficiency in interhemispheric communication. This in turn may be responsible for the struggle that these patients have with symbolization, fantasy activities, and the ability to verbalize their own feelings or emotions. During manic episodes, on the other hand, patients are able to be more creative. We suggest that this may be due to higher production of ACTH, which in turn fosters communication between hemispheres, thus enhancing the aspects of the manic state that facilitate creative productivity. This possibility jibes with Russ's hypothesis (1993) that creativity is enhanced in individuals who are more emotional.

A comparison may be drawn to Wallas's stages of incubation and illumination, in terms of low and high ACTH production. In the incubation stage, when the conscious mind is less active, less ACTH is secreted. This "downtime" may allow the brain to regenerate the ACTH that ushers forth creative ideas in the illumination stage. The unconscious mind is dominant in the incubation stage, which is when the individual must refrain from focusing on the task or challenge at hand. Figure 10.3 portrays this relationship between cognitive arousal and incubation. It indicates that when cognitive arousal (and ACTH) is high, incubation is low, and vice versa.

If, as Wallas suggested, incubation precedes illumination as a necessary step in the creative process, then it seems reasonable to assume that ACTH secretion would escalate during periods of actual creative output. As bipolar research indicates, however, it is likely that if arousal becomes too high, creative production will be hampered, and actual output will be lowered (see also the Chapter Six section on calming the nervous system).

**Figure 10.3. Relationship Between Incubation Stage
and Cognitive Arousal.**

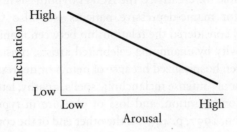

Unlike the negative connection between arousal and incubation, however, we would expect the relationship between arousal and illumination to be more curvilinear. That is, illumination is highest when cognitive arousal is moderate, and illumination declines when arousal is either high or low. Figure 10.4 depicts the situation.

Further evidence for the ACTH hypothesis comes from Martindale, Hine, Mitchell, and Covella (1984), who found that during states of low cortical arousal, creative individuals are more likely to experience a decrease in conscious attention (probably what Wallas meant by his incubation stage). Martindale contended that during this state of "defocused attention," neurons are simultaneously activated, interacting with other neurons in ways that are considered critical for the formation of new ideas. This period of low arousal also depends on low interest in environmental stimuli, such as when a person is daydreaming or is just about to fall asleep. At such times, unobstructed access to the unconscious allows individuals to tap into old ideas or fantasies that can provide fertile ground for creative insights. These findings are in line with the hypothesis represented in Figure 10.2.

Russ (1993) discovered that this period of low arousal is usually followed by increased levels of physiological arousal. Again, this notion supports Wallas's concept of an illumination stage. Russ hypothesized that once ideas have had an opportunity to incubate in the unconscious, there is sufficient motivation or arousal for ideas to become integrated. When ideas become integrated, illumination may occur, and the creator may become consciously aware of an innovation. ACTH is secreted in response to excitation or stimulation, so it may be secreted in the illumination stage. Therefore, Russ's notion fits the ACTH model, by proposing that there is a process in which an initial state of low arousal is followed by excitation.

Figure 10.4. Relationship Between Illumination Stage and Creative Arousal.

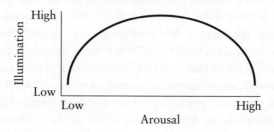

A study conducted by Molle and associates (1996) suggested a similar relationship between arousal and the creative process. In this study, electroencephalogram (EEG) responses were recorded during divergent thinking, convergent thinking (defined in Chapter Nine), and mental relaxation tasks. He perceived convergent thinking as "a process of analytical thought" (p. 61). The subjects in this study were given hypothetical scenarios similar to those suggested by Guilford in his prior studies of divergent thinking (1962, 1975). For example, subjects were presented with hypothetical situations such as, "Due to a new scientific breakthrough, humans no longer need to eat food to survive." They were told to think of unique consequences of such statements. The convergent-thinking task in this study contained arithmetic and logic-based word problems. The mental relaxation task instructed subjects to fantasize about "lying on a beach while the sun is shining" (Molle & others, 1996).

EEG results of the study showed that complexity in the frontal cortex was similar during divergent thinking and relaxation, whereas the EEG's complexity was reduced during convergent thinking. Molle theorized that the EEG's complexity during divergent tasks reflected "higher degrees of freedom in the competitive interactions among cortical neuron assemblies" (p. 61). The similarities between the EEGs of divergent-thinking and mental relaxation tasks further emphasize that a state of low arousal or some relaxing of focused control actually facilitates the creative process.

Miller and others (1996) examined three subjects who experienced heightened periods of artistic creativity when a disease caused degeneration in their temporal lobes. All of the subjects were recognized as "skillful painters," even though their temporal lobes were not functioning. Miller and colleagues suggested that the deficiency of temporal lobe function enabled the subjects to experience visual and memory sensations that were not subject to any filtering process. Their experiences appear similar to the brain activity that occurs during low arousal and similar to unconscious brain activity that is part of the creative process.

In summary, the stage of low arousal allows relevant thoughts to be generated in the unconscious mind. When these thoughts are relevant to the specific problem or task at hand, motivation and renewed interest in the topic cause them to become conscious. A moderate level of ACTH is secreted, and this neurophysiological environment fosters bilateral communication between the hemispheres, which leads to illumination (see Mednick's remote associates theory in Chapter Eight).

Relationships Among Neurotransmitters, Learning, and Other Cognitive Variables

Simonton (1993) speculated that creativity is associated with learning and education. A high level of learning or education does not necessarily produce creative behavior, however. In fact, too much learning in a particular domain may well inhibit it. Furthermore, deWeid's animal research (1995) emphasized that ACTH can stimulate the learning process. Similarly, experiments with human subjects have confirmed that ACTH facilitates positive modifications in motivation, attention, concentration, arousal, and vigilance. All of these qualities are important to learning and creativity.

Spence (1996) has questioned the concept that hormones play so large a part in thinking, from the standpoint of free will. He proposed that a conscious free will is inconsistent with the findings of neuroscience, and he cited previous studies that determined that measured brain activity is preceded by predictive neural activity. This means that whenever conscious choices are made, even simple ones such as when to move a finger, they are preceded by detectable neurological impulses of which the person is unaware. Furthermore, Spence argued that free will is more of a belief than a voluntary action. Thus, conscious will may act more as a volitional check on choices *after* they are made unconsciously than as the direct cause of all behavior. Although it is only a hypothesis at this time, confirmation of Spence's view would support the ACTH theory.

The hypothesis that low and then moderate secretions of ACTH facilitate the creative process has an interesting counterpart in the evolutionary theory of creativity of Findlay and Lumsden (1988a). These researchers have based their concept on "current theories of biocultural dynamics, leading to the hypothesis that creative activity is an evolved strategy" (p. i). That is, they argue that creativity is primarily a function of biological factors (genes, hormones, and so forth) that have evolved slowly over the millennia in reaction to cultural forces. This biopsychosocial theory has generated a number of interesting hypotheses about the relationships between creativity and age, environmental complexity, and the sociocultural environment.

Of primary importance is Findlay and Lumsden's hypothesis that creative activity occurs because "there are collections of neurons that are innately predisposed to respond to particular patterns of electrochemical excitation" (p. ii). Creation comes about as a result of new connections among nodes in the existing structure, as a consequence of "a novel sequence of group selection events" (p. ii). We will discuss the fascinating ramifications of this theory in Chapter Twelve, which presents our own biopsychosocial explanation of the creative act.

The exact role that ACTH plays in the creative process is not clear. The numerous studies cited in this chapter support the hypothesis that ACTH acts as a catalyst or agent for interneuronal communication, including that between the two cerebral hemispheres (see Chapter Eleven). One direction for future research may be to determine the extent to which individuals might consciously manipulate ACTH secretion. It may even become possible to ingest some synthetic product that controls ACTH secretion. If it does become possible to control it, perhaps interhemispheric communication can also be manipulated or enhanced. Another focus for future research is to examine the possibility of a sensitive period in creative development during which particular cycles of ACTH secretion must occur in order for interhemispheric communication to develop fully. Finally, it could be that individual rhythms of ACTH secretion prove useful as an indirect measure of creative potential.

It is clear, however, that neurobiological theories can explain only part of the creative process. The hypotheses suggested in this chapter do not provide definitive answers but serve as starting points from which researchers can strive to explore the role of neurophysiology in the creative process. In the next chapter, we turn to the larger biological picture, the interaction of the brain's two hemispheres and the resulting implications for creative thought.

11

THE HEMISPHERES
OF THE BRAIN

CREATIVE THINKERS OFTEN SHIFT the emphasis from the logical, linear processing style of the left hemisphere to the more holistic style of the right hemisphere, in which intuitive thinking plays a larger part. . . .

At the anatomical level, the right hemisphere is uniquely suited for creativity, since it occupies a larger volume in the "association cortex," where the most complex levels of information processing and integration are carried out. . . . But one must be careful of oversimplifications. The brain always works as a unit; therefore, to imply that in the ordinary person [that is, not brain-injured], the right hemisphere can somehow be separated from the left is inaccurate and misleading [Restak, 1991].

⟶○

Restak's warning against oversimplification is important, because until recently, research has indicated that creativity is primarily a right-hemisphere affair. This has led to such erroneous generalizations as the belief that most left-handers are highly creative. Here is a brief review of the facts.

The cerebral cortex (that convoluted one-inch-thick layer on the top of the brain in which thinking, sensation, and perception occur) is divided into two halves, or hemispheres. In most people, one side is more dominant. The vast majority of us are right-handed, so we tend to be dominated by the left lateral side of the brain. This was first learned when it was noticed that damage to one side of the brain usually impairs the functioning of the body's opposite side. This relationship is known as hemispheric dominance (also called lateral dominance). Figure 11.1 illustrates this concept.

Figure 11.1. Hemispheric Dominance.

Source: *Dacey, 1989b.*

Hemispheric Dominance

Soon after children are born, their undifferentiated movements develop into a pattern of preference for one hand, one eye, and one foot over the other. Because most people have a preferred side, their brain may be said to be dominated by the hemisphere on the opposite side of their body. Although each hemisphere has overlapping functions with the other, the left side is primarily concerned with language. The right is more involved in nonverbal functions such as dance and music. There is some evidence, and much speculation, that the right half also has primary responsibility for creative thinking. The speculation has far outrun the evidence, however, leading to what has been called "dichotomania," a mania for splitting up all kinds of mental functions and assigning them to one of the two hemispheres. A list of the most commonly seen labels used to describe the left and right hemispheres has been adapted from Springer and Deutsch (1981, 1993) and is presented below in the form of dichotomous adjectives.

LEFT HEMISPHERE	RIGHT HEMISPHERE
Verbal	Nonverbal, visuospatial
Digital	Analog
Logical, analytical	Gestalt, synthetic
Rational	Intuitive
Western oriented	Eastern oriented
Intellectual	Intuitive, sensuous, emotional
Convergent	Divergent
Inductive	Deductive
Rational	Metaphoric, intuitive
Horizontal	Vertical
Discrete	Continuous
Concrete	Abstract
Realistic	Fantastic
Directed	Free
Differential	Existential
Sequential	Multiple
Historical	Timeless
Explicit	Implicit, tacit
Objective	Subjective
Successive	Simultaneous

Although there is some evidence for most of these dichotomies, they are more the result of imaginative guesses than of hard research. Springer and Deutsch have noted that using such labels to describe particular hemispheric processes raises numerous questions: Are these labels simply convenient descriptions of the manner in which hemispheres process information? Are these labels meant to suggest that each hemisphere is unique in its style of thinking? Most intriguingly, does all creative thought involve each of these dichotomous relationships at some stage of the process?

For example, creativity is often described as a trait that combines two aspects of mental functioning: being imaginative but also being right. A number of those who have investigated hemispheric dominance have suggested that these two functions tend to occur in opposite sides of the brain. Accuracy (also called "convergent thinking") and originality (referred to as "divergent thinking") appear to be opposite cognitive processes (see Chapter Nine). It has been hypothesized that convergent thinking is primarily a left-side function and that divergent thinking is chiefly a right-side function.

Research Evidence of Hemispheric Dominance

The notion that one side of the brain could more powerfully direct mental processes in some people came about in the late nineteenth century when it was learned that equal amounts of brain lesion (abrasion of cortical tissue due to injury) do not cause equal amounts of disruption in functioning. The discovery of apraxia, the inability to perform physical functions such as combing one's hair, also led to many new hypotheses.

Eventually, it was accepted that most people are right-handed because their left hemispheres are dominant. It was concluded that the right side had few important functions, serving mainly as a backup to the more powerful left. Not until the 1930s did some scientists begin to suspect that the influence of culture, with its emphasis on logic and language, has made the left side so important. New right-side functions, especially nonverbal ones, were uncovered as Penfield and Roberts (1959) experimented with electrically stimulating spots in the brain.

There are some obvious cognitive asymmetries (unevenness in mental function between the hemispheres). The left hemisphere is dominant for many facets of language, perception of phonetics, use of syntax, and some aspects of semantic analysis. The right hemisphere is dominant for many aspects of visuospatial processing, such as perceiving objects, recognizing three-dimensional objects in unusual orientations, and recognizing obscured visual stimuli.

Some evidence also points to chemical asymmetries that may be responsible for cognitive, emotional, and behavioral asymmetries. An example of this is that dopamine is more prevalent in the left hemisphere and that norepinephrine is more prevalent in the right hemisphere (Hellige, 1993). The effects of such asymmetry must be tested thoroughly, but it is reasonable to speculate that such chemical asymmetries in the human brain have consequences for creativity. For example, scientists are now looking to see whether highly creative people have similar ratios of these brain chemicals.

The greatest spur to our understanding of hemispheric functions has come from reactions to having the brain "split" by the cutting of the *corpus callosum*, the thick bundle of nerves that connects the brain's two hemispheres. The ability to communicate between hemispheres and the subsequent effects on creativity have been examined by TenHouten (1994), who studied the creative abilities of normal patients and of those diagnosed with alexithymia. *Alexithymia* is a disorder in which a person has difficulty expressing feelings or emotions, an inability to fantasize, and feelings of social insufficiency.

Such a person often exhibits indiscriminate emotions and thinking (Reber, 1985). For the purposes of Reber's study, the alexithymic patients were also "split-brain" patients. In other words, the corpus callosum of the alexithymic patients had been severed, which prevented any inter-hemispheric communication. We would expect this to limit creative ability severely.

The design of Reber's study followed a procedure whereby all subjects viewed a three-minute videotape. The video used visual images and music to depict the deaths of a baby and a boy. After the video, subjects answered several questions and wrote four sentences about their reactions to the video. Reber hypothesized that the split-brain patients would exhibit an inability to talk (a left-hemisphere activity) about their feelings (a right-hemisphere activity). As predicted, split-brain patients exhibited significantly more alexithymic behavior than the control subjects in terms of speech and the ability to associate meaning with fantasy and symbols in the video. These subjects were described as dull, unexpressive, passive, and unimaginative.

Describing creativity as a "magic synthesis" of the two cerebral planes, Hoppe and Kyle (1990) produced findings similar to Reber's. Hoppe also studied alexithymic patients and found them to be impeded in hemispheric bisociation; they could only follow a fixed set of rules in the left hemisphere and were inhibited in "inner speech," the conversations we have with ourselves. Clearly alexithymia is antithetical to creative thinking.

Roger Sperry and his associates were the first to discover the functions of the corpus callosum, which earned Sperry a Nobel Prize in 1981 (Restak, 1984). Sperry studied split-brain patients in order to learn about interhemispheric connections. The dramatic asymmetries he observed in such patients contributed to the furor over hemispheric asymmetry. Asymmetry has been hypothesized to produce performance differences, depending on the visual field stimulated. For example, split-brain patients can name objects seen by the right eye, because the naming function is usually located in the left hemisphere. When using the left eye, the patients report seeing nothing (Restak, 1984).

Thus, perception is affected by the hemisphere that receives direct stimulation and carries out necessary functioning. Certain tasks may require that processing occur in a particular hemisphere, regardless of which hemisphere is stimulated. This leads to greater activation of the more involved hemisphere. It is hypothesized that over time, when hemispheres are unequally activated, attention becomes more easily directed to the hemisphere that was directly activated, which results in better performance when it receives a stimulus. This may have important implications for handedness and therefore for creativity.

Left-Handedness and Creativity

If left-handers are right-dominated, and if the right side is all that is suggested above, they should be more creative. Many famous left-handers certainly were—Leonardo da Vinci, Benjamin Franklin, and Michelangelo, to name a few. But is this so for the general population?

First of all, it should be noted that left-handers have been viewed throughout the ages as being unsavory characters and as perhaps being in league with the devil. In French, the word for left is *gauche,* which means "crude" in English. Among its definitions of *left-handed,* the *American Heritage Dictionary* includes "awkward, maladroit (against the right), obliquely derisive, dubious, and insincere, as in left-handed flattery." Numerous biblical allusions show a bias against anything on the left. The Latin word *sinister,* the Spanish word *siniestro,* and the Italian word *sinistro* all mean "left."

This general suspicion may not be entirely without substance (Gabrielli & Mednick, 1980). Left-handed individuals tend to be more emotional and impulsive and less analytical. Gabrielli and Sarnoff noted that left-handers are also overrepresented in the delinquent population, as ascertained in a study conducted by Schalling (1978). If left-handers are more creatively productive, it certainly has not been recognized historically!

Despite early beliefs in the sinister causes of being left-handed, today's scientists identify two primary causes. In some cases genetic inheritance is probably the cause, especially when it occurs in several generations of a family. In other cases, it may come about as a result of minimal brain damage to the left hemisphere, probably during birth. Because of this damage, the person comes to rely more heavily than usual on the right side and has to use more cross-hemispheric activity for language as well as for other functions (Casey, Nuttall, & Pezaris, 1997; Hellige, 1993). Handedness also serves as a marker for other facets of hemispheric asymmetry. At the present time, however, it has not been demonstrated that handedness is related to asymmetric arousal of the hemispheres or the hemispheres' ability to communicate.

Studies of twins provide interesting information about handedness. Only about 10 percent of the population is left-handed (this figure used to be 5 percent, which was no doubt due to the practice in many schools of discouraging left-handed writing). One member of a set of twins, however, is left-handed 25 percent of the time. This is true for both monozygotic (identical, single-egg) and dizygotic (fraternal, two-egg) twins. Minimal brain damage has been given as one reason; twins may be squeezed together during gestation, and thus one of the pair is more likely to suffer slight brain lesions. Another theory argues that in monozygotic twins, there is a mirror-imaging effect in which each twin has some features that are opposite from the other. Included are the whorls in fingerprints and in hair on top of the head. This might be true with handedness, at least in some of the cases. This explanation offers no help with dizygotic twins, however.

Before surgeons operate on the brain, they sometimes perform tests of hemisphericality using a sodium amytal procedure. This chemical can anesthetize one hemisphere at a time, so the doctor can determine where language and other functions are centralized. For right-handers, language is nearly always left-brained, and for more than half of left-handers, this is also true. Thus, the early presumption that all left-handed people are right-dominant is simply not true. For other mental functions, the situation becomes even more complicated. In fact, researchers must be cautious even with how they determine such an apparently obvious trait as handedness, because so many individuals who write with their left hand are really ambidextrous, and some right-handers "hook" their hands from above when writing. This latter group appears also to be right-hemisphere dominant (Casey, Nuttall, & Pezaris, 1997). In fact, only direct observation is reliable.

Levy and Reid (1976) found that inversion is a better predictor of dominance than handedness alone. Nevertheless, like the other predictors above, it certainly is not perfect. This leaves us with the question, "Are left-handers generally more creative than right-handers?"

From the standpoint of intelligence, there is no question that left-handers are often disadvantaged. For instance, they suffer a higher incidence of retardation and reading disability. Levy (cited in McKeever & VanDeventer, 1977) hypothesized that this is because language and visuospatial abilities compete for neural tissue (as may well be the case for left-handers) and that language will usually win. Levy predicted that if given an IQ test, left-handers will not score lower than right-handers on verbal tests but will have a deficit on performance tests. She tested a large group on the Wechsler Adult Intelligence Test (the standard in the field of IQ tests) and found her hypothesis supported.

According to these results, the left-handed are less competent than their counterparts in the very skills (such as determining relationships between objects and recognizing patterns) in which the right hemisphere is supposed to excel, but they suffer no linguistic loss. The most important conclusion is the one indicated before—there is no benefit in being left-handed when it comes to standard mental tasks, and there is probably some deficit. The one plus indicated over and over again, though, is the increased hemispheric communication that the left-handed seem to have.

Perhaps the first study to look explicitly at the relationship between handedness and actual creative achievement is the research by Dacey (1989b, 1989c), which examined the families of highly creative individuals. Although 10 percent of the general population is left-handed on average, Dacey found that 20 percent of the most creative people are left-handed (out of a sample of 125 people). This is not definitive, but it offers some evidence in favor of the theory that left-handedness should be more common among the highly creative.

Hemisphericality and Gender Differences

Hellige (1993) noted that more females than males tend to be left-handed. There is some suggestion that male brains and female brains have a somewhat different asymmetry. The relationship of gender differences to hemispheric dominance has been the subject of great interest in recent research.

It is generally agreed that a raised level of testosterone while the fetus is in utero accelerates the development of the brain's right hemisphere and possibly delays the development of the left hemisphere (Reite & others, 1995; Voyer, 1994). Reite and associates concluded that another sex difference appears in the isthmus of the corpus callosum, which connects the temporoparietal (upper and lower rear) regions of both hemispheres. Generally, this region of the brain is larger in females.

If interhemispheric communication is important to creativity and if the corpus callosum is larger in females, their potential for creativity should also be greater. This somewhat contradicts the notion that testosterone affects handedness and that there are more left-handed women than men. It follows that women would have more opportunities for creative thought, given the larger corpus callosum and the larger number of left-handed females. The typically higher level of testosterone in males would seem to enhance their creative potential more than that of females.

Reite and associates (1995) proposed a possible resolution to this contradiction by suggesting that there is a general verbal superiority for females and a visuospatial superiority for males. The authors noted that certain measures of verbal and spatial performance appear to be associated with location of neural activity in the right hemisphere for both males and females.

In a study that is unusual for investigating all three aspects of the biopsychosocial approach, Casey, Nuttall, and Pezaris (1997) sought to explain the superiority of males on the Mathematics Scholastic Aptitude Test (SAT-M). Some scholars have argued that this perennial result is due to a male genetic advantage in doing math, whereas others have attributed it to female math anxiety, which girls learn early in life. Casey and associates measured the relationships among sex and spatial skills (innate traits), math self-confidence and geometry knowledge (psychological variables), and math anxiety (a socially induced trait). It should be noted that the sources of each of these variables are themselves biopsychosocial, at least to some degree. Through a complex statistical technique known as path analysis, the researchers established that attitudinal variables accounted for only 36 percent of the variation in SAT-M scores and that spatial skills accounted for 64 percent. This study validates the hypothesis of Reite and associates.

Another perspective has been offered by Voyer (1994), who studied handedness in relation to spatial ability in males and females. Voyer distinguished between two types of hemispheric dominance (standard and anomalous) that affect handedness and that are caused by the presence or absence of testosterone in utero. Voyer defined standard dominance as "strong left hemisphere dominance for language and handedness, and strong right hemisphere dominance for other functions" (p. 212). He defined anomalous dominance as "any deviation from the standard form" (p. 212). For example, this would occur when language ability is located relatively equally in each hemisphere. According to Voyer, left-handed individuals and right-handed people with left-handed relatives are more likely to have anomalous dominance than other people.

Voyer acknowledged that if anomalous dominance is caused by fetal testosterone and that if males are usually exposed to higher levels of this hormone than females, then anomalous dominance is more likely to occur in males. He noted, however, that this hypothesis does not explain why anomalous dominance is not present in all males even though they are all exposed to fetal testosterone in substantial amounts.

As a result of meta-analysis, Voyer found that individuals with anomalous dominance are more likely to exhibit superior right-hemisphere functions than people with standard dominance. It was not clear, however, whether sex differences in spatial abilities were accounted for by sex differences in laterality. The purpose of Voyer's commentary was primarily to present a different perspective on the theory that brain development (and therefore creativity) is somehow linked to the effects of fetal testosterone.

Hemispheric Dominance and Emotional Disturbance

Emotional disturbance may also be affected by hemispheric dominance. Mandal, Asthana, Pandey, and Sarbadhikari (1996) stated that affective processing is generally considered to be a function of the right hemisphere, which might account for its having such an important effect on creativity. The left hemisphere tends to be superior for cognitive functions. One characteristic of depressive illness is right-hemisphere dysfunction, according to the authors, although they admitted that such claims are not universally accepted. One of the reasons for the controversy over this topic is that the relationship between affective processing and emotional illness is not easily understood.

Interhemispheric Coordination

Citing the early finding of the Russian neuropsychologist Luria (1973) that electrically weak neural stimuli can evoke strong responses, Arieti (1976) stated that some people's brain hemispheres are unusually capable of intercommunication as a result of very weak neural charges. Because of this, they are able to come up with remote, but highly interesting, associations that evade the rest of us. On the basis of his own research, he drew the following conclusion: "In the creative person, too, a weak stimulus, such as a characteristic of an object, may become a strong one when used as a metaphor. A weak stimulus such as a falling apple may evoke the concept of the force of gravity. . . . The apple and the moon not only have the common quality of being attracted by the earth; they are part of the class of gravitational bodies, a new engram [neural memory] appearing for the first time in the mind of Newton. In these cases of creativity the old meanings, by being interconnected and interpreted, form a new meaningfulness" (pp. 397–398).

When considering hemispheric asymmetry, it is important to keep in mind the brain's unity. Both cerebral hemispheres are involved to some extent in all behavior. The left and right hemispheres, along with the corpus callosum, other neocortical commissures, and subcortical structures, form a single integrated information-processing system. Although it is not clear whether the corpus callosum provides an excitatory or inhibitory influence, it does play an important part in transferring a variety of information from one hemisphere to the other.

Herrmann (1981) offered a description of the probable relationships between laterality and the whole brain, as they affect creative problem solving. His ideas also are in accord with those of Wallas, discussed in Chapter Two. According to Herrmann,

> If you think through a creative process consisting of interest, preparation, incubation, illumination, verification, and exploitation, then it becomes clear that the process itself has left-brained, right-brained and whole-brained phases to it. If you started with interest being the first stage, then I would speculate that would be whole-brained. Preparation is clearly left-brained. That means doing the rigorous task of defining a problem and specifying it in its essence. Incubation, on the other hand, is clearly right-brained. It involves getting away from the problem and engaging in an activity that permits the effortless, natural processes of the right brain to mull over the complexities of the problem, so as to permit the mind to come up with new combinations that could lead to a solution. The illustration stage is where this kind of "Aha" can occur, which produces one or more possible ideas or potential solutions. The verification stage, then, is the critical left-brained analysis of the idea or potential solution against the specifications of the problem. The final stage could be called "exploitation," which is the putting to use or applying the solution which emerges from the previous stages. Exploitation is probably whole-brained [p. 13].

Herrmann's theory offers an intriguing speculation on hemispheric relationships, although today we would not expect the differences in hemispheric function to be as discrete as he surmised. He has continued to test his hypotheses through the use of an instrument he designed, the Herrmann Brain Dominance Instrument (HBDI).

Payne and Evans (1985) studied the correlation of SAT scores with self-report subscales from the HBDI. The purpose was to determine if there is a link between hemispheric dominance and academic aptitude. The authors noted that the right hemisphere is often linked with spatial and holistic operations, such as skills related to the integration of stimuli and nonverbal or metaphoric thought processes. The left hemisphere is linked with sequential and analytical operations, such as reading, writing, and computing.

Payne and Evans found a significant relationship between HBDI right cerebral and total cerebral scores and SAT math, verbal, and total scores.

The findings suggested the importance of the whole brain in academic aptitude, for neither hemisphere score of the HBDI showed any significant relationship, whereas measures that reflect functions of the individual cerebral and limbic lobes did indicate statistical significance. This is further support, albeit indirect, for some of Herrmann's ideas.

Lateral eye movements refer to shifts in the gaze, either to the left or right, that occur when people engage in reflective thinking. A substantial body of evidence suggests that reflective thinking involving the left hemisphere produces lateral eye movements to the right, whereas thinking engaging the right hemisphere results in lateral eye movements to the left (Bakan, 1969; Kinsbourne, 1972; Kocel, Galin, Ornstein, & Merrin, 1972).

Falcone and Loder (1984) found that subjects scoring high on Guilford's Uses Test (Chapter Nine) tended to gaze to the left more often and for a longer duration while taking that test than did subjects who scored low. The researchers found no difference in the direction of lateral eye gaze when subjects were taking Mednick's Remote Associates Test (see Chapter Eight for more on this test). Falcone and Loder attribute the different results to the different natures of the two tests. Whereas Guilford's Uses Test clearly involves divergent thinking and visual imagery, the Remote Associates Test initially involves divergent processes but then requires the subject to use convergent thinking in order to recognize the particular overlapping associations.

Brain hemisphericality can also be directly measured by comparing EEG readings of the brain's two sides during creative activity. If the brain's right side gains dominance during creative thinking, then it is reasonable to expect that EEG measurements will indicate this. Martindale, Hines, Mitchell, and Covella (1984) did find that highly creative subjects, as assessed by a variety of measures, do exhibit more right-hemisphere EEG activity than subjects who rank lower in creativity. This pattern of activity was not found during the performance of a noncreative task.

Katz (1983) took subjects who had been classified into two groups of high and low creativity and had them perform a number of tasks known to engage one hemisphere over the other. In addition to lateral eye movement exercises, the subjects performed visual field and dichotic listening tasks. In visual field tasks, items are presented only to the subject's left or right visual field, and subjects then identify them. In dichotic listening tasks, two items (either words or melodies) are simultaneously presented into each ear through headphones, and subjects are then asked to recall or recognize the items. In both tasks, superiority in performance in either the right visual field or the right ear indicates greater left-hemisphere processing, and vice versa. The author found that by knowing only the scores on the hemispheric tasks, one could predict 75 percent of the time whether a subject could be retroactively classified into a low- or high-creativity group. Tagano, Fin, and Moran (1983) found a similar relationship between divergent thinking and hemispheric dominance as measured by a dichotic listening task.

Finke (1997) concluded that creative thinking cannot reside solely in the right hemisphere, because the left cerebral hemisphere plays an important role in generating and assembling a mental image. For example, damage to posterior regions of the left hemisphere can affect image generation while leaving other types of visual skill intact. Also, electrophysiological studies have shown increased activity in the left hemisphere during image generation.

Findings from studies that involve split-brain patients have shown that the left hemisphere is superior to the right hemisphere for many types of imagery tasks. Finke noted that studies of split-brain patients that include imagery tasks entailing the generation of highly detailed images or the use of spatial versus categorical information make particular use of the left hemisphere. The strongest evidence, however, suggests that creative imagery probably involves interactions between both hemispheres.

Isaksen and Dorval (1992) also investigated the relationship between imagery and creativity. Their study examined the results of 154 college students (43 males and 111 females) on the Kirton Adaptation-Innovation Inventory (on preferred styles of problem solving) and on Paivio's Individual Differences Questionnaire (on the preferred mode of symbolic representation). Although the Adaptors and Innovators fell into a normal distribution, there was a general preference for conscious visual representation. According to the researchers, this finding "may suggest that visual imagery is the most preferred mode of conscious representation" (p. 274).

Significant differences were found between the mean scores of the Adaptors and Innovators on both imaginary and verbal scores, so that participants with an innovative cognitive style showed stronger preferences for using conscious symbolic representation than those with an adaptive style. Gender as a covariate did not affect the results. Isaksen and Dorval stated that clearer relationships between imagery and creativity variables emerge when definite distinctions are made between variables that examine ability and those that examine preference. Because this research was correlational, the authors suggested that replications of their study incorporate experimental designs that could examine the actual usefulness of imagery in creative problem-solving performance.

Zamb's research (1970) with writers and psychotherapists indicated that during the first incubational phase of the creative process, there is a paucity of interhemispheric communication. This coincides with the idea that ACTH production is low in the first phase (see Chapter Ten). She believed that incubation fosters creative thinking by allowing the right hemisphere maximum autonomy to explore ideas without interference from the left. In her work, she has had success in increasing creative productivity by encouraging vivid imagery that stimulates right-hemisphere activity. The goal of this activity is to produce the transformational intercollosal process that Hoppe called "symbollexia" (1988, p. 430).

Some Caveats About Brain Research and Creativity

Although researchers have observed a correlation between stages in the creative process and the duality of cognitive functions based in different brain regions, no well-controlled study has been published that assesses hemisphericity in actual creators (Katz, 1997). There are a number of questions about just how studies should be conducted and many possible ways to study this connection. Katz examined empirical evidence for a link between hemisphericity and creativity, addressing issues of measuring hemispheric specialization and measuring creativity. In his summary of the field today, he concluded that three definitions of creativity are represented in empirical work:

1. The performance of actual people who have been identified as creative

2. People's performance on psychometric instruments constructed to measure assumed components of creativity

3. The use of cognitive functions associated with creativity (for example, fantasy) or engagement in creative activities (for example, art, music, science)

These definitions may be used in conjunction with three different areas of hemisphericity research:

1. Direct measures of brain activity in normal humans or in those with particular brain lesions

2. Indirect measures of brain activity, such as performance on propositional-appositional cognitive tests

3. Research that examines changes in creativity correlated with procedures that can be demonstrated to incorporate the brain's hemispheres in various ways

Despite the absence of a well-controlled study that addresses hemisphericity in actual creators, there are some "suggestive case studies" of creative people who have suffered some form of brain damage. Such studies provide insight into this area of investigation and provide conclusions that Katz organized into three categories:

1. High-level creative performance uses both hemispheres of the brain.

2. Different cognitive skills are required by different creative activities.

3. These skills may involve the two hemispheres in different ways. For example, an artist who suffers unilateral right-hemisphere damage may still produce art but may tend to produce paintings that are drastically different from those seen prior to the brain injury.

The significance of Katz's observations is that without some sort of organized methodology to examine hemisphericity accurately, we may be led to false conclusions about the function of the two hemispheres. Katz cited the work of Hines (1991), who argued that to propose that creativity is localized in only one hemisphere could lead to a foolish argument such as, "Beethoven would have been as great a composer and Titian just as great a painter had their left hemispheres been removed" (p. 223). Perhaps there exists a certain "privileged role" in creativity that draws more from the right hemisphere, but researchers today recognize that creativity is a complex activity that employs numerous cognitive processes. Productive thought may best be executed by either the left or the right hemisphere or a combination of the two.

Katz further concluded that virtually every measure used in the suggestive case studies has been questioned by some researcher for various reasons. He acknowledged that identifying behaviors as creative is tricky, for no one can be certain that a particular behavior is unique to creativity and not related to some noncognitive factor, such as self-esteem. If it were possible to examine EEGs of eminent creators (or some other brain measures, such as positron-emission tomography, or PET, scans) while they were solving problems in their own field of expertise and in a different field, then perhaps the function of each hemisphere would be visible to a greater degree. At present, researchers in this field must rely on previous studies or instruments developed by fellow researchers that might provide insight into the question of hemisphericity.

Bryden and Bulman-Fleming (1994) provided suggestions for future methodology. They examined methods of studying relationships between normal subjects' cerebral hemispheres and concluded that hemispheres may process certain material with different levels of efficiency. A particular task may require interhemispheric coordination, however. Therefore, they suggested, bilateral visual tasks (tasks in which stimuli are presented to the two hemispheres to promote interaction) may be preferable ways to study interhemispheric communication.

Finally, a critical review of empirical evidence (Loverock & Modigliani, 1995) has revealed a trend away from an emphasis on hemispheric specialization and toward models that include both sides of the brain as an integrated structure. The authors concluded that although it is not yet possible to identify the areas of the brain in any presumed component of imagery processing with accuracy, there is no longer any question that the left hemisphere plays a part in this process. They noted that in real life, imagery processes are more complex than can possibly be examined in a controlled experiment, adding that "as difficult as this might be, there is a need to balance experimental control with approaches that are ecologically relevant" (p. 125).

PART FIVE

INTEGRATION

A NEW BIOPSYCHOSOCIAL
EXPLANATION OF CREATIVITY

AFTER TEN CHAPTERS in which we have summarized research on the most salient biological, psychological, and social influences on the creative process, we will now offer our own integrative explanation of the creative process. Furthermore, we will demonstrate the usefulness of this explanation by suggesting ways in which it intersects with J. P. Guilford's insightful model of creative problem solving. We believe that, together, these ideas form a new theory of the nature of the creative process. Before launching into this enterprise, however, we think it will be enlightening to examine an earlier biopsychosocial model of creativity—the evolutionary model of Scott Findlay and Charles Lumsden (1988a, 1988b).

These researchers approached the question of how creativity works from the standpoint of sociobiology, as it has been pioneered by E. O. Wilson (1975, 1978; Lumsden & Wilson, 1983). Sociobiologists are mainly biologists who wish to inquire into the interactive effects of environments on biological processes. The Findlay and Lumsden model reflects this bent. They described their goal (1988a) by asserting the following:

> A productive characterization of the creative process cannot be stated solely by reference to a single level of organization. . . . Our system concept is then integrated with current theories of biocultural dynamics, leading to the hypothesis that creative activity is an evolved strategy in which rules of cognitive development act through the joint inheritance of genetic and cultural information. . . . We suggest that creative potential in particular problem domains relates to the organization of semantic networks through the forging links among previously dissociated elements. Formulation of this *linking thesis* in turn generates several quantitative predictions about domain specificity,

the relationship between creative potential and age, environmental complexity and various aspects of the sociocultural environment [italics theirs, p. 3].

Findlay and Lumsden (1988a) offered their model because of the problems that other approaches presented. They summarized the views of how creativity works from eight major disciplines—history, sociology, cultural anthropology, neurobiology, evolutionary biology, artificial intelligence, cognitive psychology, and social psychology—and then pointed out weaknesses in each. This review is quite valuable in itself. They then produced their own theory, which is represented in its most fundamental form in Figure 12.1.

As this diagram shows, they viewed creativity as resulting from a sequential interaction among four variables:

○ The genotype, which is the person's genetic constitution

○ Brain development

○ The cognitive phenotype, which is the genetically and environmentally determined manner of thinking that the person has developed

○ The physical and sociocultural environment

Each of these elements is influenced by the others to various degrees.

Furthermore, Findlay and Lumsden divided creativity into three stages: the mental process; the discovery, which may or may not result from the mental process; and the innovation, which may or may not result from the discovery. Each of these stages may also have a retroactive effect on the four elements that caused them to occur in the first place. For example, an innovation may alter the physical or sociocultural environment so that through natural selection, more people with creatively predisposed genes will be likely to be born and to survive. The interaction of outer and inner forces also explains why some periods seem to be conducive to musical innovation, whereas others promote political change, and still others appear to have fostered no innovation at all. Hence, their theory is an early exemplar of contextualism (which will be elucidated below).

Wilson evaluated this model in the following way: "At the very least, Findlay and Lumsden have provided a first framework that simultaneously incorporates both biological and cultural evolution in the explanation of the creative process" (1988, p. 1). Their model infuses much-needed evolutionary science into the creativity picture. With the model's "linking" hypothesis, it incorporates the similar cognitive ideas

Figure 12.1. The Gene-Culture Coevolutionary Circuit.

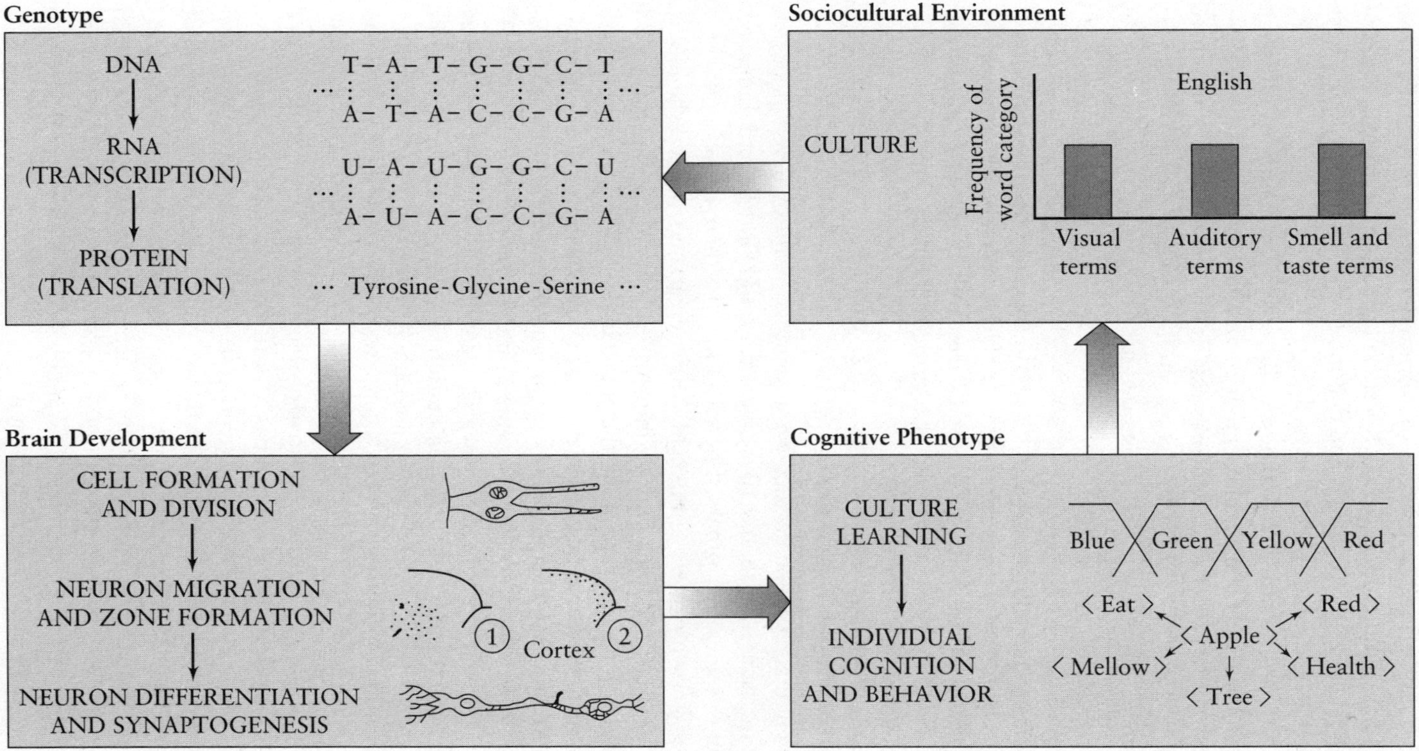

Source: *Findlay and Lumsden, 1988a. Used by permission of the publisher Academic Press.*

of Campbell (1960: blind variation and selective attention), Mednick (1962: remote associates), Koestler (1964: bisociation), Rothenberg (1979: Janusian thinking), and deBono (1984: lateral thinking). In short, their model is a big step forward.

It is not without its weaknesses, however. For one thing, although the sociobiological evolutionary point of view is elegantly presented and although the larger environment's role is integrated well, factors between these two are inadequately considered. As Amabile and Cheek (1988) stated, "Most notably it [the model] has little to say about the intermediate levels of analysis, particularly the cognitive phenotype (including personality) and the intermediate social environment" (p. 57). In addition, Gardner (1988b) felt that the criteria for including or excluding theoretical points of view are not clear. He wondered, for example, at the absence of the neuropsychological research of Geschwind and Sperry (Gardner, 1988b). Gardner also criticized Findlay and Lumsden's approach to some areas of cognition: "For instance, while endorsing modularity, they continue to speak of processes like learning and memory, with the clear implication that these processes occur in the same way across different materials—a decidedly non-modular point of view" (p. 91).

In their 1988 book *The Creative Mind,* Findlay and Lumsden admirably included others' brief reactions to their model of thirty-three well-known experts in the field. Most researchers praised the model but also suggested some way to improve it. Since then, however, we have found only one article about the model in the psychological and social literature. In that article, Moneta (1993) demonstrated that although the model treated divergent thinking, it ignored convergent thinking, which has been shown to play a commensurately important role in creativity. This dearth of subsequent research using the model as a basis is perhaps the model's most significant limitation.

At any rate, we have taken a decidedly different path in our approach to the interactive causes of creativity. We believe that three features of our model—its biopsychosocial approach, its contextual emphasis, and its application to Guilford's creative problem-solving (CPS) model—make it worthy of consideration as a basis for further research. In Figure 12.2, we offer our model of the creative process. The items in parentheses are major examples, but they are not the only ones. The major premise of the model is that, for creativity, the biopsychosocial approach reveals a five-layer system of causation in which each layer interacts with and bidirectionally affects the other four. A sixth variable, time, runs across the whole, such that whatever the state of the interactions were at one time, they might well have changed at a later time.

Figure 12.2. The Dacey-Lennon Model of Creativity's Biopsychosocial Sources.

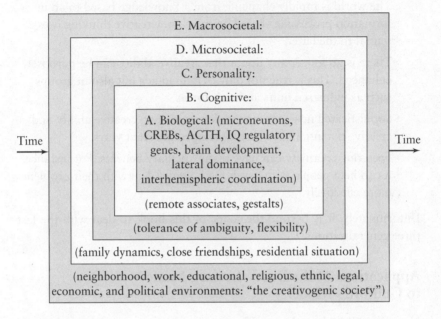

E. Macrosocietal:

D. Microsocietal:

C. Personality:

B. Cognitive:

A. Biological: (microneurons, CREBs, ACTH, IQ regulatory genes, brain development, lateral dominance, interhemispheric coordination)

Time →

Time →

(remote associates, gestalts)

(tolerance of ambiguity, flexibility)

(family dynamics, close friendships, residential situation)

(neighborhood, work, educational, religious, ethnic, legal, economic, and political environments: "the creativogenic society")

Generalizations About Our Biopsychosocial Approach

Our model and its application to Guilford's model comprise our new explanation of creativity. This elucidation offered by the model is designed to reflect the basic biopsychosocial generalizations that we can now make about the creative process:

○ Being creative is not simply a case of having high intelligence. Although having above-average intelligence is necessary, being an intellectual "genius" is not.

○ In addition to mental ability, creativity depends on certain physical, personality, and motivational variables, as well as on certain environmental circumstances.

○ All people are born with the ability to be creative at some level, although whether this ability exists on a continuum or whether it is qualitatively different at the highest levels is still a matter of debate.

○ The "nature versus nurture" debate is over. There is now little doubt that three factors—biological, psychological, and social—play a role in every creative act.

○ Creativity tends to follow developmental trends over the life span and may be most readily cultivated during peak periods of life.

○ The world is rapidly changing from a knowledge-based to an information processing–based orientation. Creative thinking is essential to the latter.

○ There is no longer any doubt that creative ability can be purposely enhanced. This is true not only of individuals but also of groups such as industrial units and task forces.

○ Sophisticated new instruments for measuring creative ability and creative potential have been developed in recent years.

○ Fostering creativity can have many ancillary benefits. For instance, it can help people with psychopathologies deal with their problems more effectively.

Unfortunately, it is beyond the scope of this book to deal with the last three generalizations.

Applications of the Dacey-Lennon Model to Guilford's Model

Now we will look at the specific ways in which our model enriches and expands on Guilford's CPS model (discussed in Chapter Nine). It should be stated at the outset that although all of the variables included in the processes we will describe have been reasonably well established in the research literature, in many cases the processes themselves (the variables' interactions) and our allegations of bidirectional causation among them are still theoretical. These allegations should be viewed as hypotheses that await confirmation through additional research. Nevertheless, they do compose a new theory of the creative thought process.

The four tables that follow show how the major variables discussed thus far in the book relate to each of Guilford's five stages. For convenience of presentation, we have divided the factors from the Dacey-Lennon model into biological (cellular and hemispheric), personality, cognitive, and social categories. Each table covers one category. The variables appear alphabetically within each table, and their relative levels are indicated. We will start with Table 12.1, which examines biological factors in creativity.

Table 12.1. Biological Factors.

Biological Factors	Stage I: Filter	Stage II: Cognition I	Stage III: Production I	Stage IV: Cognition II	Stage V: Production II
ACTH (Chapter Ten)	Low	Moderate	Moderate	High	High
Bipolar activity (Chapters Seven, Ten)	High (depression)	Low: inactive	Low: inactive	Low: inactive	High (hypomania)
CREBs (Chapter Ten)	Low to Moderate	High	Moderate	High	Moderate
Interhemispheric coordination (Chapter Eleven)	Independent activity	Independent activity	Independent activity	Coordinated activity	Coordinated activity
Microneuronal development (Chapter Ten)	Low	Moderate	Moderate	High	High

ACTH

When the hypothalamus stimulates the pituitary gland, the hormone ACTH is produced. ACTH secretion increases in response to stress and other external stimuli. In turn, it stimulates the adrenal gland's outer layer, which secretes a number of hormones into the bloodstream. The presence of ACTH directly affects both biological and mental functions. At high levels of stimulation, a higher level of ACTH is secreted, which stimulates communication between the hemispheres of the brain.

Specifically, ACTH neuropeptides act to facilitate communication between neurons, which results in higher levels of cognition and significantly greater productivity. When an individual is in the filtering stage, there is no need for high communication between hemispheres, because the person is functioning unconsciously. As the person's stimulation increases throughout the next four stages of creativity, the levels of cognition and production reflect the amount of ACTH that is secreted. When interhemispheric communication is most needed—in the Production II stage—ACTH secretion is at its highest.

Bipolar Activity

Disorders such as bipolar disease (manic depression) provide an example of how creativity may progress in stages that are closely linked to biopsychosocial factors. When an individual is depressed, it follows that internal stimulation is at a low level. In the first stage, the individual's conscious processing is depressed; there may be periods of apathy and lethargy. A lack of enthusiasm for otherwise enjoyable events may encourage the filtering process.

It may well be that the "downtime" that occurs during periods of depression allows the mind to regenerate and refuel. Depression and mania do not appear to play significant roles in the creative process either during the early stages of cognition and production or in the second phase of cognition.

Hypermanic episodes consist of energy surges, sleeplessness, high productivity, and fluid interchange of thoughts or ideas. Creative expression in the last stage may be facilitated by a high level of hypermania, as it seems to foster the illumination and expressive ability that can result in creativity.

CREBs

Creative persons have superior memory functions. They have not only a high-level ability to remember but also the capacity to recognize what is worth remembering and what to avoid storing in the first place. This ability functions at a low to moderate level, albeit without awareness, in Stage I and at a moderate level at both production stages. CREBs' main contribution comes at the cognition stages, particularly Cognition II. In this stage, the great breadth of previously stored information contributes to an excellent organization of problem parameters, which in turn enhances the superior production of solutions.

Interhemispheric Coordination

There is evidence that certain human functions are controlled by one side of the brain more than the other. An accurate account of the creative process, however, must take into consideration the qualities that each hemisphere shares with the other.

During the filtering stage, there is not much interaction between the two hemispheres. The brain's left and right sides function autonomously, according to the type of unconscious procedure in which a person may be involved. The separation of the hemispheres continues throughout the second and third stages, when there is less integration of cognition and production. During Stages 4 and 5, cognition and production interact more as the result of greater hemispheric coordination. In this mode, individuals are able to be not only original but also logical, and they achieve a higher quality of solutions than in earlier stages.

Microneuronal Development

Unlike macroneurons, which are present at birth, microneurons continue to develop throughout one's lifetime. The way in which these minuscule neurons develop depends greatly on many biological, psychological, and social factors. They function as alternative pathways between macroneuronal channels. Thus, a complex microneuronal system makes it possible to generate more creative ideas.

Similar to the production of ACTH, microneuronal activity is low in the filtering stage and increases over the next four stages. It is likely that fewer pathways are necessary for functioning in Cognition I and Production I, but the increased number of pathways in the later stages inevitably offers a greater potential for creative output.

Having discussed the biological factors of creativity, we now move on to personality factors, which are depicted in Table 12.2.

Collective Unconscious

The unconscious memories that humans share relate to Guilford's CPS model in an interesting way. We believe that such memories play an important role in the filtering process, because they contain many deep fears and anxieties that we wish to avoid. Because thoughts in the first levels of cognition and production are logical and relatively unimaginative, reliance on the collective unconscious is low. It becomes highly active again as the creative thinker digs deep for understandings and associations in Stages 4 and 5.

Courage

Because the function of the filter is to avoid conflict, courage will be inactive in Stage I. It will play only a minimum role in Cognition I and Production I. At the higher levels of cognition and production, however, it becomes vital. Made up of such characteristics as "having a passionate love for something," "not being afraid to be alone," and "daring to go against the crowd," courage is essential to the creative act.

Delay of Gratification

There is no need for delay of gratification at the filtering stage, where the unconscious desire is to expunge the disturbing problem as quickly and effectively as possible. The willingness to endure the stress of prolonged effort so as to reap higher pleasures in the long run begins to come into play at the lower levels of cognition and production. Then, delay of gratification becomes truly vital at the higher levels. This is so because Stage IV and V processes require much harder work with no immediate reinforcement. The creative person must have a vision of the goal in order to muster the strength needed to prevail during these demanding processes.

Ego Strength

Ego strength is active in both conscious and unconscious modes, so it functions at the filtering stage. As the goal of this stage is problem avoidance, however, we can assume that ego strength is low here.

Because the function of the lower levels of cognition and production is to generate acceptable solutions, ego strength is only needed moderately at these stages. Its role is greatest at the fourth and fifth stages, which are concerned with "the primitive, the uncultured, the naive, the magical, the nonsensical."

Flexibility

Flexibility refers not only to a lack of personal rigidity but also to the ability to attend to all aspects of a problem, without trying to find the "one right answer." Therefore, flexibility is inactive in the filtering stage and is used only moderately in the lower levels of cognition. The free-ranging mind, the curiosity about each feature of a new problem, the hunger to understand everything—these are the aspects of flexibility that contribute so much in Stages 4 and 5.

Functional Freedom

People who possess functional freedom can imagine many uses for objects and can visualize many different outcomes in situations. Their view of the way things work is not fixed in narrow ruts. In the filtering stage, this trait is inactive, because the person is not attempting to find new approaches to the problem but rather to evade it. Functional freedom is needed to a slight extent in the first cognitive and production stages, because any solution will require a new look at the functions of its components. Only in Cognition II and Production II will functional freedom become essential, however. There, the ability to restructure a situation drastically and to make intuitive leaps between obvious and remotely possible functions can bring forth truly creative solutions.

Gender-Role Stereotyping

Gender-role researcher Sandra Bem has found that most societies have pathologized gender deviance by "naturalizing what is essentially just conformity to the cultural requirement that the sex of the body match the gender of the psyche" (1993, p. 5). Many problems involve some aspect of gender conflict. Since the major purpose of filtering is to avoid conflict, we expect that gender-role stereotyping will not be active in this stage. It will operate at a moderate to high level in Stages 2 and 3, and Stages 4 and 5 will find the creative thinker to be nearly free of it.

Table 12.2. Personality Factors.

Biological Factors	Stage I: Filter	Stage II: Cognition I	Stage III: Production I	Stage IV: Cognition II	Stage V: Production II
Collective unconscious (Chapter Seven)	High	Low	Low	High	High
Courage (Chapter Five)	Low	Low	Low	High	High
Delay of gratification (Chapter Five)	Low	Low	Low	High	High
Ego strength (Chapter Seven)	Low	Moderate	Moderate	High	High
Flexibility (Chapter Five)	Inactive	Moderate	Moderate	High	High
Functional freedom (Chapter Five)	Inactive	Low	Low	High	High
Gender role stereotyping (Chapter Five)	High	Low	Low	High	High
Perseverance (Chapter Five)	Inactive	Low	Low	High	High
Preference for disorder (Chapter Five)	Inactive	Low	Low	Moderate	High
Regression (Chapter Seven)	High	Low	Low	High	High

Biological Factors	Stage I: Filter	Stage II: Cognition I	Stage III: Production I	Stage IV: Cognition II	Stage V: Production II
Repression (Chapter Seven)	High	Low	Low	Inactive	Inactive
Risk taking (Chapter Five)	Inactive	Low	Low	Moderate	High
Self-control (Chapter Six)	Inactive	Low	Low	High	High
Stimulus freedom (Chapter Five)	Inactive	Low	Moderate	High	High
Sublimation (Chapter Seven)	Inactive	Inactive	Inactive	Moderate	High
Tolerance of ambiguity (Chapter Five)	Inactive	Low	Moderate	High	High

Perseverance

According to our model, perseverance results from having faith in one's plan, in oneself, and possibly in the assistance of some higher power. Thus, this characteristic plays no role in Stage I and only a slight part in Stages II and III. Perseverance is essential, however, in the last two stages. There, an individual will feel quite tempted to eschew the hard work of repeatedly reexamining the problem and generating more unusual solutions. Only those with the stamina and intrinsic motivation for a creative project are likely to persevere and thus to succeed.

Preference for Disorder

The stereotype that creative individuals are messy, unreliable, and disorganized has been shown to be false. No one who is capable of the highest levels of original productivity can afford to be guilty of these "sins." Creative thinkers, however, do seem to enjoy engaging in problems that are complex, multileveled, and, at first sight, completely disorganized. Such thinkers derive great pleasure in resolving problems by imposing their own imaginative organization on them (Barron, 1995).

Thus, preference for disorder is irrelevant in Stage I, and it functions at a low level in the next two stages. In Cognition II, it becomes of moderate importance, but the need to make sense of the problem still predominates. In Production II, a high tolerance for complex disarray is vital, as the thinker wanders through uncharted territories in search of the most appropriate solution.

Regression

The levels of regression in Guilford's five stages appear at first to be curious. Regression has a high status in most filtering functions, for its essence is to keep any unpleasant thoughts away from consciousness. This defense mechanism is often seen in children, who have not yet developed self-control skills. Regression operates at a much lower plane in the first stages of cognition and production, which are concerned with approaching the problem from a simple, conscious perspective.

Regression is frequently used at high levels in Stages IV and V, but for different reasons than at the filtering stage. At these loftier levels of imagination, the ability to play around with ideas, to regress in the service of the ego, as Kris put it, is invaluable. The thinker often reverts to childlike attitudes, forsaking the seriousness of the professional for the naïveté of the novice. Thus, a relaxed regression to puerile viewpoints can often result in brilliant new cognitions and the production of wondrously appropriate solutions.

Repression

Because it is a defense mechanism and therefore operates unconsciously, repression is most active in the filtering process. In fact, it is probably the primary method by which problems are excluded from being dealt with consciously. Repression is likely to occur in Stages II and III as well but only in the background when the mind seeks to avoid confronting a problem of which it has become conscious. Because the person is so mentally alert and self-aware in Stages IV and V, repression is inactive at these levels of CPS.

Risk Taking

Highly creative people are in no way similar to compulsive gamblers. They certainly take risks in originating creative products, but these are moderate, calculated risks, not all-out wagers. Nevertheless, few innovations have come about without the willingness to chance losing fortune, reputation, or self-esteem. Risk taking is inactive in the filtering process, because the point of the process is to protect the ego from awareness of the problem. The cautious approach of the second and third stages ensures a low level of risk. Chance taking increases somewhat in Cognition II and reaches its highest level in Production II.

Stimulus Freedom

In general, stimulus freedom is a most salient factor in creative thinking. It refers to the ability to resist two natural human tendencies: (1) to obey rules to the letter so as to avoid punishment and (2) to assume the existence of guidelines when a situation is actually ambiguous. Thinkers low in creativity tend to be bound by what they believe are the circumstantial parameters of a problem, and they therefore fail to produce high-level solutions.

The individual stuck at the filtering stage is stimulus bound and is thus unlikely to want to attend to the problem. Stimulus freedom is low in Stage I. It is only slightly more in evidence in the traditionalistic thinking that tends to take place in Cognition I and Production I. Stages IV and V require a high level of stimulus freedom in order to achieve the rarefied air of the great idea.

Sublimation

Freud believed that sublimation comes into play when individuals are unable to fulfill their sex drives. They typically make up for the deficit by being creative in some artistic way (for example, becoming a great violinist). Modern theorists such as Oremland and Whitebook have reinterpreted sublimation by saying that it need not be socially acceptable. That is, a person is still compensating for a lack of sexual fulfillment, but he or she may do so in ways that are as culturally acceptable as playing a violin. Creativity, they maintain, must by its nature be free to choose any outlet, not just one that is guaranteed instant praise. Thus, Whitebook defines *sublimation* as a "process through which genetic material, with all its contingency, privacy, and particularity, is transformed into cultural objects such as paintings, political constitutions, mathematical proofs, musical compositions, scientific theories . . . which can claim public validity in their respective domains" (1994, p. 94).

If we accept this more modern view, sublimation will be avoided at the filter stage, because it is not a way of filtering out the problem but is rather a means of unconsciously addressing it. Sublimation does not function in the highly conscious processes of Cognition I and Production I. It will come into the picture moderately in Cognition II, and it may be used fully in Production II.

Tolerance of Ambiguity

We have suggested that if there is a master trait in the psychology of creativity, including both personality and cognitive aspects, it is a tolerance of ambiguity. All people tend to be bored by the familiar and frightened by the strange, and this is true of creative people as well. They differ from their less imaginative peers in that they are interested in the unfamiliar to a greater extent and in that it takes a much higher degree of strangeness to frighten them. Creative thinkers are more tolerant of the ambiguous, the unusual, the bizarre.

We expect to find this trait inactive in Stage I and low in Stage II. It should be present at a moderate level in Stage III, because some tolerance of ambiguity is required even for lower forms of problem solving. The trait is most valuable, however, when the thinker reaches the loftier planes of Cognition II and Production II.

We now move on to Table 12.3, which looks at the cognitive factors involved in creativity.

Cognitive Mobility

A creative individual can successfully operate complex mental processes or more primitive mental processes, depending on the situation. *Cognitive mobility* is the term used to describe this flexibility. Although some problems may require a high level of field independence (see Chapter Eight), a creative individual is able to recognize when a problem requires a different kind of approach.

High levels of cognitive mobility are not necessary in the early stages of creativity. In Cognition II, moderate levels of cognitive mobility are necessary for recognizing that a problem may involve various mental processes. The highest level of cognitive mobility is at work in Production II, because such production requires flexibility among available processes.

Convergent Thinking

Convergent thinking works best to produce a right answer for a question that can have only one answer. Such thinking helps to identify the most appropriate or useful solution to a problem in the process of creative problem solving.

Convergent thinking is inactive in the unconscious filtering stage. It is low in the early stages of cognition and production, as this is when rational, more ordinary solutions originate. It is highest in Stage IV, which requires an advanced way of structuring the problem. During the second production stage, convergent thinking returns to a moderate level, serving to select the best solution from among those generated.

Divergent Thinking

Divergent thinking is essential in generating a wide range of ideas. It involves an attempt to think in different directions as one searches for a variety of answers to questions.

In the filtering stage, divergent thinking is inactive. The level of divergent thinking over the next four stages is the inverse of the level of convergent thinking, as they have opposite, though complementary, functions.

Table 12.3. Cognitive Factors.

Biological Factors	Stage I: Filter	Stage II: Cognition I	Stage III: Production I	Stage IV: Cognition II	Stage V: Production II
Collective unconscious (Chapter Seven)	High	Low	Low	High	High
Cognitive mobility (Chapter Eight)	Low	Low	Low	Moderate	High
Convergent thinking (Chapter Nine)	Inactive	Low	Low	High	Moderate
Divergent thinking (Chapter Nine)	Inactive	High	Moderate	Moderate	Low
Ego control (Chapter Eight)	Inactive	Moderate	Moderate	High	High
Ego resilience (Chapter Eight)	Inactive	Low	Moderate	Moderate	High
Field independence (Chapter Eight)	Low	Low	Moderate	Moderate	High
Lateral thinking (Chapter Nine)	Low	Low	Low	Moderate	High
Remote associates (Chapter Eight)	Low	Moderate	Moderate	High	High
Use of metaphor (Chapter Eight)	Low	Moderate	Moderate	High	High

Ego Control

Ego control refers to the extent to which a person can express or restrain impulses, feelings, and desires. This factor is related to delay of gratification and avoidance of distraction, which in turn depend on self-control. Ego control is therefore important in terms of providing the discipline required to carry out a task.

Ego control is inactive during the filtering stage of creativity because its function requires conscious awareness. In the early stages of cognition and production, the level of ego control is moderate, as the individual attempts to wrestle with a problem and develop solutions. In the second stages of cognition and production, a high level of ego control is required. Not only must a person actively avoid distractions and focus on the task at hand, but he or she must harness problem-solving skills and apply them to that task.

Ego Resilience

Ego resilience refers to a person's ability to modify his or her level of ego control to meet a situation's demands. This factor also relates to the ability to handle anxiety under stress. Ego-resilient individuals can skillfully adapt to changing circumstances, carefully evaluate a situation, and capitalize on the problem-solving strategies available to them. Such individuals are more flexible in their thinking and are therefore more creative.

Ego resilience is inactive in the filtering stage of creativity, as the individual does not actively seek to solve a problem at this time. A low level of ego resilience is at work in the first stage of cognition, as the individual begins to evaluate a particular situation. The level increases in Stages 3 and 4 as the person begins adapting to the demands of the situation. At the highest level, in the fifth stage, ego resilience is in full force, so to speak. The creative person can successfully adapt to the situation and make use of several problem-solving strategies that have been generated in previous stages.

Field Independence

Field independence involves the ability to look at a whole picture or problem and break it up into smaller parts. An individual is then able to attend to the more relevant parts while ignoring the less important parts. A task that might strike many people as insurmountable will be recognized by a more creative person as a series of several smaller, quite manageable tasks.

In the filtering stage, the individual does not actively attempt to examine the larger picture, as he or she is making no effort to solve a problem. In the second and third stages of the model, the individual begins actively seeking answers to problems but does not take the extra steps required to break a larger problem into smaller parts. In these stages, many people stop the problem-solving process before they have seen the larger picture. Creative individuals are able to recognize the steps required to reach a goal. In Stages IV and V, their field independence is high. These individuals are able to see the problem in a way others cannot envision.

Lateral Thinking

Similar to cognitive mobility, lateral thinking requires flexibility. Rather than examining a problem from a vertical perspective that simply involves moving between lower- and higher-level concepts, a person using lateral thinking looks for diverse ways of interpreting or solving a problem. Whereas lateral thinking functions at low levels in the first three stages of creativity, in the higher levels of cognition and production, lateral thinking increases to moderate and then high levels of functioning.

Remote Associates

Mednick believed that creativity is the process of associating ideas that already exist in the mind in unusual, original, and useful combinations. When people think about solving a problem, they search their mind for an association that might serve as a solution. Whereas many people are willing to accept the first idea that comes to mind, more creative individuals tend to search further for more unusual and higher-quality associations.

During the filtering stage, remote associations are low, because the individual is not actively searching for associations but rather letting the associations take place indiscriminately. As the person moves into the stages of early cognition and production, he or she makes more associations, but they are not far-reaching enough to stimulate new connections and new meaning. In the later stages of cognition and production, the individual actively delves into remote regions of the mind in search of associations that result in high-quality creative ideas.

Use of Metaphor

The use of metaphors involves the ability to see a relationship between seemingly dissimilar things. Rather than seeing only one relationship between items, creative thinkers can find relationships between those items that most people would overlook, and they are able to compare them in unique, qualitatively different ways.

The use of metaphors operates at a low level in the filtering stage of creativity. The individual may be aware of relationships between a problem's variables but he or she will not actively look for them. In the early stages of cognition and production, the individual needs moderate levels of metaphor use to envision relationships between things and to make initial attempts at creative output. Stages 4 and 5 require the highest amount of metaphor use. At these levels, the most unique and remote connections between things are made, which lead to the most creative products.

We will now look at Table 12.4, which examines the social factors in creativity.

Being Later Born

Although a large body of early research on birth order found that first-born children and only children were most likely to be successful at many endeavors, more recent research suggests that later borns are more likely to be unconventional and therefore more creative than firstborns or only children. An only child or firstborn interacts mainly with adults from birth, whereas a later born child has at least one other child who is a major influence on his or her intellectual development. Because of their closer identification with parents and parental values, only children and firstborns are more likely to be traditional in their approach to problems. Therefore, the model posits that firstborns will be most vulnerable to the filtering process and will tend to be satisfied with Cognition I and Production I answers. Later borns are less interested in pleasing authority figures (firstborns have that "all sewn up"). Therefore, they are better able to conceptualize and produce creative solutions.

High Family Socioeconomic Status

The majority of eminent creators were born into families who had significant economic resources or who sacrificed greatly to provide resources and opportunities to nurture the creators' talents. Creative potential is probably normally distributed across all social and economic levels, but

Table 12.4. Social Factors.

Biological Factors	Stage I: Filter	Stage II: Cognition I	Stage III: Production I	Stage IV: Cognition II	Stage V: Production II
Being later born: positive effects (Chapter Two)	Low	Low	Low	High	High
High family socio-economic status: positive effects (Chapter Three)	Low	Moderate	Moderate	High	High
Innovative educational environment: positive effects (Chapter Four)	Low	Low	Low	Moderate	Moderate
Nurturing parenting style: positive effects (Chapter Three)	Low	Moderate	Moderate	High	High
Reinforcement in work environment: negative effects (Chapter Four)	Inactive	Low	Low	High	High
Supportive political climate: positive effects (Chapter Four)	Low	Moderate	Moderate	High	High

those who have more resources to develop those qualities are more likely to reach their potential.

In terms of the model, high socioeconomic status will have little effect on the filtering process. Economic advantages are most likely to affect conscious efforts to be productive (for example, having training and appropriate tools). Those with moderate advantages are more likely to be able to operate at the Cognition I and Production I stages, and those with extensive financial and educational resources will probably feel freest to go to the creative stages of Cognition II and Production II.

Innovative Educational Environment

Traditional educational models promote the quest for approval and thus cause many to be unable to go beyond filtering or to settle for the first stages of cognition and production. Those whose educational environments encourage independent thinking and inventiveness pass out of these early stages into creative cognition and production.

Dacey's study (1989c) of the families of creative adolescents strongly suggests, however, that rigid schooling may not have as baleful an effect on creativity as it would first appear. Neither the parents nor the children in this study regarded their schools as having a great impact on their creativity, regardless of whether their particular school happened to be traditional or innovative. They believed that the home is far more influential. Thus, at best, the positive effects of an innovative educational environment on CPS are only moderate.

Nurturing Parenting Style

If a person's parents were authoritarian (strict and controlling), the filtering process will most likely be strong, largely because a fear of making mistakes will cause a person to avoid the problem situation. If the parenting is permissive (low control), the person is likely to lack the self-control needed to contend with the problem effectively. At the first cognition and production stages, those reared by authoritative (midway between controlling and permissive) parents will be predisposed to treat the problem superficially; in line with the conventional bent of their upbringing, they will tend to produce conventional solutions. Those with nurturing parents (parenting by means of modeling and effective discussion), however, tend to have the greatest advantage at the Cognition II stage and will likely find a truly creative solution in Production II.

Reinforcement in Work Environment

Recent research has examined the impact of work environments on adults' creativity on two levels: that of the individual worker's immediate environment and that of the organization itself, including the ways in which rewards operate in this environment. Amabile (1996, 1997; Amabile, Goldfarb, & Brackfield, 1990; Amabile, Hill, Hennessey, & Tighe, 1994) has distinguished between *creativity* and *innovation,* defining *creativity* as "the production of novel and appropriate ideas by individuals or small groups of individuals working closely together" (Amabile, 1996, p. 3) and *innovation* as "the successful implementation of ideas by an organization" (Amabile, 1996, p. 3). She and her colleagues have discovered many workplace characteristics that stifle creativity. Probably the most significant obstacle is management's reinforcement of the types of thinking that it defines as creative.

Reinforcement in the workplace cultivates filtering in employees who lack imagination. They are frustrated by their inability to acquire those reinforcements and therefore eschew the competition. Employees with moderate creativity are stimulated by the reinforcing environment, because they believe they can discover which so-called innovations will receive management's approval and they then seek to produce them. Reinforcement is a distinct obstacle at the height of creative thinking (which takes place in Stages 4 and 5), however, because creativity absolutely requires an atmosphere of freedom from coercion.

Supportive Political Climate

Highly repressive political forces (those that threaten any challenge to the status quo) tend to suppress an open examination of problems and therefore encourage filtering. If the political climate is moderately supportive, people tend to use Cognition I and Production I solutions, as they are more likely to consider innovative thoughts, but they will still fear reprisals if their thinking deviates too much from traditional modes. In times of freely supportive political regimes, people (especially creative ones) are much more likely to use Cognition II and Production II solutions.

Contextual Aspects of This New Theory of Creativity

In this section, we will summarize the tenets of the contextual approach. We will follow the summary of each aspect of contextualism with examples of how that aspect applies to our theory.

Contextualism is a relatively new approach to theory building that has important applications to our theory of creative problem solving. *Contextualism* refers to a set of assumptions about reality that make for a more complex but ultimately more useful understanding of human thought and behavior than we have had before. The concept of contextualism has been evolving for some years, but its tenets have been championed of late, primarily by Richard Lerner (1995, 1996, forthcoming; Lerner & Simi, 1997), as well as by Muuss (1996). Lerner's viewpoint is having a considerable impact on the field of human development in particular and on social science in general.

Contextualism holds that any model of human development in any area of human endeavor should incorporate four contextual traits: bidirectional causation, relative plasticity, historical embeddedness, and diversity and individual differences in development. We will describe these traits and then give biological, personality, cognitive, and social examples drawn from our model of the creative process.

Bidirectional Causation

Imagine a study that looks at how students' creative ability is affected by the type of classroom in which they study. According to Lerner, not only are pupils affected by the way their classroom is arranged and by its atmosphere but the classroom in turn is affected by the types of students and the teacher in it. The presence of highly creative children will push the class toward exploration and innovation rather than absorption of knowledge. Their presence also tends to affect how the other children in the classroom think and behave, whose reactions in turn affect their peers.

A major basis for change lies in the multiple levels of the individual's interactions with other individuals. This special case of bidirectional causation is called "relationism."

A third aspect of bidirectional causation is known as "goodness of fit." This aspect of the contextual approach refers to the relationships among the individual's traits and the biological, psychological, and social demands of the environment in which that person is found. Thus, contextualism moves away from concern over what variables are to blame for behavior and toward the idea of how well matched they are. If the person's traits fit well with the psychosocial environment, the person will experience healthy development and will fulfill her or his creative potential, but if this fit is negative, then mental or physical illness is likely to result.

BIOLOGICAL FACTORS. Bipolar disorder is a good example of a biological factor in creativity that calls for bidirectional research. The hypomanic stage has been identified as one that may produce a wealth of creative ideas, but both full-blown mania and depression interfere with the person's attempt to implement any of them. The standard goal of psychopharmacological treatment for bipolar disorder is to modify the person's moods to prevent both highs and lows. Creative people are often resistant to or noncompliant with treatment for bipolar disorder, because they feel it makes them dull and uninspired. Research might be done on how to modify treatments to allow a controllable level of hypomania in those who can use this stage productively and to discover whether the professionals in charge of treatment would consider such modification an acceptable option.

PERSONALITY FACTORS. One personality factor that research has identified as key to creativity is tolerance of ambiguity. Looking at this trait from the opposite direction, new research might be conducted to discover how others react to a person who has a strong tolerance of ambiguity and whether their interactions with the person help preserve this tolerance or tend to discourage it. For example, do most teachers find it exhilarating or frustrating to have such a student in their classes?

COGNITIVE FACTORS. A cognitive example of bidirectional causation is cognitive mobility, the ability to use both complex and primitive mental processes. This trait is influenced by the situation and will in turn influence it, either in the direction of change and growth or in the maintenance of the status quo. In a society that remains primitive, such as that of rural Papua New Guinea, people lead a subsistence-level existence, which is dominated by activities like carrying water and gathering firewood and which therefore requires a very narrow range of cognitive mobility. In turn, the society itself is very traditional and slow to make any kind of change.

On the other hand, in an advanced technological society such as our own, people need a broad range of thinking skills to organize and accomplish many necessary daily tasks in both workplaces and households. The complex demands made on the individual increase as more is expected of them in both areas. Mothers who work professionally while their children are young must be able to use several cognitive skills in keeping abreast of advances within their careers and in caring physically for their children while also nurturing their family's emotional and intellectual growth. In turn, the atmospheres of the workplace and the home are both changed in this bidirectional interaction.

SOCIAL FACTORS. The research that Dacey and colleagues (1989a, 1989b) did on the families of creative adolescents, which was discussed in Chapter Three, identified many characteristics of home environments that allow creativity to blossom in children, such as the imposition of few or no rules. From a bidirectional standpoint, further research might seek to discover how having a creative child shapes the way parents are able to interact with that child. For example, it is possible that having such a child causes at least some people to revise their parenting strategies extensively.

Relative Plasticity

One of the most hotly debated issues in psychology over the years has been the question of whether human development tends to be relatively stable over the life span or whether it is marked by plasticity in response to environmental and somatic influences. *Plasticity* is essentially the potential for change in a given context. Contextualism sides with the view that the individual always has the potential for change, although past and contemporary contextual conditions may oppose severe limitations.

In terms of people's relative plasticity, the Dacey-Lennon model is a good example of the contextual standpoint. Plasticity is not just a matter of inherited temperament or of psychological tendency; the environment can cultivate it powerfully. This is critical to our hopes for the future of our world, because individuals with greater adaptability tend to be more creative.

BIOLOGICAL FACTORS. A major contributor to plasticity is coordination between the brain's two hemispheres. The right hemisphere may be more open to innovative ideas than the left hemisphere, and to the extent that a society values creativity, these ideas may be put into effect. All of the biological variables reviewed in this book—ACTH, CREBs, microneurons—foster greater plasticity of human development and thus creative achievement.

COGNITIVE FACTORS. The cognitive factor of ego resilience involves the ability to adapt to changing circumstances, to analyze a situation, and to incorporate problem-solving strategies. As a result, one can turn a problem situation into a creative solution. The saying "When life hands you lemons, make lemonade" is an example of ego resilience. Creative individuals can bounce back from adversity and turn the situation to their advantage.

An example of this may be seen in the number of new ideas created during the period when the Declaration of Independence was drafted. In the time of the Revolutionary War, when change was the goal and motivation behind the generation of new ideas, the laws and standards created exemplify the use of interhemispheric communication. The new laws illustrate a change from the English monarchy's old governance to the new and revised laws that center around personal freedom. The recognition that different contexts may require different laws illustrates the effect of ego resilience on cognitive plasticity.

PERSONALITY FACTORS. Several aspects of one's personality may influence the extent to which life tends to be characterized by change. Tolerance of ambiguity, risk taking, stimulus and functional freedom, ego strength, and flexibility are examples of such personality traits. A note of caution here: the personality that is oriented toward change is not always more likely to produce creative ideas. For example, too much flexibility can lead to an inability to make decisions. The point is that unless plasticity is the prevailing tendency, creativity is impossible.

SOCIAL FACTORS. There is evidence that certain educational environments may suppress some individuals' creative impulses. The opposite may also be true when educational environments actively encourage creative production. Classrooms that feature whole language and inventive story writing are social elements that are likely to cultivate plasticity.

Classroom teachers who use whole language in their curricula allow students to write freely without worrying about correct spelling and grammar. The students can generate creative stories and ideas and feel proud of their accomplishments. Meanwhile, the teacher facilitates learning by providing ample opportunities for the students to encounter correct spelling and grammar in other situations, such as reading and phonetic exercises. Children in such classrooms are able to learn by doing and are therefore free to create without fear of failure.

Historical Embeddedness

No human behavior occurs as an isolated activity. All actions are meaningful only in the context of the historical time in which they occur. The goal of contextualist researchers is to improve our understanding of the interactions between the environment and the person's internal state. The theory emphasizes that these two general factors (the external and the internal) are not only constantly affecting each other; each is actually embedded in the other's history. They cannot be understood except in terms of their constant interactions, which are forever undergoing change.

BIOLOGICAL FACTORS. Interhemispheric coordination is itself an example of embeddedness, as both hemispheres of the brain continually interact with one another. One might think that in a period such as the Renaissance, a heavy emphasis on visual arts required more extensive reliance on visualizing and imaging, with logical and mathematical functions acting in a supporting role. In our own time, one might hypothesize that the emphasis on scientific and technological progress encourage a reversal of this, involving greater use of "left-brain" strengths, with the other hemisphere's functions in a more secondary position.

The roles of the two hemispheres cannot really be so clearly separated, however. The functioning of one hemisphere has no meaning except in the context of the other. Even if two individuals' left hemispheres were identical, they would not operate in the same way, because the outcomes would rely and would be embedded in the operations of their different right hemispheres.

PERSONALITY FACTORS. An aspect of personality that greatly affects and that is affected by environmental influences is gender-role stereotyping. In the Victorian period, for example, when a woman was expected to be the "angel in the house," it was far more difficult than it is today for her to choose options such as being single or childless, options that might better foster her creativity. The internal state of a talented woman would often be at odds with the press of her environment, which would be embedded within her sense of herself. At the present time, there is more support for both men and women to aspire to the highest levels of achievement in their chosen fields.

COGNITIVE FACTORS. The cognitive skill of divergent thinking is much more likely to be encouraged today in environments such as schools and workplaces than was true in previous centuries. Even in our own century, though, schooling has largely been directed to learning "the right answer," and business has been oriented toward "the right way" of doing things, as exemplified by the production methods and employee relations of Henry Ford. Hence, the very center of the person's approach to thinking about the world is profoundly embedded in an era's zeitgeist.

SOCIAL FACTORS. Children with unique interests and abilities affect their families in many ways, just as families influence the development of children. As an example of how behavior is embedded in the historical context of the larger family unit, consider a child born with a proclivity toward music. The most prolific musical family in history was the Bach family, which was prominent for seven generations. The most influential member, J. S. Bach, was born into the fifth generation. Twice married, he was the father of twenty children, four of whose work is played to this day. Clearly, as proficiency in music was expected and highly valued in this family, the physical and psychological means for its development were readily available to the children. In northern Germany, during the time in which the Bachs lived, the composition and performance of music was financially supported by the courts, municipalities, and churches, so that a musician might expect to make a solid living from music.

What about children born today with musical potential equivalent to that of J. S. Bach? How might the context affect their development? If the parents valued the arts and played instruments themselves, they would be far more likely to be alert to the child's possible musical abilities than if they had entirely different interests. If a child with great musical aptitude (such as perfect pitch or a lovely singing voice) were born into a family that for generations has considered music a frivolous luxury, the outcome would likely be very different.

Diversity and Individual Differences in Development

In the past, developmental psychology has emphasized the ways in which all humans are alike (that is why we have behaviorist and stage theories). More and more, the emphasis is on the variety of ways in which individuals learn to cope with themselves and their environments.

Contextualism maintains that there are four major factors in development:

1. The physical setting (for example, the classroom or the battlefield).

2. The social environment (the teachers and peers with whom a child interacts in the classroom environment, for instance).

3. An individual's personal characteristics (physical appearance and manner of speaking would be examples).

4. Time (in the short term, the person's daily schedule, and in the long term, the effects of history on the physical and social setting). Contextualism argues that any statements about developmental patterns

are suspect because the context in which these patterns occur is always being altered over time.

Thus, development cannot be seen in a simplistic way. Lerner argues that we must no longer subscribe to theories that claim to be universal and timeless. The way in which a person develops will depend on each of the four factors cited. To be accurate, a description of development during an age period (life stage) must be decidedly more intricate than was previously thought to be true in the unidimensional theories of the past.

Contextualism highlights the idea of individual differences and pays particular attention to the rich and beneficial diversity that exists among ethnic groups. In a world in which the number of nonwhite persons is rapidly ascending, this is a most relevant distinction. In his book *Theories of Adolescence* (1996), Muuss articulates the relevance of this implication: "As children possess different genetic dispositions, grow up in diverse settings, and contribute uniquely to their own development, these contextual factors do shape children differently, thus turning the focus towards diversity. . . . Each individual child is unique and becomes increasingly more unique as development progresses through the course of life" (p. 351).

This emphasis on the importance of diversity in understanding human development is particularly crucial at this point in American history. For example, there is considerable evidence that psychology has paid disproportionate attention to the developmental patterns of white middle-class children and has neglected children of color (Lerner & Miller, 1994; Muuss, 1996). Of great concern is the finding that African Americans in particular are being studied less and less. Compared with whites, African American teens experience more of the risk factors that psychologists most commonly study, such as delinquency, dropout rates, and drug abuse. Therefore, it is vital to understand the unique contexts of African Americans in order to help them fulfill their creative potential, which is an essential part of producing solutions to the many problems they face.

In many ways, an acceptance of diversity and individual difference has increased recently, creating an atmosphere that encourages growth within individual social and environmental contexts. This increased tolerance provides more opportunities for creative output, because an appreciation of diversity allows a greater number of creative products to be produced and accepted.

BIOLOGICAL FACTORS. Biological contextualism may be seen in those people who experience the ups and downs involved with bipolar disorder. They seem to have a higher creative output than other individuals.

Although manic-depressive mood swings are not a requirement of creativity, the symptoms of depression and mania may mirror the incubation and generation processes inherent in the creative process. Many creative individuals experience a period of "downtime" when creative ideas may be formulated, which are then enhanced and expressed in the following stage of production.

During the early years of Pablo Picasso's painting, he experienced his "blue period," when he was known to suffer from depressions that were reflected in his artwork. Many of the paintings from this period were painted with a cool palette of blues and feature dark, shadowy images that depict loneliness, exhaustion, and hunger. Art historians recognize this period as a positive step toward maturity for Picasso. Only a few years later, he was recognized as a leading member of the artistic front, having produced hundreds of paintings, sketches, and sculptures. This increased diversity of ideas led to the development of cubism, which revolutionized Western painting.

PERSONALITY FACTORS. Several personality factors contribute to healthy development. Among them are delay of gratification and perseverance. These factors are similar, in that an individual who visualizes a desired goal may decide to work harder for a longer period of time in order to achieve that goal. Only with the extreme commitment that these factors can produce are truly diverse creative products likely to result.

COGNITIVE FACTORS. The use of metaphor is a cognitive factor that varies according to individuals' developmental levels. Young children are more apt to use metaphors than older children, who may seek concrete relationships between objects or concepts. In a more sophisticated way, adults are able to capitalize on the ability to see relationships between seemingly dissimilar things and are better able to use metaphoric thinking to generate multiple creative solutions.

SOCIAL FACTORS. The concept of reinforcement in the workplace has been understood to mean that certain behaviors or levels of performance are rewarded, based on compliance with standards that higher management sets. Employees who deviate from these standards are therefore not reinforced. Because most employees strive for positive reinforcement, usually in the form of monetary rewards or promotions, their creative efforts will be restricted to what they believe the upper-level management really wants. This approach stifles the natural diversity of their thinking, and ultimately of their overall development. Development of benefits packages and employee-training programs, however well meant, will lead to lower levels of creative suggestions on the job.

Probabilistic View of Causation

The contextualist posits that statements about causation must be probabilistic. We may no longer make simplistic statements such as, "This causes that." The more accurately we can define the four developmental factors, the more confident we may be in our predictions about how a person is likely to behave. Of course, we can never know everything about these factors. Probabilistic statements can only be made about the course that any particular person's life is likely to take: "People like Jimmy are 80 percent more likely to quit smoking as a result of Program X than if they receive no help."

Lerner's contextual approach forces us to look more carefully at these and many other heretofore neglected developmental variables. His approach helps us to think about creativity in a more accurate, realistic way. We sincerely hope that the same might be said of our model of creativity and of the way in which we have applied it to Guilford's CPS model to form a new explanation of creativity.

REFERENCES

Abra, J. (1989). Changes in creativity with age: Data, explanations, and further predictions. *International Journal of Aging in Human Development, 28*(2), 105–126.

Adler, A. (1917). *A study of organ inferiority and its psychical compensation.* New York: Nervous and Mental Diseases Publishing.

Adorno, T. W., Frankel-Brunswick, E., Levinson, D., & Sanford, R. (1950). *The authoritarian personality.* New York: HarperCollins.

Aguilar-Alonso, A. (1996). Personality and creativity. *Personality and Individual Differences, 21*(6), 959–969.

Albert, R. (1992). A developmental theory of eminence. In R. Albert (Ed.), *Genius and eminence* (2nd ed.). New York: Pergamon Press.

Albert, R. (1996a). Presidential address to Division Ten of the American Psychological Association: What the study of eminence can teach us. *Creativity Research Journal, 9*(4), 307–315.

Albert, R. (1996b). Some reasons why childhood creativity often fails to make it past puberty into the real world. In M. A. Runco (Ed.), *Creativity from childhood through adulthood: The developmental issues.* San Francisco: Jossey-Bass.

Albert, R., & Runco, M. A. (1997). A history of research on creativity. In R. Sternberg (Ed.), *Handbook of creativity.* Cambridge, England: Cambridge University Press.

Altman, J. (1967). Postnatal growth and differentiation of the mammalian brain with implications for a morphological theory of memory. In G. C. Quarton (Ed.), *The neurosciences: A study program.* New York: Rockefeller University Press.

Amabile, T. (1982a). Children's artistic creativity: Detrimental effects of competition in a field setting. *Personality and Social Psychology Bulletin, 8,* 573–578.

Amabile, T. (1982b). Social psychology of creativity: A consensual assessment technique. *Journal of Social Psychology, 43,* 997–1013.

Amabile, T. (1983a). *The social psychology of creativity.* New York: Springer-Verlag.

Amabile, T. (1983b). Social psychology of creativity: A componential conceptualization. *Journal of Personality and Social Psychology, 45,* 357–377.

Amabile, T. (1989). *Growing up creative: Nurturing a lifetime of creativity.* Buffalo, NY: Creative Education Foundation Press.

Amabile, T. (1996). *Creativity in context.* Boulder, CO: Westview Press.

Amabile, T. (1997). Entrepreneurial creativity through motivational synergy. *Journal of Creative Behavior, 31*(1), 18–26.

Amabile, T., & Cheek, J. M. (1988). Microscopic and macroscopic creativity. In C. S. Findlay & C. Lumsden (Eds.), *The creative mind.* Orlando, FL: Academic Press.

Amabile, T., Conti, R., & Collins, A. (1996). Frank Barron's influence on current and future generations of creativity researchers: Some personal reflections. In A. Montuori (Ed.), *Unusual associates: A Festschrift for Frank Barron.* Cresskill, NJ: Hampton Press.

Amabile, T., DeJong, W., & Lepper, M. (1976). Effects of externally-imposed deadlines on subsequent intrinsic motivation. *Journal of Personality and Social Psychology, 34,* 92–98.

Amabile, T., & Gitomer, J. (1984). Children's artistic creativity: Effects of choice in task materials. *Personality and Social Psychology Bulletin, 10,* 209–215.

Amabile, T., Goldfarb, P., & Brackfield, S. (1990). Social influences on creativity: Evaluation, coaction, and surveillance. *Creativity Research Journal, 3*(1), 6–21.

Amabile, T., Hennessey, B., & Grossman, B. (1986). Social influences on creativity: The effects of contracted-for reward. *Journal of Personality and Social Psychology, 50,* 14.

Amabile, T., Hill, K., Hennessey, B., & Tighe, E. (1994). The work preference inventory: Assessing intrinsic and extrinsic motivational orientations. *Journal of Personality and Social Psychology, 66*(5), 950–967.

Ansbacher, H. L., & Ansbacher, R. R. (Eds.). (1956). *The individual psychology of Alfred Adler.* New York: Basic Books.

Arieti, S. (1976). *Creativity: The magic synthesis.* New York: Basic Books.

Arlin, P. K. (1975). Cognitive development in adulthood: A fifth stage? *Developmental Psychology, 11,* 602–606.

Atkinson, J. (1964). *An introduction to motivation.* New York: American Book.

Bailin, S. (1994). *Achieving extraordinary ends: An essay on creativity.* Norwood, NJ: Ablex.

Bakan, P. (1969). Hypnotizability, laterality of eye movement and functional brain asymmetry. *Perceptual and Motor Skills, 28,* 927–932.

Bandura, A. (1997). *Self-efficacy: The exercise of control.* New York: Freeman.

Barron, F. (1968). *Creativity and personal freedom.* New York: Van Nostrand Reinhold.

Barron, F. (1988). Putting creativity to work. In R. Sternberg (Ed.), *The nature of creativity: Contemporary psychological perspectives.* New York: Cambridge University Press.

Barron, F. (1995). *No rootless flower: An ecology of creativity.* Cresskill, NJ: Hampton Press.

Barron, F. (1997). Introduction. In F. Barron, A. Montuori, & A. Barron (Eds.), *Creators on creating.* New York: Putnam.

Barron, F., & Welsh, G. S. (1952). Artistic perception as a factor in personality style: Its measurement by a figure preference test. *Journal of Psychology, 33,* 199–203.

Barzun, J. (1964). *Science: The glorious entertainment.* New York: Basic Books.

Baumrind, D. (1989). Rearing competent children. In W. Damon (Ed.), *Child development today and tomorrow.* San Francisco: Jossey-Bass.

Begley, S. (1997, Spring–Summer). How to build a baby's brain. *Newsweek,* 28–32.

Bem, S. (1975). Androgyny versus the tight little lives of fluffy women and chesty men. *Psychology Today, 17,* 351–358.

Bem, S. (1993). *The lenses of gender: Transforming the debate on sexual inequality.* New Haven, CT: Yale University Press.

Benassi, V., Mahler, H., & Asdigian, N. (1993). The mindfulness of ostensibly thoughtless action. *Journal of Social Behavior and Personality, 8*(6), 67–82.

Benson, H. (1975). *The relaxation response.* New York: Morrow.

Benson, H. (1984). *Beyond the relaxation response.* New York: Morrow.

Berdyaev, N. (1954). *The meaning of the creative act* (D. Lowrie, Trans.). New York: HarperCollins. (Original work published 1914)

Beritoff, J. S. (1965). *Neural mechanisms of higher vertebrate behavior.* Boston: Little, Brown.

Berlas, S., Amabile, T., & Handel, M. (1979). *Effects of evaluation on children's artistic creativity.* Paper presented at the meeting of the American Psychological Association, New York.

Bernstein, D. (1990). Of carrots and sticks: A review of Deci and Ryan's intrinsic motivation and self-determination in human behavior. *Journal of the Experimental Analysis of Behavior, 54*(3), 323–332.

Besemer, S., & O'Quin, K. (1993). Assessing creative products: Progress and potentials. In S. Isaksen, M. Murdock, R. Firestien, & D. J. Treffinger (Eds.), *Nurturing and developing creativity: The emergence of a discipline.* Norwood, NJ: Ablex.

Bieri, J., Bradburn, W., & Galinski, M. (1958). Sex differences in perceptual behavior. *Journal of Personality, 26,* 1–12.

Bito, H., Tsien, R. W., & Deisseroth, K. (1996). Signaling from synapse to nucleus: Postsynaptic CREB phosphorylation during multiple forms of hippocampal synaptic plasticity. *Neuron, 1,* 89–101.

Block, J., & Block, J. H. (1980). The role of ego-control and ego-resiliency in the organization of behavior. In W. A. Collins (Ed.), *Minnesota symposia on child psychology.* Vol. 13. Hillsdale, NJ: Erlbaum.

Bloom, B. (1985). *Developing talent in young people.* New York: Ballantine Books.

Bloomberg, M. (1971). Creativity as related to field independence and mobility. *Journal of Genetic Psychology, 118,* 3–12.

Bond, A. (1995). Virginia Woolf: Manic depressive psychosis and genius. In B. Panter, M. Panter, E. Virshup, & B. Virshup (Eds.), *Creativity and madness: Psychological studies of art and artists.* Burbank, CA: Aimed Press.

Boorstin, D. (1992). *The creators: A history of heroes of the imagination.* New York: Random House.

Breuer, J., & Freud, S. (1917/1957). *Studies on hysteria.* New York: Basic Books.

Briggs, J. (1988). *Fire in the crucible: The alchemy of creative genius.* New York: St. Martin's Press.

Bruner, J. (1973). *Beyond the information given: Studies in the psychology of knowing.* New York: Norton.

Bryden, M. P., & Bulman-Fleming, M. B. (1994). Laterality effects in normal subjects: Evidence for interhemispheric interactions. *Behavioural Brain Research, 64,* 119–129.

Bucci, W. (1993). The development of emotional meaning in free association: A multiple code theory. In A. Wilson & J. Gedo (Eds.), *Hierarchical concepts in psychoanalysis: Theory, research, and clinical practice.* New York: Guilford Press.

Cameron, J., & Pierce, W. D. (1994). Reinforcement, reward, and intrinsic motivation: A meta-analysis. *Review of Educational Research, 64*(3), 363–423.

Campbell, D. (1960). Blind variation and selective retentions in creative thought as in other knowledge processes. *Psychological Review, 67,* 380–400.

Casey, M. B., Nuttall, R., & Pezaris, E. (1997). Mediators of gender differences in mathematics college entrance test scores. *Developmental Psychology, 33*(4), 669–680.

Chi, M. (1997). Creativity: Shifting across ontological categories flexibly. In T. Ward, S. Smith, & J. Vaid (Eds.), *Creative thought: An investigation of conceptual structures and processes.* Washington, DC: American Psychological Association.

Cicone, M., Gardner, H., & Winner, E. (1981). Understanding the psychology in psychological metaphors. *Journal of Child Language, 8*(1), 213–216.

Claridge, G. (1993). When is psychoticism psychoticism? And how does it really relate to creativity? *Psychological Inquiry, 4*(3), 184–188.

Cohen-Shalev, A. (1989). Old age styles: Developmental changes in creative production from a life-span perspective. *Journal of Aging Studies, 3*(1), 21–37.

Cohn, V. (1975). *Sister Kenny: The woman who challenged the doctors.* Minneapolis: University of Minnesota Press.

Coney, J., & Serna, P. (1995). Creative thinking from an information processing perspective: A new approach to Mednick's theory of associative hierarchies. *Journal of Creative Behavior, 29*(2), 109–131.

Connelly, M., Harris, R., Dacey, J., & King, J. (1995). *An evaluation of the effectiveness of a program of instruction in aggression control designed for inner city seventh grade students.* Unpublished manuscript, Boston College, Chestnut Hill, MA.

Conti, R., Coon, H., & Amabile, T. (1996). Evidence to support the componential model of creativity: Secondary analyses of three studies. *Creativity Research Journal, 9*(4), 385–395.

Cox, M., Owen, M., Henderson, V., & Margand, N. (1992). Prediction of infant-father and infant-mother attachment. *Developmental Psychology, 28*(3), 474–483.

Crain, W. (1980). *Theories of development: Concepts and applications.* Englewood Cliffs, NJ: Prentice Hall.

Cropley, A. (1997). Fostering creativity in the classroom: General principles. In M. A. Runco (Ed.), *The creativity research handbook.* Vol. 1. Cresskill, NJ: Hampton Press.

Crovitz, H. F. (1970). *Galton's walk.* New York: HarperCollins.

Csikszentmihalyi, M. (1990). *Flow: The psychology of optimal experience.* New York: HarperCollins.

Csikszentmihalyi, M. (1993). *The evolving self: A psychology for the third millennium.* New York: HarperCollins.

Csikszentmihalyi, M. (1994). The domain of creativity. In D. Feldman, M. Csikszentmihalyi, & H. Gardner (Eds.), *Changing the world: A framework for the study of creativity.* New York: Praeger.

Csikszentmihalyi, M. (1996). *Creativity: Flow and the psychology of discovery and invention.* New York: HarperCollins.

Csikszentmihalyi, M. (1997). *Finding flow.* New York: Basic Books.

Csikszentmihalyi, M., & Rathunde, K. (1993). Developmental perspectives on motivation. In J. Jacobs, (Ed.) *Nebraska symposium on motivation:*

Current theory and research in motivation, 40, 57–97, Lincoln, NE: University of Nebraska Press.

Csikszentmihalyi, M., Rathunde, K., & Whalen, S. (1993). *Talented teenagers: The roots of success and failure.* Cambridge, England: Cambridge University Press.

Dacey, J. (1976). *New ways to learn.* Stamford, CT: Greylock.

Dacey, J. (1986). *Adolescents today* (3rd ed.). Glenview, IL: Scott, Foresman.

Dacey, J. (1989a). Discriminating characteristics of the families of highly creative adolescents. *Journal of Creative Behavior, 23*(4), 263–271.

Dacey, J. (1989b). *Fundamentals of creative thinking.* San Francisco: Jossey-Bass.

Dacey, J. (1989c). Peak periods of creative growth across the lifespan. *Journal of Creative Behavior, 23*(4), 221–247.

Dacey, J., Amara, D., & Seavey, G. (1993, Fall). Reducing dropout rate in inner city middle school children through instruction in self control. *Journal of Research on Middle Level Education, 20*(2), 91–102.

Dacey, J., deSalvatore, L., & Robinson, J. (1997, Fall). The results of teaching middle school students two relaxation techniques as part of a conflict prevention program. *Research in Middle Level Education, 23.*

Dacey, J., & Gordon, M. (1971, February). *Implications of post-natal cortical development for creativity research.* Paper presented at the American Education Research Association Convention, New York City.

Dacey, J., Madaus, G., & Crellin, D. (1968, November). *Can creativity be facilitated? The critical period hypothesis.* Paper presented at the Ninth Annual Convention of the Educational Research Association of New York State, Kiamesho Lake.

Dacey, J., & Packer, A. (1992). *The nurturing parent: How to raise creative, loving, responsible children.* New York: Simon & Schuster.

Dacey, J., & Ripple, R. E. (1967). The facilitation of problem solving and verbal creativity by exposure to programmed instruction. *Psychology in the Schools, 4*(3), 240–245.

Dacey, J., & Travers, J. (1996). *Human development across the lifespan* (4th ed.). New York: McGraw-Hill.

Damon, W. (1995). Greater expectations: Overcoming the culture of indulgence in America's homes and schools. New York: Free Press.

Davidson, J., Deuser, R., & Sternberg, R. (1994). *Metacognition: Knowing about knowing.* Cambridge, MA: MIT Press.

Dawson, C. (1954). *Medieval essays.* New York: Image Books.

deBono, E. (1970). *Lateral thinking: Creativity step by step.* New York: HarperCollins.

deBono, E. (1971). *New think.* New York: Avon.

deBono, E. (1984). *The CORT thingking skills program.* New York: Pergamon Press.

deBono, E. (1992). *Serious creativity.* New York: HarperCollins.

Deci, E. (1971). Effects of externally mediated rewards on intrinsic motivation. *Journal of Personality and Social Psychology, 18,* 105–115.

Deci, E. (1975). *Intrinsic motivation.* New York: Plenum Press.

Del Vecchio, M., Zhou, H., Tully, T., & Yin, J. C. (1995). CREB as a memory modulator: Induced expression of a dCREB2 activator insoform enhances long-term memory in drosophila. *Cell, 81*(1), 107–115.

Dennis, W. (1956). Age and achievement. *Journal of Gerontology, 2,* 331–333.

Dennis, W. (1966). Creative productivity between twenty and eighty years. *Journal of Gerontology, 21,* 1–8.

Derks, P. (1985). Abstract: Creativity in Shakespeare's humor. *Journal of Creative Behavior, 19*(3), 218.

deWeid, D. (1995). ACTH neuropeptides, learning, and creativity. In N. E. Spear, L. P. Spear, & M. L. Woodruff (Eds.), *Neurobehavioral plasticity.* Hillsdale, NJ: Erlbaum.

Diamond, S. (1996). *Anger, madness, and the daimonic: The psychological genesis of violence, evil, and creativity.* New York: SUNY Press.

Dudek, S. (1993). Creativity and psychoticism: An overinclusive model. *Psychological Inquiry, 4*(3), 190–192.

Dudek, S., & Hall, W. (1992). Personality consistency: Eminent architects twenty-five years later. In R. Albert (Ed.), *Genius and eminence* (2nd ed.). New York: Pergamon Press.

Duncker, K. (1945). On problem solving (L. S. Lees, Trans.). *Psychological Monographs, 58*(Whole No. 270).

Durrheim, K., & Foster, D. (1997). Tolerance of ambiguity as a content specific construct. *Personality and Individual Differences, 22*(5), 741–750.

Ehrenzweig, A. (1975). *The psychoanalysis of artistic vision and hearing* (3rd ed.). London: Shelton.

Eisenberger, R., & Cameron, J. (1996). Detrimental effects of reward: Reality or myth? *American Psychologist, 51*(11), 1153–1166.

Eisenberger, R., & Cameron, J. (1998). Reward, intrinsic interest, and creativity: New findings. *American Psychologist, 53*(6), 676–679.

Eisenberger, R., & Selbst, M. (1994). Does reward increase or decrease creativity? *Journal of Personality and Social Psychology, 66*(6), 1116–1127.

Eisenman, R. (1997). Mental illness, deviance, and creativity. In M. A. Runco (Ed.), *The creativity research handbook.* Vol. 1. Cresskill, NJ: Hampton Press.

Eisenstadt, J. M. (1994). Parental loss and genius. In R. Frankiel (Ed.), *Essential papers on object loss.* New York: New York University Press.

Elkind, D. (1989). *The hurried child* (Rev. ed.). Reading, MA: Addison-Wesley.

Epstein, S. (1995). Elizabeth Layton: Life-long depression with healing in later life. In B. Panter, M. Panter, E. Virshup, & B. Virshup (Eds.), *Creativity and madness: Psychological studies of art and artists.* Burbank, CA: Aimed Press.

Epstein, R. (1996). *Cognition, creativity, and behavior.* New York: Praeger.

Esquivel, G. (1995). Teaching behaviors that foster creativity. *Educational Psychology Review, 7*(2), 185–202.

Eysenck, H. (1992a). *The decline and fall of the Freudian empire.* Washington, DC: Scott-Townsend.

Eysenck, H. (1992b). The definition and measurement of psychoticism. *Personality and Individual Differences, 13,* 757–785.

Eysenck, H. (1993a). Creativity and personality: An attempt to bridge divergent traditions. *Psychological Inquiry, 4*(3), 238–246.

Eysenck, H. (1993b). Creativity and personality: Suggestions for a theory. *Psychological Inquiry, 4*(3), 147–178.

Eysenck, H. (1994). The measurement of creativity. In M. Boden (Ed.), *Dimensions of creativity.* Cambridge, MA: MIT Press.

Eysenck, H. (1995). *Genius: The natural history of creativity.* Cambridge, England: Cambridge University Press.

Eysenck, H. (1996). Creativity and psychopathology: Answer to a paradox. In A. Montuori (Ed.), *Unusual associates: A Festschrift for Frank Barron.* Cresskill, NJ: Cresskill Press.

Eysenck, H. (1997). Creativity and personality. In M. A. Runco (Ed.), *The creativity research handbook.* Vol. 1. Cresskill, NJ: Hampton Press.

Falcone, D., & Loder, K. (1984). A modified lateral eye-movement measure, the right hemisphere, and creativity. *Perceptual and Motor Skills, 58*(3), 823–830.

Feldhusen, J., & Goh, B. (1995). Assessing and accessing creativity: An integrative review of theory, research, and development. *Creativity Research Journal, 8*(3), 231–247.

Feldman, D. (1980). *Beyond universals in cognitive development.* Norwood, NJ: Ablex.

Feldman, D., Csikszentmihalyi, M., & Gardner, H. (1994a). *Changing the world: A framework for the study of creativity.* New York: Praeger.

Feldman, D., Csikszentmihalyi, M., & Gardner, H. (1994b). A framework for the study of creativity. In D. Feldman, M. Csikszentmihalyi, & H. Gardner (Eds.), *Changing the world: A framework for the study of creativity.* New York: Praeger.

Findlay, C. S., & Lumsden, C. (1988a). *The creative mind.* Orlando, FL: Academic Press.

Findlay, C. S., & Lumsden, C. (1988b). The creative mind: Toward an evolutionary theory of discovery and innovation. *Journal of Social and Biological Structures, 11,* 3–55.

Finke, R. (1997). Mental imagery and visual creativity. In M. A. Runco (Ed.), *The creativity research handbook*. Vol. 1. Cresskill, NJ: Hampton Press.

Fowler, J. (1991). Stages in faith consciousness. In J. Fowler (Ed.), *Weaving the new creation*. San Francisco: HarperCollins.

Frankland, P. W., & others (1997). Spaced training induces normal long-term memory in CREB mutant mice. *Current Biology, 7*(1), 1–11.

Freeman, M. (1993). *Finding the muse: A sociopsychological inquiry into the conditions of artistic creativity*. Cambridge, England: Cambridge University Press.

Fromm, E. (1941). *Escape from freedom*. New York: Farrar, Straus & Giroux.

Fromm, E. (1959). The creative attitude. In H. H. Anderson (Ed.), *Creativity and its cultivation*. New York: HarperCollins.

Gabrielli, W. F., Jr., & Mednick, S. A. (1980). Sinistrality and delinquency. *Journal of Abnormal Psychology, 89*(5), 654–661.

Galton, F. (1870). *Hereditary genius*. Englewood Cliffs, NJ: Appleton-Century-Crofts.

Galton, F. (1879). Psychometric experiments. *Brain, 2*, 148–162.

Gamble, K., & Kellner, H. (1968). Creative functioning and cognitive regression. *Journal of Personality and Social Psychology, 9*, 266–271.

Garbarino, J. (1975). The impact of anticipated reward upon cross-age tutoring. *Journal of Personality and Social Psychology, 32*, 421–428.

Gardner, H. (1982). *Art, mind, and brain: A cognitive approach to creativity*. New York: Basic Books.

Gardner, H. (1988a). Creativity: An interdisciplinary perspective. *Creativity Research Journal, 1*, 8–26.

Gardner, H. (1988b). The need for more specificity. In C. S. Findlay & C. Lumsden (Eds.), *The creative mind*. Orlando, FL: Academic Press.

Gardner, H. (1991). *The unschooled mind: How children think and how schools should teach*. New York: Basic Books.

Gardner, H. (1993a). *Creating minds: An anatomy of creativity seen through the lives of Freud, Einstein, Picasso, Stravinsky, Eliot, Graham, and Gandhi*. New York: Basic Books.

Gardner, H. (1993b). *Multiple intelligences: The theory in practice*. New York: Basic Books.

Gardner, H. (1997a). *Extraordinary minds*. New York: Basic Books.

Gardner, H. (1997b). Six afterthoughts: Comments on "Varieties of intellectual talent." *Journal of Creative Behavior, 31*(2), 120–124.

Gardner, H., & Winner, E. (1982). Autumn leaves and old photographs: The development of metaphor preferences. *Journal of Experimental Child Psychology, 34*(1), 135–150.

Gardner, H., & Wolf, C. (1994). The fruits of asynchrony: A psychological examination of creativity. In D. Feldman, M. Csikszentmihalyi, & H. Gardner (Eds.), *Changing the world: A framework for the study of creativity.* New York: Praeger.

Gardner, K., & Moran, J. (1990). Family adaptability, cohesion, and creativity. *Creativity Research Journal, 3*(4), 281–286.

Gedo, J. (1996). *The artist and the emotional world: Creativity and personality.* New York: Columbia University Press.

Gedo, J. (1997). Psychoanalytic theories of creativity. In M. A. Runco (Ed.), *The creativity research handbook.* Vol. 1. Cresskill, NJ: Hampton Press.

Gerrard, G., Poteat, G. M., & Ironsmith, M. (1996). Promoting children's creativity: Effects of competition, self-esteem, and immunization. *Creativity Research Journal, 9*(4), 339–346.

Getzels, J. (1975). Creativity: Prospects and issues. In I. A. Taylor & J. W. Getzels (Eds.), *Perspectives in creativity.* Hawthorne, NY: Aldine de Gruyter.

Getzels, J., & Csikszentmihalyi, M. (1975). From problem solving to problem finding. In I. A. Taylor & J. W. Getzels (Eds.), *Perspectives in creativity.* Hawthorne, NY: Aldine de Gruyter.

Getzels, J., & Jackson, P. (1962). *Creativity and intelligence: Explorations with gifted students.* New York: Wiley.

Ghiselin, B. (1952). *The creative process.* Berkeley: University of California Press.

Gibbs, R. (1997). How language affects the embodied nature of creative cognition. In T. Ward, S. Smith, & J. Vaid (Eds.), *Creative thought: An investigation of conceptual structures and processes.* Washington, DC: American Psychological Association.

Gillette, E. (1992). Psychoanalysts' resistance to new ideas. *Journal of the American Psychoanalytic Association, 40,* 1232–1235.

Goertzel, M. G., Goertzel, V., & Goertzel, T. G. (1978). *Three hundred eminent personalities.* San Francisco: Jossey-Bass.

Golden, C. J. (1975). The measurement of creativity by the Stroop Color-Word Test. *Journal of Personality Assessment, 39,* 502–506.

Goodwin, F., & Jamison, K. R. (1990). Manic-depressive illness, creativity, and leadership. In F. Goodwin & K. R. Jamison (Eds.), *Manic-depressive illness.* Oxford, England: Oxford University Press.

Gordon, W. J. J. (1961). *Synectics: The development of creative capacity.* New York: HarperCollins.

Gordon, W. J. J. (1972). On being explicit about the creative process. *Journal of Creative Behavior, 6,* 295–300.

Gould, R. (1978). *Transformations.* New York: Simon & Schuster.

Gray, C. (1966). A measurement of creativity in Western civilization. *American Anthropologist, 68,* 1384–1417.

Greenberg, M. E., & Frank, D. A. (1994). CREB: A mediator of long-term memory from mollusks to mammals. *Cell, 79*(1), 5–8.

Greene, D., & Lepper, M. R. (1974). Effects of extrinsic rewards on children's subsequent intrinsic interest. *Child Development, 45,* 1141–1145.

Gruber, H. (1981). *Darwin on man: A psychological study of scientific creativity.* Chicago: University of Chicago Press.

Gruber, H. (1988). The evolving systems approach to creative work. *Creativity Research Journal, 1,* 27–51.

Gruber, H. (1995). Insight and affect in the history of science. In R. Sternberg & J. Davidson (Eds.), *The nature of insight.* Cambridge, MA: MIT Press.

Gruber, H., & Davis, S. (1988). Inching our way up Mount Olympus: The evolving-systems approach to creative thinking. In R. Sternberg (Ed.), *The nature of creativity: Contemporary psychological perspectives.* Cambridge, England: Cambridge University Press.

Gruber, H., Terrell, G., & Wertheimer, M. (Eds.). (1964). *Contemporary approaches to creative thinking.* Rockaway Beach, NY: Lieber-Atherton.

Grzeskowiak, S. (1996). Curiosity in small children and the childrearing style of their mothers. In A. Cropley & D. Dehn (Eds.), *Fostering the growth of high ability: European perspectives.* Norwood, NJ: Ablex.

Guilford, J. P. (1957). A revised structure of the intellect. *Report of Psychology, 19,* 1–63.

Guilford, J. P. (1962). Factors that aid and hinder creativity. *Teachers' College Record, 63,* 391.

Guilford, J. P. (1967). *The nature of human intelligence.* New York: McGraw-Hill.

Guilford, J. P. (1970). A multivariate analysis of some controlled-association tasks. *Journal of General Psychology, 83*(1), 119–134.

Guilford, J. P. (1975). Creativity: A quarter century of progress. In I. A. Taylor & J. W. Getzels (Eds.), *Perspectives in creativity.* Hawthorne, NY: Aldine de Gruyter.

Gustafson, R. (1991). The effect of alcohol on the quantity of creative production. *Psychological Reports, 69*(1), 83–90.

Gustafson, R., & Norlander, R. (1994). Effects of alcohol on persistent effort and deductive thinking during the preparation phase of the creative process. *Journal of Creative Behavior, 28,* 124–132.

Gustafson, R., & Norlander, R. (1995). Effects of creative and non-creative work on the tendency to drink alcohol during the restitution phase of the creative process. *Journal of Creative Behavior, 29*(1), 25–35.

Hadas, M. (1965). The Greek paradigm of self control. In R. Klausner (Ed.), *The quest for self control.* New York: Free Press.

Hallman, R. (1967). Techniques of creative teaching. *Journal of Creative Behavior, 1*(3), 325–330.

Hammer, E. F. (1984). *Creativity, talent, and personality.* Malabar, FL: Krieger.

Harrington, D. (1990). The ecology of human creativity: A psychological perspective. In M. A. Runco & R. Albert (Eds.), *Theories of creativity.* Thousand Oaks, CA: Sage.

Harrington, D., Block, J., & Block, J. H. (1983). Predicting creativity in preadolescence from divergent thinking in early childhood. *Journal of Personality and Social Psychology, 45*(3), 609–623.

Harrington, D., Block, J. H., & Block, J. H. (1992). Testing aspects of Carl Rogers' theory of creative environments: Child-rearing antecedents of creative potential in young adults. In R. Albert (Ed.), *Genius and eminence* (2nd ed.). New York: Pergamon Press.

Harth, E. (1993). *The creative loop: How the brain makes a mind.* Reading, MA: Addison-Wesley.

Hellige, J. (1993). *Hemispheric asymmetry: What's right and what's left.* Cambridge, MA: Harvard University Press.

Helson, R. (1992). Which of those young women with creative potential became productive? Personality in college and characteristics of parents. In R. Albert (Ed.), *Genius and eminence* (2nd ed.). New York: Pergamon Press.

Helson, R. (1996). In search of the creative personality. *Creativity Research Journal, 9*(4), 295–306.

Helson, R., & Crutchfield, R. (1970). Mathematicians: The creative researcher and the average Ph.D. *Journal of consulting and clinical psychology, 34,* 250–257.

Helson, R., Roberts, B., & Agronick, G. (1995). Enduringness and change in creative personality and the prediction of occupational creativity. *Journal of Personality and Social Psychology, 69*(6), 1173–1183.

Hennessey, B. (1989). The effect of extrinsic constraints on children's creativity while using a computer. *Creativity Research Journal, 2,* 151–168.

Hennessey, B. (1995). Social, environmental, and developmental issues and creativity. *Educational Psychology Review, 7(2),* 163–183.

Hennessey, B., & Amabile, T. (1998). Reward, intrinsic motivation, and creativity. *American Psychologist, 53*(6), 674–675.

Herrmann, N. (1981). The creative brain. *Training and Development Journal,* 11–16.

Herrmann, N. (1991). The creative brain. *Journal of Creative Behavior, 25*(4), 275–295.

Hersch, C. (1962). The cognitive functioning of the creative person: A developmental analysis. *Journal of Projective Techniques, 26,* 193–200.

Hines, T. (1991). The myth of right hemisphere creativity. *Journal of Creative Behavior, 25*(3), 223–227.

Hoppe, K. (1988). The present state of research on alexithymia: Critique of an "instrumentalizing" critique. *Psyche: Zeitschrift fuer Psychoanalyse und ihre Anwendungen, 43*(11), 1029–1043.

Hoppe, K. D., & Kyle, N. L. (1990). Dual brain, creativity, and health [Special Issue: Creativity and Health]. *Creativity Research Journal, 3*(2), 150–157.

Hunt, J. M. (1969). Has contemporary education failed? Has it been attempted? *Harvard Educational Review, 39*(2), 278–300.

Isaksen, S. (1983). Toward a model for the facilitation of creative problem solving. *Journal of Creative Behavior, 17*(1), 18–31.

Isaksen, S., & Dorval, K. (1992). Mode of symbolic representation and cognitive style. *Imagination, Cognition, and Personality, 11*(3), 271–277.

Isaksen, S., Dorval, K., Noller, R., & Firestien, F. (1993). The dynamic nature of creative problem solving. In S. Gryskiewicz (Ed.), *Discovering creativity.* Greensboro, NC: Center for Creative Leadership.

Jackson, P. W., & Messick, S. (1965). The person, the product, and the response: Conceptual problems in the assessment of creativity. *Journal of personality, 33*(3), 309–329.

James, W. (1880). Great men, great thoughts, and the environment. *Atlantic Monthly, 46,* 441–459.

James, W. (1890). *The principles of psychology.* New York: Henry Holt.

Jamison, K. R. (1993). *Touched with fire: Manic-depressive illness and the artistic temperament.* Toronto: Free Press.

Jamison, K. R. (1995, February). Manic-depressive illness and creativity. *Scientific American,* 62–67.

Jamison, K. R. (1997). Manic-depressive illness and creativity [Special Issue]. *Scientific American,* 44–49.

Jaquish, G., & Ripple, R. E. (1980). Divergent thinking and self-esteem in preadolescents and adolescents. *Journal of Youth and Adolescence, 9*(2), 143–152.

Jay, E., & Perkins, D. (1997). Problem finding: The search for mechanism. In M. A. Runco (Ed.), *The creativity research handbook.* Vol. 1. Cresskill, NJ: Hampton Press.

Jensen, A. (1969). How much can we boost IQ and scholastic achievement? *Harvard Educational Review, 39,* 1–123.

John-Steiner, V. (1997). *Notebooks of the mind: Explorations of thinking* (Rev. ed.). Oxford, England: Oxford University Press.

Jung, C. G. (1933). *Modern man in search of a soul.* Orlando, FL: Harcourt Brace.

Jung, C. G. (1956). *Two essays on analytical psychology.* New York: Meridian Books.

Jung, C. G. (1960). *The structure and dynamics of the psyche.* Princeton, NJ: Princeton University Press.

Jung, C. G. (1966). *The spirit in men, art, and literature.* New York: Bollingen Foundation.

Kaestner, K. H., & others. (1996). Targeting of the CREB gene leads to up-regulation of a novel CREB mRNA insoform. *EMBO Journal, 15*(5), 1098–1106.

Kamino, K., & others. (1997). Elevated amyloid beta protein (1–40) level induces CREB phosphorylation at serine-133 via p44/42 MAP kinanse (Erk1/2)-depeearch. *Biochemical and Biophysical Research Communications, 232*(3), 637–651.

Katz, A. (1997). Creativity and the cerebral hemispheres. In M. A. Runco (Ed.), *The creativity research handbook.* Vol. 1. Cresskill, NJ: Hampton Press.

Katz, A. N. (1983). Creativity and individual differences in asymmetric cerebral hemispheric functioning. *Empirical Studies of the Arts, 1*(1), 3–16.

Keirouz, K. (1990). Concerns of parents of gifted children: A research review. *Gifted Child Quarterly, 34*(2), 56–63.

Kemple, K., David, G., & Wang, Y. (1996). Preschoolers' creativity, shyness, and self-esteem. *Creativity Research Journal, 9*(4), 317–327.

Kernberg, O. (1993). The current status of psychoanalysis. *Journal of the American Psychoanalytic Association, 41,* 45–62.

Kernoodle-Loveland, K., & Olley, J. (1979). The effect of external reward on interest and quality of talk performance in children of high and low intrinsic motivation. *Child Development, 50,* 1207–1210.

Kerr, B., Schaffer, J., Chambers, C., & Hallowell, K. (1991). Substance use of creatively talented adults. *Journal of Creative Behavior, 25,* 145–153.

Kiebler, M., & others. (1996). Nitric oxide acts directly in the presynaptic neuron to produce long-term potentiation in cultured hippocampal neurons. *Cell, 87*(6), 1025–1035.

Kimball, R. (1993). *You the creator.* Portland, ME: Green Timber.

King, D. (1995). Applied spirituality: Expressing love and service. In R. J. Kus (Ed.), *Spirituality and chemical dependency.* Binghamton, NY: Haworth Press.

Kinsbourne, M. (1972). Eye and head turning indicates of cerebral lateralization. *Science, 176,* 539–541.

Kocel, K., Galin, D., Ornstein, R., & Merrin, E. L. (1972). Lateral eye movement and cognitive mode. *Psychonomic Science, 27*(4), 223–224.

Koestler, A. (1964). *The act of creation.* New York: Macmillan.

Koestner, R., Ryan, R., Bernieri, F., & Holt, K. (1984). Setting limits on children's behavior: The differential effects of controlling versus informational styles on intrinsic motivation and creativity. *Journal of Personality, 52,* 233–248.

Kogan, N. (1983). Stylistic variation in childhood and adolescence: Creativity, metaphor, cognitive styles. In P. H. Mussen (Ed.), *Handbook of child psychology.* Vol. 3. New York: Wiley.

Köhler, W. (1925). *The mentality of apes* (E. Winter, Trans.). Orlando, FL: Harcourt Brace.

Köhler, W. (1929). *Gestalt psychology.* New York: Liveright.

Kohn, A. (1993a). *Punished by rewards.* Boston: Houghton Mifflin.

Kohn, A. (1993b, September–October). Why incentive plans cannot work. *Harvard Business Review, 71,* 56–63.

Kokot, S., & Colman, J. (1997). The creative mode of being. *Journal of Creative Behavior, 31*(3), 212–226.

Konorski, J. (1967). *Integrative activity of the brain.* Chicago: University of Chicago Press.

Kris, E. (1952). *Psychoanalytic explorations in art.* New York: International Universities.

Kris, E. (1965a). On inspiration: Preliminary notes on emotional conditions in creative states. In H. M. Ruitenbeek (Ed.), *The creative imagination.* Chicago: Quadrangle Books.

Kris, E. (1965b). Psychoanalysis and the study of creative imagination. In H. M. Ruitenbeek (Ed.), *The creative imagination.* Chicago: Quadrangle Books.

Kroeber, A. (1944). *Configurations of culture growth.* Berkeley: University of California Press.

Laing, R. D. (1970). *Self and others.* New York: Pantheon Books.

Langer, E. (1993). A mindful education. *Educational Psychologist, 28*(1), 43–50.

Langer, E. (1996). *The power of mindful learning.* Reading, MA: Addison-Wesley.

Lapp, W., Collins, R., & Izzo, C. (1994). On the enhancement of creativity by alcohol: Pharmacology or expectation? *American Journal of Psychology, 107*(2), 173–206.

Lawson, A. E. (1976). Formal operations and field independence in a heterogeneous sample. *Perceptual and Motor Skills, 42,* 981–982.

Lehman, H. C. (1953). *Age and achievement.* Princeton, NJ: Princeton University Press.

Lehman, H. C. (1962). The creative production rates of present versus past generations of scientists. *Journal of Gerontology, 17,* 409–417.

Lehman, H. C. (1966). The psychologist's most creative years. *Psychology, 21,* 363–369.

Leonard, L. (1990). *Witness to the fire: Creativity and the veil of addiction.* Boston: Shambhala.

Lepper, M. (1998). A whole much less than the sum of its parts. *American Psychologist, 53,* 6, 675–676.

Lepper, M., & Greene, D. (1975). Turning play into work: Effects of adult surveillance and extrinsic rewards on children's intrinsic motivation. *Journal of Personality and Social Psychology, 31,* 479–486.

Lepper, M., Greene, D., & Nisbett, R. (1983). Undermining children's intrinsic interest with extrinsic rewards: A test of the overjustification hypothesis. *Journal of Personality and Social Psychology, 28,* 129–137.

Lepper, M., Sagotsky, G., Dafoe, J., & Greene, D. (1982). Consequences of superfluous social constraints: Effects on young children's social inferences and subsequent intrinsic interest. *Journal of Personality and Social Psychology, 42,* 51–65.

Lerner, R. (1995). *America's youth in crisis: Challenges and options for programs and policies.* Thousand Oaks, CA: Sage.

Lerner, R. (1996). Relative plasticity, integration, temporality, and diversity in human development: A developmental contextual perspective about theory, process, and method. *Developmental Psychology, 32,* 781–786.

Lerner, R. (Ed.). (forthcoming). *Handbook of child psychology* (5th ed.). Vol. 1. *Theoretical models of human development.* New York: Wiley.

Lerner, R., & Miller, J. (1994). Integrating scholarship and outreach in human development research, policy, and service: A developmental contextual perspective. In D. L. Featherman (Ed.), *Life-span development and behavior.* Vol. 12. Hillsdale, NJ: Erlbaum.

Lerner, R., & Simi, N. L. (1997, May). A holistic, integrated model of risk and protection in adolescence: A developmental contextual perspective about research, programs, and policies. Paper presented at *Developmental science and the holistic approach.* Symposium conducted at the Royal Swedish Academy of Sciences, Wiks Castle, Sweden.

Levinson, D. (1978). *Seasons of a man's life.* New York: Knopf.

Levinson, D. (1997). *Seasons of a woman's life.* New York: Ballantine Books.

Levy, J., & Reid, M. L. (1976). Variations in writing posture and cerebral organization. *Science, 194,* 337.

Litterst, J., & Eyo, B. (1993). Developing classroom imagination: Shaping and energizing a suitable climate for growth, discovery, and vision. *Journal of Creative Behavior, 27*(1), 270–282.

Logue, A. W. (1995). *Self-control: Waiting until tomorrow for what you want today.* Englewood Cliffs, NJ: Prentice Hall.

Loverock, D., & Modigliani, V. (1995). Visual imagery and the brain: A review. *Journal of Mental Imagery, 19*(1–2), 91–132.

Ludwig, A. (1992). Creative achievement and psychopathology: Comparisons among professions. *American Journal of Psychotherapy, 46,* 330–356.

Lumsden, C., & Wilson, E. O. (1983). *Promethean fire: Reflections on the origin of mind.* Cambridge, MA: Harvard University Press.

Luria, A. R. (1973). *The working brain: An introduction to neuropsychology.* New York: Basic Books.

MacKinnon, D. (1964). The creativity of architects. In C. W. Taylor (Ed.), *Widening horizons in creativity.* New York: Wiley.

MacKinnon, D. (1965). Personality and the realization of creative potential. *American Psychologist, 20,* 273–281.

MacKinnon, D. (1975). IPAR's contribution to the conceptualization and study of creativity. In I. A. Taylor & J. W. Getzels (Eds.), *Perspectives in creativity.* Hawthorne, NY: Aldine de Gruyter.

MacKinnon, D. (1978). *In search of human effectiveness: Identifying and developing creativity.* Buffalo, NY: Creative Education Foundation Press.

MacKinnon, D. (1992). The highly effective individual. In R. Albert (Ed.), *Genius and eminence* (2nd ed.). New York: Pergamon Press.

Maier, N. R. F. (1970). *Problem solving and creativity in individuals and groups.* Pacific Grove, CA: Brooks/Cole.

Mandal, M., Asthana, H., Pandey, R., & Sarbadhikari, S. (1996). Hemispheric balance. *Journal of Psychology, 130*(4), 447–459.

Markman, A., Yamauchi, T., & Makin, V. (1997). The creation of new concepts: A multifaceted approach to category learning. In T. Ward, S. Smith, & J. Vaid (Eds.), *Creative thought: An investigation of conceptual structures and processes.* Washington, DC: American Psychological Association.

Martindale, C. (1990). *The clockwork muse: The predictability of artistic change.* New York: Basic Books.

Martindale, C., & Dailey, A. (1996). Creativity, primary process cognition, and personality. *Personality and Individual Differences, 20*(4), 409–414.

Martindale, C., Hines, D., Mitchell, L., & Covella, E. (1984). EEG alpha asymmetry and creativity. *Personality and Individual Differences, 5*(1), 77–86.

Maslow, A. H. (1954). *Motivation and personality.* New York: HarperCollins.

Maslow, A. H. (1962). *Toward a psychology of being.* New York: Van Nostrand Reinhold.

Maslow, A. H. (1971). *The farther reaches of human nature.* New York: Viking Press.

Masson, J. M. (1984). *The assault on truth: Freud's suppression of the seduction theory.* New York: Farrar, Straus & Giroux.

Masson, J. M. (1990). Final analysis: *The making and unmaking of a psychoanalyst.* Reading, MA: Addison-Wesley.

Mayer, R. (1995). The search for insight: Grappling with Gestalt psychology's unanswered questions. In R. Sternberg & J. Davidson (Eds.), *The nature of insight.* Cambridge, MA: MIT Press.

McWhinnie, H. (1967). Some relationships between creativity and perception in sixth-grade children. *Perceptual and Motor Skills, 25*(3), 979–980.

McGaugh, J. L., & Guzowski, J. F. (1997). Antisense oligodeoxynucleotide-mediated disruption of hippocampal cAMP response element binding protein levels impairs consolidation of memory for water maze training. *Proceedings of the National Academy of Sciences, 94*(6), 2693–2698.

McKeever, W., & VanDeventer, A. (1977). Failure to confirm a spatial ability impairment in persons with evidence of right hemisphere speech capability. *Cortex, 13*(3), 321–326.

Meador, K. (1992). Emerging rainbows: A review of the literature on creativity in preschoolers. *Journal for the Education of the Gifted, 15*(2), 163–181.

Meckstroth, E. (1990). Parents' role in encouraging highly gifted children. *Roeper Review, 12*(1), 208–210.

Mednick, S. A. (1962). The associative basis of the creative process. *Psychological Review, 69,* 220–232.

Mellou, E. (1996). The two-conditions view of creativity. *Journal of Creative Behavior, 30*(2), 126–143.

Mendecka, G. (1996). Attitudes of parents and development of creativity. In A. Cropley & D. Dehn (Eds.), *Fostering the growth of high ability: European perspectives.* Norwood, NJ: Ablex.

Michel, M., & Dudek, S. (1991). Mother-child relationships and creativity. *Creativity Research Journal, 4*(3), 281–286.

Miller, B. L., & others. (1996). Enhanced artistic creativity with temporal lobe degeneration. *Lancet, 348,* 1744–1745.

Mischel, W., Shoda, Y., & Rodriguez, M. L. (1989). Delay of gratification in children. *Science, 244,* 933–938.

Mockros, C. (1996). The social context of extraordinary individuals. *Advanced Development Journal, 7,* 19–38.

Molle, M., & others. (1996). Enhanced dynamic complexity in the human EEG during creative thinking. *Neuroscience Letters, 208,* 61–64.

Moneta, G. (1993). A model of scientists' creative potential: The matching of cognitive structure and domain structure. *Philosophical Psychology, 6*(1), 22–37.

Montour, K. (1977). William James Sidis: The broken twig. *American Psychologist, 32*(4), 265–279.

Montuori, A. (1996). Frank Barron's ecological vision. In A. Montuori (Ed.), *Unusual associates: A Festschrift for Frank Barron*. Cresskill, NJ: Hampton Press.

Montuori, A. (1997). The courage to go naked. In F. Barron, A. Montuori, & A. Barron (Eds.), *Creators on creating*. Los Angeles: Tarcher.

Moon, S., Kelly, K., & Feldhusen, J. (1997). Specialized counseling services for gifted youth and their families: A needs assessment. *Gifted Child Quarterly, 41*(1), 16–25.

Moore, A. N., Dixon, C. E., & Dash, P. K. (1995). Spatial memory deficits, increased phosphorylation of the transcription factor CREB, and induction of the AP-1 complex following experimental brain injury. *Journal of Neuroscience, 3*, 2030–2039.

Moore, M. (1967). The monkey puzzle. *The complete poems of Marianne Moore*. New York: Viking.

Moukwa, M. (1995). A structure to foster creativity: An industrial experience. *Journal of Creative Behavior, 29*(1), 54–63.

Muuss, R. E. (1996). *Theories of adolescence* (6th ed.). New York: Random House.

Neimark, E. E. (1975). Individual differences and the role of cognitive style in cognitive development. *Genetic Psychological Monographs, 91*, 171–225.

Noppe, L. D. (1985). The relationship of formal thought and cognitive styles to creativity. *Journal of Creative Behavior, 19*, 88–96.

Norlander, T., & Gustafson, R. (1996). Effects of alcohol on scientific thought during the incubation phase of the creative process. *Journal of Creative Behavior, 30*(4), 231–248.

Noy, P. (1969). A revision of the psychoanalytic theory of the primary process. *International Journal of Psycho-Analysis, 50*, 155–178.

Ochse, A. (1991). Why there were relatively few eminent women creators. *Journal of Creative Behavior, 25*(4), 334–343.

O'Quin, K., & Derks, P. (1997). Humor and creativity: A review of the empirical literature. In M. A. Runco (Ed.), *The creativity research handbook*. Vol. 1. Cresskill, NJ: Hampton Press.

Oremland, J. (1997). *The origins and psychodynamics of creativity: A psychoanalytic perspective*. Madison, CT: International Universities Press.

Orenstein, P. (1994). *School girls: Young women, self-esteem, and the confidence gap*. New York: Doubleday.

Panter, B. (1995). Vincent van Gogh: Creativity and madness. In B. Panter, M. Panter, E. Virshup, & B. Virshup (Eds.), *Creativity and madness: Psychological studies of art and artists*. Burbank, CA: Aimed Press.

Panter, B., Panter, M., Virshup, E., & Virshup, B. (Eds.). (1995). *Creativity and madness: Psychological studies of art and artists*. Burbank, CA: Aimed Press.

Parnes, S. J., & Harding, H. F. (Eds.). (1962). *Source book for creative thinking.* New York: Scribner.

Payne, D. A., & Evans, K. A. (1985). The relationship of laterality to academic aptitude. *Educational and Psychological Measurement, 45,* 971–976.

Penfield, W., & Roberts, L. (1959). *Speech and brain mechanisms.* Princeton, NJ: Princeton University Press.

Perkins, D. (1981). *The mind's best work.* Cambridge, MA: Harvard University Press.

Perkins, D. (1992). *Smart schools: From training memories to educating minds.* New York: Free Press.

Perkins, D. (1997). Creativity's camel: The role of analogy in invention. In T. Ward, S. Smith, & J. Vaid (Eds.), *Creative thought: An investigation of conceptual structures and processes.* Washington, DC: American Psychological Association.

Pesut, D. (1990). Creative thinking as a self-regulatory metacognitive process: A model for education, training, and further research. *Journal of Creative Behavior, 24*(2), 105–110.

Picariello, M. (1994). *Children's perceptions of autonomy in the classroom: Implications for intrinsic motivation, learning, and creativity.* Unpublished doctoral dissertation, Brandeis University.

Pohlman, L. (1996). Creativity, gender, and the family: A study of creative writers. *Journal of Creative Behavior, 30*(1), 1–24.

Rank, O. (1945). *Will therapy and truth and reality* (J. Taft, Trans.). New York: Knopf.

Rank, O. (1965). Life and creation. In H. M. Ruitenbeek (Ed.), *The creative imagination.* Chicago: Quadrangle Books.

Reber, A. (1985). Syntactical learning and judgment, still unconscious and still abstract: Comment on Dulany, Carlson, and Dewey. *Journal of Experimental Psychology: General, 114*(1), 17–24.

Reite, M., & others. (1995). MEG based brain laterality: Sex differences in normal adults. *Neuropsychologia, 33*(12), 1607–1616.

Restak, R. M. (1984). *The brain.* New York: Bantam Books.

Restak, R. M. (1991). *The brain has a mind of its own.* New York: Harmony Books.

Rhodes, C. (1990). Growth from deficiency creativity to being creativity. *Creativity Research Journal, 3*(4), 287–299.

Richards, R. (1993). Everyday creativity, eminent creativity, and psychopathology. *Psychological Inquiry, 4*(3), 212–217.

Richards, R. (1994). Creativity and bipolar mood swings: Why the association? In M. P. Shaw & M. A. Runco (Eds.), *Creativity and affect.* Norwood, NJ: Ablex.

Richards, R. (1996). Beyond Piaget: Accepting divergent, chaotic, and creative thought. In M. A. Runco (Ed.), *Creativity from childhood through adulthood: The developmental issues.* San Francisco: Jossey-Bass.

Richards, R., & Kinney, D. (1990). Mood swings and creativity. *Creativity Research Journal, 3*(3), 202–217.

Ripple, R. E., & Dacey, J. S. (1969). Relationships of some adolescent characteristics and verbal creativity. *Psychology in the Schools, 6*(3), 321–324.

Robertson, M. (1995). Sylvia Plath: A blind girl playing with a slide rule of values. In B. Panter, M. Panter, E. Virshup, & B. Virshup (Eds.), *Creativity and madness: Psychological studies of art and artists.* Burbank, CA: Aimed Press.

Roe, A. (1946). The personality of artists. *Educational and Psychological Measurement, 6,* 401–408.

Roe, A. (1975). Painters and painting. In I. A. Taylor & J. W. Getzels (Eds.), *Perspectives in creativity.* Hawthorne, NY: Aldine de Gruyter.

Rogers, C. R. (1938). *Client-centered therapy.* Boston: Houghton Mifflin.

Rogers, C. R. (1954). Toward a theory of creativity. *ETC: A Review of General Semantics, 11,* 249–260.

Rogers, C. R. (1959). Toward a theory of creativity. In H. H. Anderson (Ed.), *Creativity and its cultivation.* New York: HarperCollins.

Rogers, V. (1995). Elizabeth Layton: Maverick model of personality growth in later life. In B. Panter, M. Panter, E. Virshup, & B. Virshup (Eds.), *Creativity and madness: Psychological studies of art and artists.* Burbank, CA: Aimed Press.

Rosenzweig, M. (1964, June). Effects of heredity and environment on brain chemistry, anatomy and learning ability in the rat. In A. J. Edwards & J. F. Cawley (Coordinators), *University of Kansas symposium: Physiological determinates of behavior.* Lawrence: University of Kansas School of Education Publications.

Rothenberg, A. (1979). Translogical secondary process cognition in creativity. *Journal of Altered States of Consciousness, 4*(2), 171–187.

Rothenberg, A. (1990). Creativity, mental health, and alcoholism. *Creativity Research Journal, 3*(2), 170–201.

Rothenberg, A. (1993). Creativity: Complex and healthy. *Psychological Inquiry, 4*(3), 217–221.

Rothenberg, A., & Hausman, C. R. (1976). *The creativity question.* Durham, NC: Duke University Press.

Roy, D. (1996). Personality model of fine artists. *Creativity Research Journal, 9*(4), 391–394.

Runco, M. A. (1993). Creativity, causality, and the separation of personality and cognition. *Psychological Inquiry, 4*(3), 221–225.

Runco, M. A. (1994). Creativity and its discontents. In M. P. Shaw & M. A. Runco (Eds.), *Creativity and affect*. Norwood, NJ: Ablex.

Runco, M. A. (1996a). Creativity and development: Recommendations. In M. A. Runco (Ed.), *Creativity from childhood through adulthood: The developmental issues*. San Francisco: Jossey-Bass.

Runco, M. A. (1996b). Personal creativity: Definition and developmental issues. In M. A. Runco (Ed.), *Creativity from childhood through adulthood: The developmental issues*. San Francisco: Jossey-Bass.

Runco, M. A. (Ed.). (1994). *Problem finding, problem solving, and creativity*. Norwood, NJ: Ablex.

Runco, M. A., & Charles, R. (1997). Developmental trends in creative potential and creative performance. In M. A. Runco (Ed.), *The creativity research handbook*. Vol. 1. Cresskill, NJ: Hampton Press.

Russ, S. W. (1993). *Affect and creativity*. Hillsdale, NJ: Erlbaum.

Ryan, R., & Grolnick, W. (1986). Origins and pawns in the classroom: Self-report and projective assessments of individual differences in children's perceptions. *Journal of Personality and Social Psychology, 50,* 550–558.

Sadker, M., & Sadker, D. (1994). *Failing at fairness: How America's schools cheat girls*. New York: Scribner.

Sapolsky, R. (1997, October). A gene for nothing. *Discover,* 40–46.

Sarnoff, D. P., & Cole, H. P. (1983). Creative and personal growth. *Journal of Creative Behavior, 17*(2), 95–102.

Sasser-Coen, J. (1993). Qualitative changes in creativity in the second half of life: A life-span developmental perspective. *Journal of Creative Behavior, 27*(1), 18–27.

Schalling, D. (1978, August 1). *Psychopathy: A partial interhemispheric disconnection syndrome? A neuropsychological analysis*. Paper presented at the symposium Psychophysiology and Neuropsychology of Psychopathic and Antisocial Behavior, Munich.

Schank, R., & Cleary, C. (1995). Making machines creative. In S. Smith, T. Ward, & R. Finke (Eds.), *The creative cognition approach*. Cambridge, MA: MIT Press.

Schuldberg, D. (1990). Schizotypal and hypomanic traits, creativity, and physical health. *Creativity Research Journal, 3,* 218–230.

Schuldberg, D. (1996). How to do things with "health": Reflections on ego strength and the theory and measurement of psychological well-being. In A. Montuori (Ed.), *Unusual associates: A Festschrift for Frank Barron*. Cresskill, NJ: Hampton Press.

Schwartz, B. (1990). The creation and destruction of value. *American Psychologist, 45*(1), 7–15.

Selye, H. (1956). *The stress of life.* New York: McGraw-Hill.

Selye, H. (1974). *Stress without distress.* Philadelphia: Lippincott.

Selye, H. (1975, October). Implications of stress concept. *New York State Journal of Medicine,* 2139–2145.

Selye, H. (1982). History and present status of the stress concept. In L. Goldberger & S. Breznitz (Eds.), *Handbook of stress: Theoretical and clinical aspects.* New York: Free Press.

Shapiro, D., Potkin, S., Jin, Y., & Brown, B. (1993). Measuring the psychological construct of control: Discriminant, divergent, and incremental validity of the Shapiro Control Inventory and Rotter's and Wallstons' Locus of Control Scales. *International Journal of Psychosomatics, 40*(1–4), 35–46.

Shapiro, D., Sandman, C., Grossman, M., & Grossman, B. (1995). Aging and sense of control. *Psychological Reports, 77*(2), 616–618.

Shekerjian, D. (1991). *Uncommon genius: Tracing the creative impulse with forty winners of the MacArthur Award.* New York: Penguin Books.

Sheldon, K. (1995). Creativity and goal conflict. *Creativity Research Journal, 8*(3), 299–306.

Shoben, E., & Gagne, C. (1997). Thematic relations and the creation of combined concepts. In T. Ward, S. Smith, & J. Vaid (Eds.), *Creative thought: An investigation of conceptual structures and processes.* Washington, DC: American Psychological Association.

Simonton, D. K. (1992). Personality correlates of exceptional personal influence: A note on Thorndike's (1950) creators and leaders. In R. Albert (Ed.), *Genius and eminence* (2nd ed.). New York: Pergamon Press.

Simonton, D. K. (1993). Foresight in insight: A Darwinian answer. In J. Brockman (Series Ed.) *Creativity: Vol. 4. The reality club.* New York: Touchstone.

Simonton, D. K. (1994). Creativity inside out—but not upside down. *Contemporary Psychology, 39*(1), 12–13.

Simonton, D. K. (1995a). Exceptional personal influence: An integrative paradigm. *Creativity Research Journal, 8*(4), 371–376.

Simonton, D. K. (1995b). Many are called, but few are chosen. *Contemporary Psychology, 40*(8), 733–735.

Skinner, B. F. (1971). *Beyond freedom and dignity.* New York: Knopf.

Smith, G., & Amner, G. (1997). Creativity and perception. In M. A. Runco (Ed.), *The creativity research handbook.* Vol. 1. Cresskill, NJ: Hampton Press.

Smith, S., Ward, T., & Finke, R. (1995a). Cognitive processes in creative contexts. In S. Smith, T. Ward, & R. Finke (Eds.), *The creative cognition approach.* Cambridge, MA: MIT Press.

Smith, S., Ward, T., & Finke, R. (1995b). *The creative cognition approach.* Cambridge, MA: MIT Press.

Sonuga-Barke, E. J., Lea, S. E. G., & Webley, P. (1989). Children's choice: Sensitivity to changes in reinforcer density. *Journal of the Experimental Analysis of Behavior, 46,* 185–197.

Spence, S. A. (1996). Free will in the light of neuropsychiatry. *Philosophy, Psychiatry, and Psychology, 3*(2), 75–90.

Spotts, J., & Mackler, B. (1967). Relationships of field-dependent and field-independent cognitive styles to creative test performance. *Perceptual and Motor Skills, 24,* 239–268.

Springer, S. P., & Deutsch, G. (1981). *Left brain, right brain.* New York: Freeman.

Springer, S. P., & Deutsch, G. (1993). *Left brain, right brain* (4th ed.). New York: Freeman.

Stanley, J. C., George, W. C., & Solano, C. H. (1977). *The gifted and the creative.* Baltimore: Johns Hopkins University Press.

Stavridou, A., & Furnham, A. (1996). The relationship between psychoticism, trait-creativity, and the attentional mechanism of cognitive inhibition. *Personality and Individual Differences, 21*(1), 143–153.

Sternberg, R. (1997). Componential analysis: A recipe. In D. K. Detterman (Ed.), *Current topics in human intelligence.* Vol. 1. Norwood, NJ: Ablex.

Sternberg, R., & Grigorenko, E. (1997). Are cognitive styles still in style? *American Psychologist, 52*(7), 700–712.

Sternberg, R., & Lubart, T. (1992). Buy low and sell high: An investment approach to creativity. *Current Directions in Psychological Science, 1*(1), 1–5.

Sternberg, R., & Lubart, T. (1993a). Creative giftedness: A multivariate investment approach. *Gifted Child Quarterly, 37*(1), 7–15.

Sternberg, R., & Lubart, T. (1993b). Investing in creativity. *Psychological Inquiry, 4*(3), 229–232.

Sternberg, R., & Lubart, T. (1995). *Defying the crowd: Cultivating creativity in a culture of conformity.* New York: Free Press.

Sternberg, R., & Lubart, T. (1996). Investing in creativity. *American Psychologist, 51*(7), 677–688.

Stone, C., & Day, M. (1980). Competence and performance models and the characterization of formal operational skills. *Human Development, 23,* 323–353.

Storr, A. (1988). *Solitude: A return to the self.* New York: Free Press.

Swietochowski, W., & Poraj, G. (1996). Parental attitudes and Type A behavior in high and low creative adolescents. In A. Cropley & D. Dehn (Eds.), *Fostering the growth of high ability: European perspectives.* Norwood, NJ: Ablex.

Tagano, D., Fin, V., & Moran, J. (1983). Divergent thinking and hemispheric dominance for language functioning among preschool children. *Perceptual and Motor Skills, 56,* 691–698.

Tavalin, F. (1995). Context for creativity: Listening to voices, allowing a pause. *Journal of Creative Behavior, 29*(2), 133–142.

Taylor, C. W. (1964). Some knowns, needs, and leads. In C. W. Taylor (Ed.), *Creativity: Progress and potential.* New York: McGraw-Hill.

Taylor, I. A. (1975). A retrospective view of creativity investigation. In I. A. Taylor & J. W. Getzels (Eds.), *Perspectives in creativity.* Hawthorne, NY: Aldine de Gruyter.

Taylor, I. A., & Getzels, J. W. (Eds.). (1975). *Perspectives in creativity.* Hawthorne, NY: Aldine de Gruyter.

TenHouten, W. D. (1994). Creativity, intentionality, and alexthymia: A graphological analysis of split brained patients and normal controls. In M. P. Shaw & M. A. Runco (Eds.), *Creativity and Affect.* Norwood, NJ: Ablex.

Thagard, P. (1997). Coherent and creative conceptual combinations. In T. Ward, S. Smith, & J. Vaid (Eds.), *Creative thought: An investigation of conceptual structures and processes.* Washington, DC: American Psychological Association.

Torrance, E. P. (1963). *Education and the creative potential.* Minneapolis: University of Minnesota Press.

Torrance, E. P. (1968). A longitudinal examination of the fourth grade slump in creativity. *Gifted Child Quarterly, 12,* 195–199.

Torrance, E. P. (1970). Influence of dyadic interaction on creative functioning. *Psychological Reports, 26,* 391–394.

Torrance, E. P. (1974a). *Verbal test booklet A: Torrance tests of creative thinking.* Bensenville, IL: Scholastic Testing.

Torrance, E. P. (1974b). *Verbal test booklet B: Torrance tests of creative thinking.* Bensenville, IL: Scholastic Testing.

Torrance, E. P. (1975). Creativity research in education: Still alive. In I. A. Taylor & J. W. Getzels (Eds.), *Perspectives in creativity.* Hawthorne, NY: Aldine de Gruyter.

Torrance, E. P. (1979). *The search for satori.* Buffalo, NY: Creative Education Foundation Press.

Torrance, E. P. (1982). Can we teach children to think creatively? *Journal of Creative Behavior, 6,* 114–143.

Torrance, E. P. (1988). The nature of creativity as manifest in its testing. In R. Sternberg (Ed.), *The nature of creativity: Contemporary psychological perspectives.* Cambridge, England: Cambridge University Press.

Torrance, E. P. (1995a). The beyonders. In *Why fly? A philosophy of creativity.* Norwood, NJ: Ablex.

Torrance, E. P. (1995b). The beyonders after thirty years. In *Why fly? A philosophy of creativity.* Norwood, NJ: Ablex.

Torrance, E. P. (1995c). Courage. In *Why fly? A philosophy of creativity.* Norwood, NJ: Ablex.

Torrance, E. P. (1995d). *Why fly? A philosophy of creativity.* Norwood, NJ: Ablex.

Torrance, E. P., Peterson, P., & Davis, D. (1963). *Revised originality scale for evaluating creative writing.* Minneapolis: University of Minnesota Press.

Torrance, E. P., & Templeton, D. (1963). *Manual for Verbal Form A: Minnesota Tests of Creative Thinking.* Minneapolis: University of Minnesota Press.

Treffinger, D. J., Ripple, R. E., & Dacey, J. S. (1968). Teacher's attitudes toward creativity. *Journal of Creative Behavior, 2*(4), 242–248.

Tully, T., & Yin, J. C. (1996). CREB and the formation of long-term memory. *Current Opinion on Neurobiology, 6*(2), 264–268.

Urban, K. (1991). On the development of creativity in children. *Creativity Research Journal, 4,* 177–191.

Vaillant, G. (1977). *Adaptation to life.* Boston: Little, Brown.

Vare, A., & Ptacek, G. (1987). *Mothers of invention: From the bra to the bomb, forgotten women and their unforgettable ideas.* New York: Morrow.

Virshup, E. (1995). Jackson Pollock: Art versus alcohol. In B. Panter, M. Panter, E. Virshup, & B. Virshup (Eds.), *Creativity and madness: Psychological studies of art and artists.* Burbank, CA: Aimed Press.

Voyer, D. (1994). Anomalous dominance, sex, and laterality. *Brain and Cognition, 26,* 211–216.

Wallace, A. (1986). *The prodigy: William James Sidis, America's greatest child prodigy.* New York: NAL/Dutton.

Wallas, G. (1926). *The art of thought.* Orlando, FL: Harcourt Brace.

Ward, T. (1995). What's old about new ideas? In S. Smith, T. Ward, & R. Finke (Eds.), *The creative cognition approach.* Cambridge, MA: MIT Press.

Ward, T., Finke, R., & Smith, S. (1995). *Creativity and the mind.* New York: Plenum.

Warick, L., & Warick, E. (1995). Edvard Munch: A study of loss, grief, and creativity. In B. Panter, M. Panter, E. Virshup, & B. Virshup (Eds.), *Creativity and madness: Psychological studies of art and artists.* Burbank, CA: Aimed Press.

Weber, R., & Perkins, D. (1992). *Inventive minds: Creativity in technology.* Oxford, England: Oxford University Press.

Webster, R. (1995). *Why Freud was wrong: Sin, science, and psychoanalysis.* New York: Basic Books.

Welsh, G. (1959). *Figure preference test: Preliminary manual.* Palo Alto, CA: Consulting Psychologists Press.

Werner, H. (1957). The concept of development from a comparative and organismic point of view. In D. B. Harris (Ed.), *The concept of development: An issue in the study of behavior.* Minneapolis: University of Minnesota Press.

Wertheimer, M. (1945). *Productive thinking.* New York: HarperCollins.

Whitebook, J. (1994). Sublimation: A frontier concept. In A. K. Richards & A. D. Richards (Eds.), *The spectrum of psychoanalysis: Essays in honor of Martin S. Bergman.* Madison, CT: International Universities Press.

Wicker, F. (1985). A rhetorical look at humor as creativity. *Journal of Creative Behavior, 19*(3), 175–184.

Wilson, E. O. (1975). *Sociobiology.* Cambridge, MA: Harvard University Press.

Wilson, E. O. (1978). *On human nature.* Cambridge, MA: Harvard University Press.

Wilson, E. (1988). Evaluation of Findlay and Lumsden model. In C. S. Findlay & C. Lumsden (Eds.), *The creative mind.* Orlando, FL: Academic Press.

Wink, P. (1991). Self- and object-directedness in adult women. *Journal of Personality, 59,* 769–791.

Winner, E. (1996). *Gifted children: Myths and realities.* New York: Basic Books.

Witken, H., & others. (1954). *Personality through perception.* New York: HarperCollins.

Witken, H., & others. (1962). *Psychological differentiation.* New York: Wiley.

Woodman, R., & Schoenfeldt, L. (1990). An interactionist model of creative behavior. *Journal of Creative Behavior, 24*(4), 279–290.

Zamb, Z. (1970). Laterality and right-left orientation in developmental disorders of reading and writing. *Psychologia a Patopsychologia Dietata, 5*(4), 303–317.

Zerbe, K. (1992). The phoenix rises from Eros, not ashes: Creative collaboration in the lives of five impressionist and postimpressionist women artists. *Journal of the American Academy of Psychoanalysis, 20*(2), 295–315.

Zimmerman, E. (1997). I don't want to sit in the corner cutting out valentines: Leadership roles for teachers of talented art students. *Gifted Child Quarterly, 41*(1), 33–41.

THE AUTHORS

JOHN DACEY is professor and chair of the Fifth Year Program in Developmental Psychology at Boston College, where he has taught since 1966. That is also the year he received his Ph.D. from Cornell University. He is the recipient of numerous grants for the study of the cognitive development in adolescents and adults. He is the author or coauthor of eight textbooks, one trade book, and twenty-six journal articles on various aspects of creativity and self-control. He is also a psychotherapist, licensed in the Commonwealth of Massachusetts since 1973. He specializes in clients who are experiencing problems with self-control. For thirteen years, he was codirector of a weekend camp at which creative problem-solving skills were taught to teenagers, some of whom were emotionally disturbed. He is married to Linda Schulman, a professor of mathematics education at Lesley College in Cambridge, Massachusetts. They live in Lexington, Massachusetts.

KATHLEEN LENNON has had a lifelong interest in creativity. She received her bachelor's degree in fine arts and modern languages from Regis College in 1963. After a number of years spent primarily in raising her three daughters, she returned to academic pursuits and earned her M.A. in counseling psychology at Framingham State College and her Ph.D. in educational and developmental psychology at Boston College. Her other activities include performing in community theater, singing, and arranging a cappella harmony. She lives in Needham, Massachusetts, with her husband, John, a vice president and mutual funds manager at Colonial Management Associates/Liberty Financial, and with too many animals.

NAME INDEX

A

Abra, J., 87, 147
Adler, A., 39, 136–137
Adorno, T. W., 70
Agronick, G., 87, 98
Aguilar-Alonso, A., 98
Albert, R., 26, 48–50, 56, 59, 63, 87, 98
Amabile, T., 50, 51, 64, 72, 79, 80, 81, 83, 84, 108, 114, 224, 244
Amara, D., 117, 120
Amner, G., 103
Ansbacher, H. L., 56
Ansbacher, R. R., 56
Arieti, S., 89, 90–91, 92, 147, 211
Arlin, P. K., 162
Asthana, H., 210
Atkinson, J., 104

B

Bailin, S., 7
Bakan, P., 213
Bandura, A., 126, 127
Barron, F., 47, 85–86, 98, 99, 106, 148–149, 234
Barzun, J., 29
Baumrind, D., 53, 64, 117
Begley, S., 119, 192
Bem, S., 107, 110, 111, 231
Benassi, V., 178
Benson, H., 124, 125
Berdyaev, N., 25
Berlas, S., 79
Bernieri, F., 71
Bernstein, D., 81

Besemer, S., 10
Bieri, J., 160
Bito, H., 194
Block, J., 60, 163–164
Block, J. H., 60, 163–164
Bloom, B., 65
Bloomberg, M., 160
Boorstin, D., 18, 22
Bouillard, J., 30
Brackfield, S., 79, 80, 244
Bradburn, W., 160
Breuer, J., 37
Briggs, J., 140
Brown, B., 129
Bruner, J., 168
Bryden, M. P., 216–217
Bucci, W., 139
Bulman-Fleming, M. B., 216–217

C

Cameron, K., 81
Campbell, D., 224
Casey, M. B., 207, 208, 210
Chambers, C., 145
Charles, R., 104
Cheek, J. M., 224
Chi, M., 167
Cicone, M., 182
Claridge, G., 144
Cleary, C., 7
Cohen-Shalev, A., 88
Cohn, V., 113
Cole, H. P., 99
Collins, A., 98
Collins, R., 146

SUBJECT INDEX

A

Academic aptitude, neurobiological factors in, 213

Accuracy. *See* Convergent thinking

ACTH (neurotransmitting hormones), 196–200, 215, 228

Adaptation-Innovation Inventory, 214

Addiction theories of creativity, 145–147

Adler, Alfred, 39, 90–91

Aesthetic needs, 137

Age of Enlightenment, 25–26

Aging, creative productivity and, 43–44, 86–88, 147

Alcohol and drug use, creativity and, 137, 145–147

Alexithymia, 205

Ambiguity, tolerance of, 98–99, 226–227, 246

Analogy, creative cognition and, 168, 183

Apraxia, 205

Archimedes, 17

Aristotle, 17, 27

Art as catharsis, 143–144, 148, 151

Art, Mind, and Brain: A Cognitive Approach to Creativity (Gardner), 164

Art of Thought, The (Wallas), 34

Associationism, 17, 27–30, 33–34, 153–157

Asymmetry, preference for, 106

Autotelic personality, 112

B

Bach, J. S., 250

Behaviorist psychology, 127, 138

Bicameral mind, 15–18

Bidirectional causation, 246–247

Biology and creativity: genetic inheritance in, 27, 29; historical embeddedness and, 249; mental illness and, 189; nature versus nurture debate and, 8–9, 32–33, 225; relative plasticity and, 245, 247–248. *See* Brain; Neurobiological approach to creativity

Biopsychosocial research, 8–10, 25–26; Findlay-Lumsden model of, 221–224. *See also* Dacey-Lennon biopsychosocial model of creativity

Bipolar disorder, creativity and, 141–144, 197, 228, 251–252; bidirectional research and, 246

Birth order, 241

Book of Kells, 22

Boston College Conflict Prevention Program (BCCPP), 120

Brain, 189–217; alarm reaction to stress in, 122–123; cognitive and chemical asymmetries in, 205; creativity research and, 205–215; of highly creative people, 7; neurons and neurotransmitter function in, 189–194; nineteenth-century knowledge of, 30–32; role of ACTH in, 196–200. *See also* Hemispheres of the brain

Brontë family, 48, 49

C